eXtreme .NET

Microsoft .NET Development Series

John Montgomery, *Series Advisor*
Don Box, *Series Advisor*
Martin Heller, *Series Editor*

The **Microsoft .NET Development Series** is supported and developed by the leaders and experts of Microsoft development technologies including Microsoft architects and DevelopMentor instructors. The books in this series provide a core resource of information and understanding every developer needs in order to write effective applications and managed code. Learn from the leaders how to maximize your use of the .NET Framework and its programming languages.

Titles in the Series

Brad Abrams, *.NET Framework Standard Library Annotated Reference Volume 1*, 0-321-15489-4

Keith Ballinger, *.NET Web Services: Architecture and Implementation*, 0-321-11359-4

Bob Beauchemin, Niels Berglund, Dan Sullivan, *A First Look at SQL Server 2005 for Developers*, 0-321-18059-3

Don Box with Chris Sells, *Essential .NET, Volume 1: The Common Language Runtime*, 0-201-73411-7

Keith Brown, *The .NET Developer's Guide to Windows Security*, 0-321-22835-9

Mahesh Chand, *Graphics Programming with GDI+*, 0-321-16077-0

Anders Hejlsberg, Scott Wiltamuth, Peter Golde, *The C# Programming Language*, 0-321-15491-6

Alex Homer, Dave Sussman, Rob Howard, *ASP.NET v. 2.0—The Beta Version*, 0-321-25727-8

James S. Miller and Susann Ragsdale, *The Common Language Infrastructure Annotated Standard*, 0-321-15493-2

Fritz Onion, *Essential ASP.NET with Examples in C#*, 0-201-76040-1

Fritz Onion, *Essential ASP.NET with Examples in Visual Basic .NET*, 0-201-76039-8

Ted Pattison and Dr. Joe Hummel, *Building Applications and Components with Visual Basic .NET*, 0-201-73495-8

Dr. Neil Roodyn, *eXtreme .NET: Introducing eXtreme Programming Techniques to .NET Developers*, 0-321-30363-6

Chris Sells, *Windows Forms Programming in C#*, 0-321-11620-8

Chris Sells and Justin Gehtland, *Windows Forms Programming in Visual Basic .NET*, 0-321-12519-3

Paul Vick, *The Visual Basic .NET Programming Language*, 0-321-16951-4

Damien Watkins, Mark Hammond, Brad Abrams, *Programming in the .NET Environment*, 0-201-77018-0

Shawn Wildermuth, *Pragmatic ADO.NET: Data Access for the Internet World*, 0-201-74568-2

Paul Yao and David Durant, *.NET Compact Framework Programming with C#*, 0-321-17403-8

Paul Yao and David Durant, *.NET Compact Framework Programming with Visual Basic .NET*, 0-321-17404-6

For more information go to www.awprofessional.com/msdotnetseries/

eXtreme .NET

Introducing eXtreme Programming Techniques to .NET Developers

 Dr. Neil Roodyn

✦✦ Addison-Wesley

Upper Saddle River, NJ • Boston • Indianapolis • San Francisco
New York • Toronto • Montreal • London • Munich • Paris • Madrid
Capetown • Sydney • Tokyo • Singapore • Mexico City

Many of the designations used by manufacturers and sellers to distinguish their products are claimed as trademarks. Where those designations appear in this book, and the publisher was aware of a trademark claim, the designations have been printed with initial capital letters or in all capitals.

The author and publisher have taken care in the preparation of this book, but make no expressed or implied warranty of any kind and assume no responsibility for errors or omissions. No liability is assumed for incidental or consequential damages in connection with or arising out of the use of the information or programs contained herein.

The publisher offers excellent discounts on this book when ordered in quantity for bulk purchases or special sales, which may include electronic versions and/or custom covers and content particular to your business, training goals, marketing focus, and branding interests. For more information, please contact:

U. S. Corporate and Government Sales
(800) 382-3419
corpsales@pearsontechgroup.com

For sales outside the U. S., please contact:

International Sales
international@pearsoned.com

Visit us on the Web: www.awprofessional.com

Library of Congress Catalog Number:

2004110807

Copyright © 2005 Pearson Education, Inc.

Pearson Education, Inc.
Rights and Contracts Department
One Lake Street
Upper Saddle River, NJ 07458

ISBN 0-321-30363-6

Text printed in the United States on recycled paper at Phoenix BookTech in Hagerstown, Maryland.

First printing, *December 2004*

*To Jim and Michele,
who provided the environment
that made this book possible.*

Contents

Foreword   xiv

CHAPTER 0   **Setup**   xvii

CHAPTER 1   **eXtreme Programming Overview**   1

What Is eXtreme Programming?   1

Working in The Ever-Faster-Changing World   2

The Answers According to Microsoft   3

The Answers According to XP   3

How .NET and XP Fit Together   3

You Don't Have to "Believe" in XP to Learn
Something from It   4

The Roles   4

What .NET Developers Can Gain from XP Practices   5

XP Practices Covered in This Book   6

Whole Team (a.k.a. On-Site Customer)   6

Planning Game   7

Pair Programming   8

Test-Driven Development   9

Constant Refactoring   11

Spiking   12

Continuous Integration   13

Stand-Up Meetings   14

The Other Practices   15

The 4 (+ 1) Key Values   18
    Communication   18
    Simplicity   19
    Feedback   21
    Courage   23
    Respect   24
Conclusion   26

CHAPTER 2   **Pair Programming**   27
I'm Not Sitting with Him!   28
    The Professional Attitude   28
    Get With the Winning Approach   28
It's a Game   28
    Exercise 2-1: Game to Teach Pair Programming   29
    Exercise 2-2: Step-by-Step Exercise to Get a Feel for
      Pair Programming   31
Try It Together   40
    Exercise 2-3: Exercises for Two Developers to
      Work On Together   40
Conclusion   41

CHAPTER 3   **How to Solve Big Problems**   43
The Software Development Problem   43
The Genius Is in the Simplicity   44
    Big, Complex Solutions   44
    The Genius Function   45
    Example of Problem Breakdown   45
Problem Breakdown Exercise   47
    Exercise 3-1: Defining the Story   48
    Exercise 3-2: Breaking Down the Stories into
      Small Subtasks   50
    Exercise 3-3: Breaking Down the Subtasks Even Further   55
Exercises to Help You Toward Genius   56

Exercise 3-4: The Shopping Cart   56

Exercise 3-5: Derived Stock Market Data   57

Exercise 3-6: What's the Weather Like?   58

Exercise 3-7: The Unfinished Solution   59

Conclusion   60

CHAPTER 4   **Test-Driven Development**   61

Is It Possible to Write Bug-Free Code?   62

Increase the Quality of Your Code   63

The Big Why   63

Introducing NUnit   66

Creating a New Project in C# Using NUnit   66

Exercise 4-1: Get NUnit Up and Running   67

Exercise 4-2: Write a Test and Add Some Functionality   71

Exercise 4-3: Plug the Business Logic into the
    User Interface   75

Exercise 4-4: Plug the Business Logic into a
    Different User Interface   76

Exercise 4-5: Write a Test to Fix a Bug   77

Exercise 4-6: Write a Test and Then Add
    Another Function   81

Exercise 4-7: Write a Test and Then Extract the Method   83

Exercise 4-8: Add the UI for Subtraction   86

Exercise 4-9: Extract Functionality Out of the UI Layer   87

How Do You Feel About TDD?   91

Exercise 4-10: Without Tests   91

Exercise 4-11: With Tests   92

Confidence Test   93

Conclusion   94

CHAPTER 5   **Refactoring**   97

What Is Refactoring   97

Do It As You Go   98

The Importance of Tests   98

The Benefits   98

    Feedback   99

    Communication   99

    Simplicity   99

Some More Big "Why" Questions   99

    Why Should I Do It When No One Else Does?   102

    Why Do Something That Doesn't Add Any New

      Features to the Code?   102

Let's Start Refactoring   102

    Exercise 5-1: Currency Converter Refactoring   103

When Not to Refactor   121

Conclusion   122

CHAPTER 6   **Spiking**   **125**

You Can't Know Everything   125

Raise Your Confidence   126

Let's Discover Something   126

    Exercise 6-1: Spiking How Time Zone Data

      Works in Windows   127

Encode the Knowledge in Tests   135

Go Where No Man Has Gone Before   139

    Exercise 6-2: Spike Web Services Without a Web Server   139

    Exercise 6-3: Spike Session State Across Service Calls 139

    Exercise 6-4: Spike Drag and Drop Documents in a

      Rich Text Control   139

Conclusion   140

CHAPTER 7   **Automating the Build Process**   **141**

What is the Build Process?   141

What's Wrong with F5?   143

I Make Mistakes   144

If a Computer Can Do It, Then It Should   144

Do It the Old Way   145

    Exercise 7-1: Creating an Integration Build Batch File   146

Introduction to NAnt   151

Exercise 7-2: Using NAnt to Automate
  the Build Process   151
Conclusion   160

CHAPTER 8   **More Testing**   161

User-Interface Testing   161
  It's Not Possible!   162
  "We Are a Special Case"   162
An Issue of Architecture   162
  Exercise 8-1: Building a Thin GUI Layer to
    Make Testing Easier   163
  Stamper Part Two   174
  Stamper Part Three   175
  Exercise 8-2: Using Reflection to Test the GUI   175
  Exercises on Your Own   188
Testing Third-Party Libraries   188
  We All Do It   188
  The .NET Framework Is a Third-Party Library!   189
  Component-Based Software Development Is Here   189
  If It Goes Wrong, We're All in the Brown Stuff   190
  Put the Alarms in Place   190
Step-by-Step Exercises Using a Third-Party Library   190
  Exercise 8-5: Setting Up NUnit (Again!)   191
  Exercise 8-6: The Quick Breadth Test   191
  Exercise 8-7: The Functional Depth Test   194
  Exercise 8-8: Testing for Exceptions   198
  Exercise 8-9: Examining the Code   200
  Exercise 8-10: Writing a Breadth Test   202
  Exercise 8-11: Getting the Breadth Test Running   205
  Exercise 8-12: Writing a Test to Break the Code   207
  Exercise 8-13: Forcing an Intermittent Error   211
Coding with Protection   212
  Exercise 8-14: Protecting Yourself Against the Change   212
  Exercise 8-15: Plugging In the New Changed Library   213
Conclusion   214

CHAPTER 9   **Step-by-Step Development**   217
Step by Step by Step   217
A Strategy to Lower the Risk of Failure   219
   Step-by-Step Exercise to Demonstrate the
   Small-Step Approach   220
Conclusion   267

APPENDIX I   **Guideline Solutions for Task
Breakdown Exercises in Chapter 3**   269
Exercise 3-4: The Shopping Cart   269
Exercise 3-5: Derived Stock Market Data   271
Exercise 3-6: What's the Weather Like?   275
Exercise 3-7: The Unfinished Solution   277

APPENDIX II   **Building Your Own Simple Test
Framework with Excel**   281

APPENDIX III   **Recommended Reading**   285
Important Books for Software Developers
   Working in Teams   285
XP-Specific Books   285
XP-Specific Web Sites   286
Agile Techniques Books   286
Agile Web Sites   286
Agile Tools Web Sites   287
A Book About Change   287

Index   289

Acknowledgments

I WANT TO THANK THE REVIEWERS of this book who all did a sterling job in tight timeframes. Troy Magennis, thank you for being on the other end of IM conversations and helping me plot the path to completing this book. Charlie Poole, thanks for the conversations over coffee and lunch; they helped clarify some of my ideas.

Christophe Nasarre, Michael Ask, Amit Kalani, Mike Snell, and James Speer, thank you for doing an outstanding job of keeping up with the numerous iterations of this book that spewed forth during the two-month period it took to complete.

Joe Field, thanks for testing and helping to perfect many of the exercises in this book.

Keith Cline, thank you for helping to Americanize my English and making the text more readable.

The team at Addison-Wesley has provided support through this process. This team includes Stephane Thomas, who helped get the project started, and Ebony Height, who has supported the process to the end. I also want to thank Christy Hackerd, who managed the copyediting stage, Curt Johnson, for his efforts marketing the book, and Joan Murray, for coming on board at the last minute to ensure the project got completed.

Finally, a special mention must go to Jim and Michele McCarthy, to whom I have dedicated this book. The McCarthys provided the space for me to write in their home outside Seattle. They also provided immense help to get me past sticking points in the writing process. Jim, thank you for the inspired title, for teaching me about book features, and for helping me understand the editing process. Michele, thanks for the numerous ideas and playing the customer role for some of the exercises. Thank you.

Foreword

THE MOST IMPORTANT TECHNOLOGICAL CHANGES of the last century were those centered around the invention of electronic computers. These changes are largely due to the monumental improvements that have occurred in computer hardware. It is hard to believe the incredible advances made in the 60 years since the Electronic Numerical Integrator and Computer (ENIAC) first ran. This fast pace is reflected in *Moore's Law*, a reference to an observation made by Gordon Moore in 1965 about the rate of growth in the number of transistors per integrated circuit.

Improvements in computer software have been significantly more modest. There is nothing comparable to Moore's Law for the progress in software technology, but there have been advances. From the earliest patch-panel programming, software development has benefited from higher-level languages and the related tools. There have been improvements in methodologies such as structured programming and object-oriented programming as well.

eXtreme Programming—or XP, as its practitioners refer to it—focuses on the people and the processes that people use. This focus is important because to people in business—that is, the people who pay for it—software development has become synonymous with "late and over budget." The approach taken by XP represents a new set of attitudes about what is important.

These attitudes and ways of working are part of a new success formula of which every software developer ought to be aware and about which they ought to learn. These attitudes are part of a cooperative, customer-oriented focus that is important not just to programmers but also to anyone in modern society who wants to prosper. Readers will find these same attitudes in such classic business books as Tom Peters' *In Search of Excellence* (Warner Books, Inc. 1984), and in Stephen Covey's *The Seven Habits of Highly Successful People* (Free Press 2003).

Attitudes, however, are not enough because software development is a profession with a history and its own obstacles. The application of a customer focus to software development is found in the world of XP. The cooperative, team-oriented spirit is one that is at the core of XP.

In his book, Dr. Neil Roodyn takes you into this world with practical examples and real-world exercises. He shares his passion for XP with a hands-on, roll-up-your-sleeves approach. If you like to write code, you will like this book. If you love to learn practical new ways to solve old problems, then you will love this book. Dr. Neil makes the tenets of XP clear and comprehensible as well as approachable and usable in the everyday world.

Paul Yao
President
The Paul Yao Company
http://www.paulyao.com

◼0
Setup

If you are a developer using the .NET Framework, or if you are thinking of using the .NET Framework, then this book is designed for you.

I have used the material in this book in training courses for a number of years. The experience of the students in these courses range from the .NET novice to the experienced developer, but everyone benefits from the exercises. The novices learn about .NET Framework development while at the same time learning good development practices. More experienced developers work through the exercises more rapidly and are able to focus on the techniques being taught.

This book introduces you to practical techniques that you can use to improve your software development abilities. These techniques have been heavily promoted in the last few years as practices in a set of methodologies. The methodology from which I draw most of my experience is *eXtreme Programming* (XP)—hence the title of this book.

Throughout the book, you will find highlighted text accompanied by icons. The icons are there to differentiate the type of section. The three section types you will encounter are as follows:

 Story: These are tales from my experiences in developing software and training development teams.

 Discussion: These are conversations taken from the real-life experience of working with development teams.

 Future Tools: This section features plans for future versions of Visual Studio.

What Do You Want?

When you are developing software, what do you want?

- Fewer bugs
- Greater predictability
- More time (to do what you want)
- Satisfaction that you've done a great job
- Happier customers and managers

This book introduces you to a set of techniques designed to put you on the road to reach your goals.

The practices examined throughout this book are taught mainly through hands-on exercises. I strongly believe in learning by doing, and, after all, this is about programming in an extreme way.

Terminology

XP refers to a collection software development practices and is sometimes called referred to as a *methodology*. However, there is more to XP than just the practices and the values. XP creates team camaraderie. XP produces happy customers. Just following the practices and knowing the values isn't XP. The practices and values provide a vocabulary to discuss and *enact* the development of software. XP is about loving the creativity of software. XP teams embrace the changes during the development. XP teams want to ship great software products. XP helps to create a team that has the same goals. XP teams achieve their goals.

.NET (pronounced "dot net") is the colloquial term given to the Microsoft .NET Framework. In this book, I discuss software development using the .NET Framework. Developers using the .NET Framework have adopted the new technology incredibly fast. There is more to .NET development than just the framework and the tools. Developers using the .NET Framework love the product and what it can achieve. The opportunities provided by the .NET Framework have excited a large percentage of the development community.

eXtreme .NET is the term I have given to developing software using the .NET Framework and some (or all) of the XP practices. eXtreme .NET teams create high-quality solutions in short timeframes. They embrace the spirit of XP along with the excitement of developing with the .NET Framework. Above all, eXtreme .NET teams have an incredible passion for creating great software.

This book introduces the techniques used by eXtreme .NET developers.

 How I Got Here

In the beginning, I just wrote code. I programmed in BASIC and then in 6502 assembler. Then I learned C, 8086 assembler, and then Pascal. I started to understand some of the issues involved with functional programming and then procedural-based development. Most of the projects I did were small, achievable by me or with just one other programmer. The communication channels were limited, and we got software shipped. I was often a guy alone in a room.[1] My bosses at the time often let me work from home or on my own hours. Often I would start early, have a long lunch, take a nap in the afternoon, and then program until midnight. Life was good, and I worked on some really cool software. Some of this software still ships.

Then in 1991, I joined my fist big software team; there were five of us! I was the last to join the team. The project was already in full swing, and it was chaos. I was confused, afraid, sad, and mad all at the same time. The code in the source-code control database didn't all compile. There was no standard coding convention; each programmer coded with a different style. There was no form of testing. We had no idea when the system would be finished. The tasks were handed down to me as I finished the previous one. I had very little idea where I was going. We were programming in C++, and this was only my second C++ project. I was afraid that the lack of object-oriented (OO) programming in the project meant that I did not understand what OO was really about. One month after joining the team, I started to raise these issues. There was a lot of struggle and internal debate, especially about the little things such as where the curly braces should go!

Eventually we got the system in a state where the code all looked pretty much the same. We reached a point where we could compile the entire code base every night. I was realizing the importance of development practices to the team.

For a few years, I worked with a couple of teams. I helped these teams implement what I considered to be crucial aspects of the development process. In 1995, I became involved in my first start-up company. All the developers were younger than I, and by virtue of my age I was looked up to as the leader. At the same time, some interesting books were published on the development process. Notable books for me were Jim McCarthy's *Dynamics of Software Development* (Microsoft Press, 1995) and Steve McConnell's two books, *Code Complete* (Microsoft Press, 1993) and *Rapid Development* (Microsoft Press, 1996) They were inspiring; they made me realize I wasn't the only person struggling with these issues and that there were better ways to develop software. What's more, they were written by guys at Microsoft, one of the world's biggest software companies. Their strategies made even more sense to us because we were using the Visual C++ development tools, and Jim McCarthy's team wrote those tools. Well, if we could do as good a job as them, we would be okay.

That first start-up company didn't make it. We ran out of funding, and there was no real marketing effort. It was a shame we had written some excellent code that would never ship. The next step was to start up on our own. Six of us from the failed start-up banded together and decided to break out on our own. We had learned a lot of lessons, including that we needed to learn more.

Four years later, at that second start-up, someone discovered XP. It was 1999, and the dot.com buzz was in full effect. This company was delivering traditional C++ applications for the Windows desktop, using back-end databases and middle-tier COM business objects. The world had changed, and XP looked like it would help us keep up. I was intrigued, and never being far from the code, I tried some pair programming. It was fun. I bought a few copies of Kent Beck's book *Extreme Programming Explained* (Addison-Wesley, 1999) and handed them around. I worked with the team on task breakdowns. We built test frameworks and tried test-first programming. We had morning stand-up meetings to discuss progress and work out our strategy for the day. The interesting thing was that it didn't seem a very big jump from the rapid application development approaches that were introduced in the McCarthy and McConnell books.

We managed to complete a lot of work and have fun at the same time. The quality of our code also improved dramatically. The last project I worked on with this team shipped ahead of schedule and has never had any bug reports from customers. I believed I had to tell other people about what we were doing.

I had a stake in another company at that time. It was being engaged to develop some early-stage software using early versions of the .NET Framework. Much of the framework was pre beta and very flaky. I suggested they use an XP approach to help them learn the tools and protect themselves from incorrect assumptions. This worked well. I investigated further and found another company in London that was using XP. They were also doing very well. It seemed like a great way to develop software. That year I ran three courses on developing software using XP practices. The teams I worked with did a great job, and a year later I felt ready to retire. The 1990s were good to me.

A year and lot of adventures later, I found myself in Australia looking for companies that were using XP. I wanted to teach and code again. I was a believer, and I wanted to work with others who knew the "way" to develop software. Yes, I wanted to write code; it is what I do, I enjoy it. I love the creative aspect of software development. I love the purity of that creation. A Russian I once worked with used to say, "Hey, this is software; you can do anything if you have enough money." I believe he was right.

I formed the *Sydney XP Activity Club* (known as SyXPAC) and started teaching groups about the joys of XP. At the same time, Microsoft was getting ready to release the .NET Framework and the Visual Studio.NET development environment. I found myself working with the two together. I introduced them together in a course I started running called XP Techniques for .NET Developers. The result has been the creation of a number of eXtreme .NET development teams. Much of the material in this book comes from the lessons learned on those courses and the mentoring I have been doing with development teams.

How to Read This Book

Most of the chapters in this book have exercises using the .NET Framework. Chapters 1 and 3 do not. These two chapters provide background knowledge for the rest of the book.

Chapter 1 provides an overview of XP. If you have read other books on XP and feel comfortable with the practices and values, you might be tempted to skip Chapter 1. Don't! Chapter 1 also contains an exploration of how .NET and XP work together.

Chapter 2 introduces pair programming. The exercises in this chapter require two developers. From this chapter onward, you can apply the pair-programming techniques to the exercises in the rest of this book.

Chapter 3 examines techniques for breaking down problems into small easy-to-achieve tasks. The exercises in Chapter 3 will help you understand the practices explored in other chapters.

Chapters 4 through to 7 cover the XP techniques that help you to achieve the goals mentioned at the beginning of this chapter.

Chapter 8 provides a deeper examination of techniques for writing code with fewer bugs.

Chapter 9 pulls all the techniques together into a single project.

The Team

Throughout this book, you will encounter dialogue between members of a team. This team is learning to become an eXtreme .NET team. I have taken most of these conversations from real-world experiences I have had while working with software teams.

Note: I've edited out swearing for your reading enjoyment!

The members of the team are as follows:

- **eXtreme Eddie**—Eddie has been programming for more than 20 years. He has done everything from mainframe work through to embedded systems. Eddie was an early adopter of XP techniques and has been using XP in Java projects for the past couple of years. Eddie embodies the XP spirit.

- **.NET Deepak**—Deepak is a young, smart coder. He graduated last year but has been using the .NET Framework since it first went into beta. Deepak knows and loves .NET. Deepak represents all there is to love about .NET.

- **Skeptic Sue**—Sue has been in software development for 10 years. She has been mainly developing Windows software in C and C++. Sue was promoted in her previous job to project manager, which she hated. She left and joined this team so that she could get back into developing software. Sue carries the scars from many failed projects and doesn't trust new ideas.

- **Panic Pete**—Pete is very bright and comes up with amazing solutions for problems. He is the clown of the team. Pete has been writing code for 5 years but has never finished a single project he started. Pete panics when the going gets tough and verbalizes this panic. When this happens, he has previously quit.
- **Customer Chris**—Chris is the internal customer for the team. He works with marketing and the customer support team. Chris once tried to write some code on a training course. He didn't enjoy it. Chris is a people person: He loves engaging in conversation.

Conclusion

I believe that all developers can learn something from the XP practices and techniques. After reading this book, you may go on to embrace the full XP process, while other readers may feel they are not ready or that XP will not fit in their organization. Either way, XP has had a big impact on the way software is being developed, and everyone in the field of software development can learn from XP.

Software development is a career that requires constant education. XP provides a set of lessons that all software developers can benefit from learning.

I have used XP practices while writing this book. This book is Version 1.0 of what I hope to build on in the coming years. As with software, the content of future versions of the book will be dependent on the technology that becomes available. The future versions of this book will reflect the feedback from the users—that is, *you*. Therefore, please provide feedback, either directly to me via email or through the publisher, Addison-Wesley.

---

[1] McCarthy, Jim. *Dynamics of Software Development*. Redmond, Washington: Microsoft Press, 1995.

■ 1 ■

eXtreme Programming Overview

I F YOU HAVE NEVER BEFORE read anything about *eXtreme Programming* (XP), read this chapter. If you want know how XP can help you develop better code for the .NET Framework, read this chapter.

This chapter does not provide a detailed, in-depth examination of XP. It provides just enough information about XP to get you started. Also explained in this chapter is the importance of XP to .NET developers. This chapter discusses the business needs for XP techniques and how software development practices have changed to meet those needs. After all, XP has evolved in response to the changing business needs of software teams.

Because the material within this chapter is introductory in nature, I direct you to other reference material for further reading.

What Is eXtreme Programming?

XP is a formalized set of software development methods that have been shown to work well together. A central theme of XP is the idea that the cost of change on a software project does not need to rise throughout the life cycle of a project. If the cost of change can be leveled off, the attitude toward the development process can be radically rethought.

XP aims to embrace the ever-changing business needs when developing a software solution. XP is nonproprietary and doesn't involve buying any special tools. XP challenges many of the common development practices, requires an open mind, and necessitates that the development team learn new techniques. XP evolution has been driven by a groundswell of developers unhappy with the continuing failings of traditional software development methodologies.

XP is very much driven from the programmer's perspective, but never loses focus of the business aspects. Customer input is highly valued throughout the development process. In fact in an XP approach, the customer is part of the development team and thus maintains closer control of the project.

A downfall of many software projects is the "us versus them" approach taken between software developers and customers. To counter this, an important aspect of XP is that it revolves around customer satisfaction. XP draws the customer into the software development team, thereby allowing the whole team to become aligned to delivering the goal.

XP is nothing new. Many XP practices are things that developers have been doing for years. The difference is that XP pulls them all together and "turns the volume up."[1] The idea is to find the things that work well and make them work even better. This is where the *extreme* comes from, the high-intensity use of these practices.

The goal of XP for you, the developer, is to enable you to focus on the code, developing high-quality solutions in a predictable and repeatable manner. XP focuses on the use of 12 main practices. Each one of these practices is a valuable tool to have in your toolbox. Each practice supports and strengthens some of the other practices. When used together, these practices have been shown to add up to more than the sum of the parts.

The XP practices support four key values: communication, simplicity, feedback, and courage. Each of the values interacts with the other. Together these values work to create a strong foundation for developing high-quality software solutions. By using these practices and supporting these values, a team can ensure that high-quality software gets produced to meet the most pressing business needs.

Working in The Ever-Faster-Changing World

The pace of change in the business world continues to increase at a dramatic rate. Even with the downturn after the dot.com crash, the business world is moving forward at a more rapid pace than ever before. With less funding available for IT projects, more than ever is expected from software development teams. To keep up with customer and client requests, we need some help.

The Answers According to Microsoft

Microsoft's response to this need follows their line of reasoning behind tools such as Visual Basic, Visual C++, and MFC: Let us (Microsoft) worry about the plumbing, and you (the developer) can worry about solving the business problems. The .NET Framework takes this a step further than any of the offerings before. The .NET Framework provides what is, in effect, a large virtual machine for your software to run on. This framework provides a huge amount of base functionality for you to work with to meet your customer needs. It also enables you to interoperate with existing COM-based technology and write your solutions as components, with different components being written in different languages.

The Answers According to XP

Emerging almost simultaneously with the .NET Framework, with the aim of solving some of the same problems, has been the agile development movement (http://www.agilealliance.org). One of the most well-publicized and written about of the agile development methods is XP. XP aims, through the use of the practices explained in this chapter, to solve these problems of ever-changing needs and creating big, complex solutions.

How .NET and XP Fit Together

.NET is a concrete technology (a set of tools and libraries) with which we can work. XP provides us with a set of practices and techniques we can use to better develop our software.

The .NET Framework provides a rich environment for building collaborative applications. Visual Studio .NET provides a rapid development IDE to help developers create these applications. .NET is being marketed as helping developers create solutions that support their business (customers) in a more responsive way; XP practices are centered on creating predictable software for the customer. The common thread between XP and .NET is the central role played by the customer.

Together XP and .NET work well, and most of the development teams I have worked with in the past year have been using both .NET and XP techniques to enhance their offerings to their customers and users. They are what I call *eXtreme .NET teams*.

You Don't Have to "Believe" in XP to Learn Something from It

Many developers tell me that XP is "a nice idea, but it would never work in the real world." Although I disagree, because I have seen it work very well in the real world, it might be that it would never work in their world. Moving to XP can be a cultural shift and can cause massive disruption if not handled carefully. However, some of the techniques practiced by developers who use XP are incredibly powerful tools for any developer to have in his or her toolbox. So even if you are in doubt and don't believe XP is worth considering, I suggest you at least try to learn what is valuable from this set of practices.

This book teaches these XP practices for you as a developer of .NET software. I hope that you learn from each one and use XP to create great software.

The Roles

Within an XP environment, members of the team take certain roles. The following roles are the ones relevant to this book:

- Customer—The customer is the goal owner. This role does not always have to be taken by a real end user (or purchaser) of the system. Often a product manager or a person from marketing can effectively play this role. The customer must have a full understanding of what they want from the software being developed. They do not need technical savvy (necessarily), but the customer should have a good understanding of what users will want to do with the software.

  In the eXtreme .NET team introduced in the Chapter 0, Chris is the customer.

- Developer—I assume that if you are reading this book, you are a developer. It is the developer's job to work with everyone on the team to create a great piece of software. The developer's day-to-day activity should focus on writing high-quality code.

  The eXtreme .NET team has Eddie, Sue, Pete, and Deepak as developers.

- **Coach**—The coach is someone who has good people skills and can help remove blockages that are preventing the team from moving forward. The coach needs to understand the XP practices to help the rest of the team best employ them. The coach is a developer and will work on the code with the team. Most coaches are experienced developers, but they are not always the most experienced people on the team.

  Eddie is taking the role of the coach in the eXtreme .NET team we are following.

What .NET Developers Can Gain from XP Practices

Over the past few years, as always, new technologies and methods for building software have emerged. Two of the largest and most publicized have been XP and Microsoft's launch of the .NET Framework. They have both come from very different places and focus on different areas of the software development paradigm.

.NET is a brand name given by Microsoft to their latest range of development tools and frameworks. Here I focus on the use of the Microsoft .NET Framework for developing software that runs on the Common Language Runtime. Since the launch of the .NET Framework, Microsoft has been pushing hard to help companies develop software on the new platform. The success of .NET will depend on the uptake by software developers and then the clients of the software that is developed. The more software developed, and therefore available for a platform, the more attractive it becomes to utilize it, the more likely it will be that developers build software for it, and so on. Bill Gates terms this a *virtuous cycle*.

So what have these two new things in the software development world got to do with each other? When development teams move to a new language or development platform, they do so for a reason, not just because it's there! These reasons can vary, but the core theme that runs through them is "it will help us develop better software." *Better* can mean several things: faster, more robust, higher quality, more usable, greater scalability, less code to write, and so forth. Many of the teams I have worked with over the past few years have made the decision to not only adopt a new development toolkit, but also a new process for developing software. I have seen a trend emerging of teams moving both to .NET and adopting a more agile development process. These are eXtreme .NET teams.

XP Practices Covered in This Book

The following subsections examine how our eXtreme .NET team uses certain practices to develop better software. In this book not all of the XP practices are covered. I have selected the ones that I believe will add the most value to a team developing a solution using the .NET Framework.

Whole Team (a.k.a. On-Site Customer)

If you adopt the *whole team* practice, the customer is an integral part of the team. Therefore, the customer is always available to discuss issues and resolve them as they arise. This practice reduces the turnaround time for queries and prevents incorrect assumptions from being made. This practice really puts the pressure on the customer role. If a customer really wants software developed, they must put energy into the process. The concept of them being part of the team adds to the reality of one team, one goal.

Never overlook the value of an on-site customer in any project. When both the development team and the customer are discovering new features of a platform together, this practice becomes more valuable than ever before. The immediate feedback that can be provided by the customer enables the team to add really valuable functionality that they may have missed before.

Consider how this applies to our eXtreme .NET team:[2]

Deepak: Oh did you know we can do this with the .NET Framework? Would that be useful to you?

Chris: Jeez, yes! How long would it take?

Deepak: We think a day or two!

Chris: How certain are you of that?

Eddie: Pretty sure, after all we did a prototype when we were spiking that technology yesterday.

Chris: Wow, well just do it! I'll take story card[3] X away until another iteration.

If Chris hadn't been there to work with the developers, one of several things might have happened:

1. The developers might have thought "that's cool, we'll try to remember to tell Chris about that next time we see him" (and then most likely they would have forgotten).

2. The developers might have assumed Chris wouldn't want it and because timeframes were tight, not bothered to mention it in case Chris asked for it as well as everything else they were doing.

3. The developers might have assumed it was valuable for Chris and implemented it, but then not had time to finish story Y, when actually Chris would have preferred not to have story X delivered.

Any of these (or other) outcomes would have been making assumptions about what the customer actually wanted. Having the customer on site to answer these questions as they come up becomes incredibly valuable.

Planning Game

The *planning game* practice provides a mechanism for planning out the features in a piece of software. The planning game helps a team estimate timeframes for delivering the software with the features. This practice involves the whole team, including the customer. By including the whole team, the communication between the team members is enhanced. The developers sit with the customer to define the required features and prioritize them. The practice takes the form of a cooperative game. The aim for all participants is to achieve the same end goal: maximize the value of the software produced.

Consider how our eXtreme .NET team interacts during part of their planning game:

Pete: Panic! Time for another planning game.

Chris: Hi guys, I've been talking to marketing, and they've been doing some research into usage and sales of the application we're developing. They think that we need to make the application support Tablet PC features.

Sue: No way! Why Tablet PC? We already discussed doing a version for the Pocket PC at a later stage.

Chris: Many more of the users are mobile than we thought. This section of mobile PC users is moving to Tablet PCs. None of our competitors are supporting Tablet features. We can grab that share of the market if we can do this.

Deepak: Okay, a Tablet PC will run our application fine. Tablet PCs run Windows XP professional with extra bits for the tablet.

Chris: Okay that's good, but what about support for writing in the forms?

Eddie: Which forms? All of them? Where is the most value?

Chris: We think if you can get the onsite report forms and expense claim forms to support handwriting that would be a good start.

Pete: Panic! I have never done anything on the Tablet before; I have no idea how long that will take.

Deepak: Chill Pete, it's easy. The Tablet SDK just extends the .NET Framework.

Eddie: Yeah, we need to tell Chris how long it will take! Any idea Deepak?

Deepak: I reckon about a day for each form.

Chris: Okay cool, I'll expect that in the next milestone then.

Eddie: Hold on Chris. You've already given us the stories for the next milestone; If you want us to do this Tablet stuff as well, then you'll have to take something else out!

Chris: Oh yeah! Okay can you swap that with the file-backup feature we discussed last time? You said that was going to take two days.

Eddie: Fine, so we'll add Digital Ink support to the onsite report and expense claim forms, and we won't do the backup stuff for the next release.

You can see how this conversation involves all the members of the team. By involving everyone, no knowledge is hidden. Everything is out in the open. Each member of the team knows the current goals.

Pair Programming

Pair programming refers to developing code with two developers sitting at one computer. In an XP team, you work with a partner on every piece of production code.

Pair programming provides a constant peer review of the code. It helps to spread knowledge throughout the team and trains developers to communicate their intentions more fully as they work together. The aim is to increase the overall intelligence creating each part of the system. The combined intelligence of two developers should be greater than either one of them alone.

As far as information dissemination goes, I have never seen anything work as effectively and as fast as pair programming. One developer learns a new trick on the IDE while messing around after work one evening. The next morning that developer shows her partner what she has learned. The pair then splits when they have finished a task (unit of work, discussed further later on) and work with another two people whom they both show the new trick. Before lunch, four developers have all learned the new technique. By the end of the day, everyone on a team of 12 could easily have learned this new trick. Now imagine this working when each of those 12 developers is learning new things. If they all learn one new thing each evening and then spread the word the next day, the entire team is learning 12 new things a day. In reality, most developers learn more than one new thing a day when they are developing software.

This works best when you have a very dynamic environment with rapidly rotating pairs. I recommend that everyone attempt to swap pairs at least twice a day. The more the better. Some of the best eXtreme .NET teams I have worked with swap pairs between four and six times a day; this is where the *extreme* comes in!

Test-Driven Development

Test-driven development (TDD) is the practice of writing tests before writing the production code. These tests are a cornerstone that supports many of the other practices, such as refactoring and simple design. The tests communicate the intention of the code and validate that intention each time they are run. This validation helps to increase confidence in the software developed.

TDD is a fantastic example of developers providing their own safety net before walking the tightrope of a new development language or framework. Consider how our eXtreme .NET team has benefited from TDD:

Eddie: So we thought the framework provided this function to perform X.

Sue: Yes, so we wrote a few unit tests and ran them.

Eddie: And, of course, they failed because we hadn't put any code in yet.

Sue: Yeah, Eddie insists we run the tests before we fill in the code; I hate it, but I know he's right.

Eddie: So then we created a class A and called method B on it.

Sue: And one of the tests still failed!

Eddie: We couldn't work it out because that function in Java does just what we wanted, but in the .NET framework it appears to behave slightly differently.

Sue: Good thing we wrote all the tests; otherwise, we could have made a wrong assumption!

In this example, Eddie and Sue were pretty sure the class library would behave as they expected it to, based on their experiences with a different class library. The fact they wrote tests meant they could move forward quickly, fix the problems early, and learn how the class library worked.

The team had another conversation:

Sue: So the next thing we needed was to complete the X task.

Pete: Yes, Sue made us write all the tests first.

Sue: Well, Eddie always does that, and he's pretty smart, so I thought I'd copy him!

Pete: Anyway, we ran the tests, they failed, and we started coding to get them to pass.

Sue: After writing the code to make only two of the tests pass, we noticed that actually four tests had passed; somehow we had got two tests to pass without doing anything!

Pete: It turned out that the .NET class we were using already does those things for us and so saved us a load of coding.

Sue: So it was worth writing all the tests first. Thanks, Eddie!

Here Sue and Pete discovered through writing the tests some functionality that the .NET Framework classes provided. This meant they could move ahead more quickly without writing code that duplicated the functionality already provided.

The combination of TDD and pair programming meant that two members of the team learned the new feature in the .NET Framework. XP teaches that the more of the practices you use, the greater the benefit you get. The practices play off each other, and the last conversation was a good example of that in action.

Constant Refactoring

Refactoring refers to the process of changing the structure of the code without changing the behavior. Refactoring is a practice that aids the removal of duplicate code and simplifies the code base. Enhancements can be made more easily to refactored code. The practice of *constant refactoring* means that after each task is complete, the pair reviews their code to see how they might simplify the code without changing the behavior. This practice enables programmers to treat the code in a more dynamic manner. Developers describe their code as becoming more fluid after they learn to refactor effectively.

Refactoring allows an overall architecture to emerge in the system as it is being developed. This approach contrasts with the normal approach of designing the architecture up front and then developing the code to fit with the architecture.

I believe that this is a key component of XP that has really helped many of the teams I have worked with to develop new software with the .NET Framework. Instead of bringing preconceived ideas of how software should be built and trying to make the new .NET code fit into this model, the XP teams have let their architectures emerge. These teams have been able to gain advantages that they would never have gotten if they had attempted to squeeze their code into an old model. This is especially the case for developers coming from either the VB or ASP background.

Let's join Sue and Eddie as they have just finished a task to see how they use refactoring to change the design:

 Sue: Cool, we've finished that. I love the way the places all update on the map and in the drop-down list now. Let's check it in so that we can get the next task finished today.

Eddie: Hey, hold on. We have a code-duplication issue.

Sue: What?

Eddie: The code we copied from the map object into the drop-down list.

Sue: So?

Eddie: We should only have the code in one place; then if we need to change it, we only have to change it in one place.

Sue: Oh.

Eddie: We can refactor the duplicate code into a separate object that both the UI controls use.

Sue: But then the code won't be in the UI controls where it's used.

Eddie: Even better! It will be easier to test, and other non-GUI classes can use it.

Sue: I bet there is a design pattern[4] for what we are doing.

Eddie: You're right. Will you look it up?

Sue: Sure.

Teams I have worked with who have previously developed large-scale enterprise applications in Java and C++ have been both surprised and pleased with the architectures they have developed. They have told me that if they had done a big architecture design up front, they would never have built the system that way, and it would have been far more complicated than was needed.

Spiking

XP promotes a form of experimentation and research known as *spiking* or "doing a spike." Spiking is experimentation to validate a theory. When the development team needs to know something, a thin vertical slice can be "driven" into the technology to get some answers. These answers can help the project succeed. Most spiking is done without the safety harness of TDD. Spiking is often carried out by solo developers who believe they need a break from pairing. Spikes are also "driven" by the one left out of a team when there are an odd number of developers, so not everyone can pair.

Driving a spike into the area of functionality the development team is planning to work on next will often produce some valuable information. In .NET projects I have worked on I have seen spikes effectively expose new information in the following areas:

- C# performance
- Web-service compliance for Remoting servers
- Issues with COM interoperability
- Transactional support in ADO.NET

All of these examples were areas in which the development team had uncertainties. In a traditional development approach, someone would have been given the task of dealing with that particular issue. That one person would have become the specialist in that area. For some developers, this is fine because they believe they are securing their jobs in the future by being the top gun in that area. This is a false belief. They are in fact acting as a bottleneck to the team's overall knowledge attainment. By driving a spike and then reporting the result back to the team, the knowledge gets spread, and more perspective can be given to a task. Pairing with another developer to write the tests and production code after a spike is done also helps to spread the knowledge.

Here's an excerpt from a meeting with our eXtreme .NET team:

Pete: I spiked the transactions in ADO.NET yesterday, and they'll do the job fine, so I'll pair with someone to write the code for task X this morning.

Deepak: Did you think about how it works with our project? I'm worried about the threading and that some issues might arise from that.

Pete: Panic! Oh no, I didn't think of that.

Deepak: Okay, I'll pair with you this morning, and you can show me what you discovered while we spike how it works across threads.

Pete: Okay, cool.

Here this team discovered that the spike had taken them some of the way to knowing the answer, but more work still had to be done.

Continuous Integration

After each task is complete, the code written gets integrated with the entire solution. The entire code base is compiled, and all the tests are run to ensure the code just created does not break anything. This *continuous integration* practice enables the team to ship early and often and enables them to deliver the short iterations on a regular basis.

As part of this practice, automated build and test scripts are developed. These scripts compile and test the entire solution. The scripts are set up as part of the development environment to make the entire process run more smoothly. This practice eliminates the element of human error from the process.

The practices of a methodology are aimed at reducing the chances of something going wrong. In the past, many projects would design and develop modules or components of the system independently. Near the end of the project, the team would attempt to integrate these modules to produce the final solution. This has become known as the big bang approach and is often a rather painful experience—an experience that involves lots of swearing and cursing because the components do not work together as expected. The XP practice of continuous integration aims to prevent this problem from arising by insisting that developers integrate their code after each task is complete and run the entire suite of tests to ensure that their code has not broken anything.

This practice is valuable when developing systems that consist of distributed components, such as Web services, remoting, custom components, or class libraries. Solutions developed in .NET often include many of these components. Even a simple ASP.NET Web site is likely to include some user controls (ASCX files). By carrying out the continuous integrations, the developers get immediate feedback on the changes they have made. The team can then work to fix any issues that arise. When working with a new toolkit, developers are much less likely to fully understand all the implications of the changes they are making. This XP practice helps these developers to cope with this issue in a far more manageable way.

Stand-Up Meetings

The practice of Stand-Up Meetings occurs each morning. The team stands up and discusses the progress from the previous day and current work issues. Standing up keeps the meetings short and focused.

Learning is about listening and doing. The proof that you have learned something is shown by your ability to teach it to someone else. Stand-up meetings provide an opportunity to spread knowledge to the team. Each morning the team stands up and each member makes a brief statement about his or her achievements the previous day and where he or she wants to get today. This is a great forum for telling the team about some new technology or a new tool that you discovered the previous day. This discussion can then elicit ideas from other team members, as in the following example from our eXtreme .NET team:

Deepak: Yesterday evening after you all went home, I was waiting for my girlfriend…

Whole Group: Ah, how sweet.

Deepak (blushes): Yeah, yeah, anyway I was playing with putting together a simple custom Web control and I discovered this thing where you can use session states; I thought you should all know.

Sue: Wow, that could be really useful for us for the online task list system; can you pair with me this morning and show me how?

Deepak: Sure.

Eddie: If we store those session states in the SQL database, can we then somehow access the task lists from the mobile interface?

Chris: Now that would be useful for my clients! If it can be done, I think you'll see it as a story in the next iteration.

The Other Practices

The practices described so far are the ones that I focus on in this book. Other XP practices include the following:

- **Sustainable pace (a.k.a. fixed working week)**—Work fixed hours, go fast while at work, and then get out. This is based on the principle that tired developers often make costly mistakes. Therefore, stay fresh and increase the intensity. By keeping to a fixed pace, we can last longer, and our endurance will be greater. Another benefit of sticking to fixed working hours is that the pace of progress can be more easily measured and therefore estimated in the future. If every week we work a different number of hours, it becomes very hard to make anything close to accurate estimates.

- **Metaphor**—Have a way of describing the system being developed in terms of something everyone understands. For example, it is like a bakery; we take the ingredients and mix them a certain way to get the results. This is possibly the least-used practice and yet it has the potential to solve a large number of issues. Using a common vocabulary to describe the behavior of a system enables a shift from talking technical to talking about the user features of the system.

- **Simple design**—Keep the design as simple as possible. Don't gold plate or add features because you think you will need them later. This keeps the code doing just the things we need it to do now and no more. This practice helps to keep the cost of change low by not encumbering the system with unneeded features.

- **Short releases**—Release a stable working version of the software every one to three weeks for the customer to review. This allows for increased feedback as to the direction of the development. This practice supports the feedback and communication values previously mentioned. Note that it is hard to accomplish this practice without employing the practice of simple design and thus the value the simplicity. These small periods of development are called *iterations* in XP terminology. We return to the concept of iterations later in the book.

- **Coding standards**—Code written adheres to a set of guidelines so that it all has the same look and feel. This makes it harder to claim ownership of the code and so supports collective ownership. This process enables any developer (or pair) to refactor and enhance code you have written.

- **Collective ownership**—The entire system and process is owned by the team, not any one individual. This means that no one person has any more right to change a piece of code than another. This helps to enforce coding standards. The flexibility of the code is thus increased because it can be changed and enhanced by the entire team; in this way, the combined intelligence of the team can be applied to make the software better.

- **Leave baggage behind**—Do not get too attached to anything because things will change. The class library you wrote two years ago may no longer have any value. The toolkit or language you use today may well not be the one we use tomorrow. Travel light and you will travel faster.

- **Quality work**—There is no such thing as an acceptable bug. Keep the quality of your software as close to zero defect as humanly possible. Work with the broken-window[5] theory that once bugs creep into your system, they will multiply at a fierce rate. Kill them quickly before they can do this.

- **Incremental change**—Do not make big changes to a system; it will become unstable. Take it small steps at a time, and you will be more likely to succeed.
- **Honesty and openness**—Work in an environment where everyone is open and honest. Discuss issues with everyone so that everyone can help to resolve them.
- **Go with instincts**—People have gut instincts for a reason. Learn to work with them and embrace them in your environment; they add value to what the development team is producing.
- **Teach learning**—Learning is vital to longevity in the software development world. It is imperative to the long-term success of a team that it encourages learning and teaching among its members.
- **Embrace change**—The only certainty in software is that it will change. Learn to embrace this change and love the possibilities that arise from the changes made.
- **Play to win**—An attitude of success breeds success; this is very different from "playing not to lose." Build a record of success stories, and you will win more often.

In his book, *Extreme Programming Explained*, Kent Beck identified an initial 12 practices that have become the main XP practices; some teams even call this set of practices *vanilla XP*. It is often said that a team is not using XP unless they use all 12 of these practices. I think this is partly true. If you do not try something, you will not know whether it works. I think that a team can say it is an XP team if it *uses many* of the practices but has *tried all* of the practices.

The original 12 practices discussed in Kent's book are test driven development, planning game, whole team, pair programming, continuous integration, constant refactoring, short releases, simple design, metaphor, collective ownership, coding standards, and sustainable pace. As you can see, the majority of the practices covered in this book fall into the original 12 practices.

Along with these 12 practices, there exists an array of other practices often followed by XP teams. These have evolved and been adopted from other methodologies of development. These extra practices have been popularized via Web sites and forums and then adopted by teams.

Even if you do not (or cannot) use all of these practices, they independently add value to the code you are writing. Techniques such as TDD will help you focus on the task at hand and deliver higher-quality code. Refactoring will enable you to change the structure and design of your system without affecting its behavior. Breaking tasks down into smaller units will enable you to focus on solving the problem one small step at a time. Pair programming will allow two developers to solve a problem that may have caused one person difficulty; it also provides an ongoing peer review of the code. Automating steps in your development process enables you to perform more regular integrations and get more reliable and rapid feedback on the state of the system.

The 4 (+ 1) Key Values

As previously mentioned, the four key values of XP are communication, simplicity, feedback, and courage. Kent Beck, one of the creators of the term *eXtreme Programming* and author of the first book on XP, has also added *respect* as the fifth of the key values. The following subsections briefly discuss each of these values.

Communication

Problems often result because people are not communicating. This is especially true in efforts that are team focused, such as software development. When the team is not openly communicating, the information flow that keeps the team moving forward is damaged.

Bad communication happens for a reason. Communication is not generally seen as an important skill for developers to obtain. In fact, many developers have previous poor experiences of communication. Managers often do not want to hear what is being said. Other developers have their own issues to contend with and do not want to hear about your issues. This experience does not encourage developers to speak out when things need to be said. A few of these experiences may lead to an environment in which communication is at best limited and at worst nonexistent. A junior developer joining such an environment would not know anything was amiss. His lack of experience could lead to the belief that poor communication is how software should be developed.

The proponents of XP (myself included) claim that communication is vital to develop software of value. The information flow created by ongoing communication allows all members of the team to contribute to the final results. This enables a group of individuals to behave as a team with the goal of developing great software.

Many of the XP practices force communication to be prevalent among the development team. Some of these practices such as the planning game, pair programming, and stand-up meetings are obvious mechanisms, but others such as coding standards and refactoring also lead to greater communication, as you will see in later chapters. An XP team uses the role of the coach to police the communication, ensure it is occurring, and encourage the use of practices to overcome any barriers.

Simplicity

"What is the simplest thing that could possibly work?" is a cry often heard in XP teams. This means to do the simplest thing that will enable you to move forward in the right direction.

 Simple is Smart

I often equate the value of simplicity with math problems. I remember at school struggling with a few tricky equations, and then slapping myself on the forehead when I found the answer (because it was so simple). It often takes real genius to create a simple solution from a complex problem. Most people create a complex solution from simple problems and think they must be pretty smart because of the complexity they have created. In fact, the aim is to be as close to genius as possible and try to create simple solutions for the most complex problems. On my own, I have a lot of difficulty trying to be a genius at any time, but with a team of smart people, we can get a lot closer to genius on a regular basis.

Don't plan the future! The future will happen regardless of whether you plan it. By planning the future, you are always avoiding the present. You are avoiding the present now by planning. You are avoiding the present that will be by focusing on where you are in your plan. A common response I get to this is a declaration of my madness.

"Of course you have to plan for the future and design the system first; otherwise, how would you ever be able to write the code? Don't be crazy!" This is so difficult for developers that it is one of the biggest hurdles to overcome when moving into an XP environment.

As you will learn in this book, XP does not promote detailed upfront design of the entire system. The design is done a small part at a time, allowing for greater flexibility in the software being developed. By developing one small piece of functionality at a time, testing first and constantly refactoring, you do not need to design the system; it will design itself! The designs will emerge as an outcome of taking a disciplined approach to using the practices. The team needs to have experience with object-oriented coding and design patterns so that they can see these patterns emerge and work with them. For this reason, tools such as UML are still incredibly valuable; they enable communication of the patterns as they emerge in the system.

The point of keeping things simple is to code for now rather than never. By this I mean that we should code to solve today's problems for your customers, not problems in the future that might or might not come up. Doing this gives you a far greater chance of solving those problems more rapidly and providing the customer with some value in the short term. If every day you produce something of value for the customer, then after several weeks the software you are building will have a culmination of all that value. This is often a sticking point for developers.

To see how this is possible, you need to understand how the practices enable us to treat the code in a different way than traditional approaches. The unit tests provided by TDD and refactoring techniques enable us to change code more readily. Creating a more fluid code base means we do not need to be concerned if the decisions we make early on are absolutely correct. We can change the design of the entire system more easily than ever before.

This simple code that you (and your team) have written will ship quicker because less can go wrong. Shipping more quickly enables you to get the value to the customer more rapidly and solicit feedback (see next section) more readily.

Simpler code means less to communicate. By keeping the solution as simple as possible, you are aiding the first value we discussed. Having less to communicate means it is easier to communicate and explain what the code is doing and the emerging design.

One final point: Simple does not mean easy. Developers who are starting out often misinterpret this as "Do the easiest thing you can possibly do." This is incorrect; simple is often a lot harder to achieve than complicated. As you work through this book, you should start to see how by keeping the task you are working on simple you can build more complex solutions. An example presented later in this book is replacing a switch statement with polymorphic behavior. The switch statement is easier to write, but the polymorphism provides a simpler solution.

Feedback

Feedback on your progress enables you to adjust your actions to better meet the goals of the project. Feedback leads to a greater understanding of the state of the system being developed. This understanding tells you exactly what you have done right and what you need to work on. Knowing what you need to work on is incredibly valuable. The feedback acts as a guide for the next set of tasks. Understanding an issue early often averts a potential crisis later on.

If you ask an XP team how they are coming along, you might get a response such as "don't ask me, ask the system." XP teams build feedback systems into their software using tests, profiling tools, and automated builds. The results from these are generally posted in very public places, providing feedback on their progress for all to see.

The granularity of the feedback cycles goes from minutes to months. The following identifies some of the practices that support these different timescales.

- **TDD**—Developers drive the code development by writing tests first and then the code to make the tests pass. This leaves test code in the system that provides feedback on the stability of the system. An XP team will receive this feedback at intervals of minutes as they work on the code throughout the day.
- **Customer user stories**—The practice of letting customers define the functionality their users require on story cards, typically index cards. These story cards are discussed further with the customer when the time comes to implement that functionality. This provides the customer with up-to-the-minute

feedback on what is being worked on. (Customer user stories are discussed more in the next chapter.) Most customers will check completed stories daily.

- **Stand-up meetings**—When a customer story is completed, the customer is informed. Often the customer will get a demo of the system within a day of a story being completed. This helps to obtain more rapid feedback. The meetings occur daily, and so again this is daily feedback.

- **Short releases**—Within the first month or two, an early working version of the software should be ready to ship. This is a goal that every XP team I have worked with has managed to reach. This shipment might be to only a few friendly parties (usually chosen by the customer). Shipping will allow the developers to receive feedback as to the usefulness of the system being developed and the correctness of the functionality. The timeframe for feedback from short releases is in terms of weeks and months.

Ship it Quick, Ship it Often

Until it ships, you know nothing! I have personally worked on projects with large scopes where the business needs were not clearly understood. The project managers refused to give the customer anything early on in the development life cycle. The managers would say, "It's not ready, and they won't understand that these functions are missing." This was a flaw in the development life cycle. The development team was coding blind. If we had given the software to the customers earlier on in the process, we could have received feedback on our progress. We were not getting feedback from what we had already developed, and this ultimately led to a failure in the project delivering what the customers wanted.

It is worthwhile shipping the simplest system that makes sense. This simple system forces feedback from the customer, and you can use that feedback to improve the software.

Simplicity, communication, and feedback create a self-supporting cycle; feedback leads to more communication, communication leads to understanding what to test, simple systems are easier to test, easier to test means more feedback, and so on, as shown in Figure 1-1.

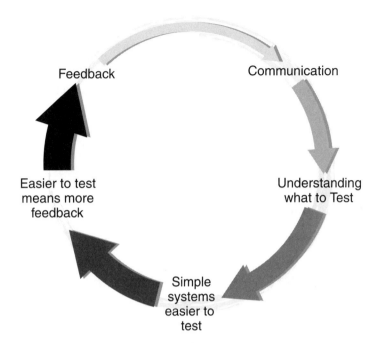

Figure 1-1   The self-supporting cycle.

Courage

To use the practices prescribed by XP and get the full value from doing so takes courage. Many of the practices are difficult, and if taken at face value, they don't seem to make sense. It is this courage to take up the practices and make the results happen that contributes to the *extreme* in XP.

By employing the safety harnesses provided through the use of the practices, developers can increase the intensity of their work. They can go fast and furious at cutting code that solves the problems at hand. By doing this, developers will find they get more produced but may tire more easily; this is called *upping the burn rate and lowering the hours*. It is about working hard and fast while at work and then getting out to relax and enjoy life. All of these things take courage to do.

Other aspects that require courage include making changes when needed, not before, and being prepared to throw code away. Both of these practices are alien to many developers and might require a change in the way you think about the code you are writing. As mentioned previously, one of the themes of XP is to lower the cost of change. Writing code that we might need in the future actually increases the cost of change. Code you do not need now is code that we are not using but that needs to be changed. The cost of change can be lowered by not including code until it used. The tests help us to validate this; if we find code that is not being used, we should throw it away because it is encumbering the system needlessly.

Employing just courage alone without the safety nets and harnesses provided by the other values and through following the practices is dangerous, often lethal, to the project. Take care and allow your confidence to grow as you follow the practices so that you can have the courage to communicate new ideas. To ensure these new ideas, keep the system simple. Experiment with new ideas and get feedback on new ideas. These ideas will become the code in your software.

Respect

One of the least-discussed and yet most important values of XP is respect. This is mainly applied on a human level to the people we work and live with. It is through respect that we can learn how other people think. Knowing how people think enables us to adjust our own behaviors to better work together to accomplish the goals for which we are aiming. Let's start with our own team of developers. The respect for other developers in our team and other teams around us is vital to the health of our environment. Showing humility for other developers will enable us to learn from them.

Although this book is not about building teams, I recommend that every developer who works in a team of more than one person find out more about team-based behaviors. If every developer did this, the world's software teams would be much more productive.

I believe every member of a team has some value to offer that team, and it often takes work to instill that belief in other members of the team. Showing disrespect for a member of the team is akin to what is described by Jim McCarthy[6] as "flipping the bozo bit"; each team member has a bozo bit. Initially, none of us is a bozo, and the bits are all off. When you flip the bit on, that person becomes a bozo and has to work hard to switch the bit off. It is important to respect our fellow team members and not "flip the bit" on them.

Working Together

When I work with development teams, I often hear developers make comments along the lines of "the customer is an idiot; he doesn't know what he wants, so we're developing this system that we know he really wants." It astounds me that such arrogance can really exist in a business environment and people get paid for it (often large sums of money!). Respect for the customer is vital to a successful project. The customer is the person with authority to make decisions, such as whether the team gets paid for doing this work. The problem often stems from the belief that because the customer "can't count in binary on his fingers," the customer is "a total loser." It is true that many customers do not have technical skills, but that is not their job. They are part of the team to bring an understanding of how to create business value from the software being developed. This is a communications issue. It is the job of the development team to work with the customer, in partnership, to produce what the customer does want and ensure that it adds value to the customer's business.

The management in an organization has a job to do. It often does not include writing code, but this does not make them any less valuable to the project. The management is there to help make your life easier so you can accomplish the job at hand. Have respect for the managers. They are often under pressure to perform and deliver. If you have respect for this, you can work together as a team to accomplish far more than is possible by working against each other.

Finally, it is imperative to respect the users of your software. In one survey done on a piece of software that had been released, 500 users were asked to carry out tasks with the software. The results were disappointing; more than 90 percent of the users failed to carry out all the tasks. The developers, when told this, responded with, "Where did you find so many stupid users?" This lack of respect for the users led to the creation of a piece of software that had all the functionality but was incredibly hard to use; this was not valuable for their business or the customer's business and the software had to be changed to make it more user friendly. It is important to respect the users and understand how they will use the software.

Conclusion

You should now have a better idea of what XP is and what you can gain from it. XP might not be for all of us, and some areas of business may never find it suitable for their development methodology. However, we can all learn things from the XP practices. The rest of this book takes you through the techniques you can apply every day, even if you are not working in an XP development team. In the next chapter, we start this process by learning pair programming and how two developers can work together to solve problems and write better code.

[1] "Turning the volume up" means taking something that works well and making it work even better.

[2] The eXtreme .NET team is introduced in Chapter 0.

[3] Story cards are explained in Chapter 2.

[4] Gamma, Erich, Richard Helm, Ralph Johnson, and John Vlissides. *Design Patterns*. Reading, Massachusetts: Addison-Wesley Professional, 1995.

[5] Gladwell, Malcolm. *The Tipping Point*. Boston, Massachusetts: Back Bay Books, 2002. This book describes the broken-window theory.

[6] McCarthy, Jim. *Dynamics of Software Development*. Redmond, Washington: Microsoft Press, 1995.

2

Pair Programming

THIS IS A CHAPTER FOR YOU TO FOLLOW if you have a partner to pair with. If you do not have someone with whom you can work through this chapter, go find someone. Recruit a friend, work colleague, or a fellow student.

This chapter provides a series of exercises that encourage you and your partner to take turns in typing the code and thinking about the problems. This chapter emphasizes the benefit of programming with a buddy and how much fun this type of development can be. It also shows you how business benefits can be gained from development in pairs and how you might best promote these ideas to your organization.

As discussed in Chapter 1, pair programming is the practice of developing all production code with two developers sitting at one machine. This goal of this practice is for developers to help each other create something far greater than one developer alone could do alone.

Pair programming may be the hardest of the XP techniques. It certainly raises the most concern among the software development community. As software developers, we are typically taught to program on our own. I expect that (like myself), the self-taught programmers have spent many hours on their own, playing with code and working out how to make some software do something. Even the education system tends not to encourage software to be developed by groups or teams, measuring success by the work of an individual.

However, as an average individual (which, of course, you and I are not!), my IQ is around 100. Surely if I work with someone else who is also average, our combined

IQ should be somewhat higher. It is unlikely that we can get close to 200 because much of our intelligence overlaps, but hopefully we could get to 130 or more. In *Software for Your Head*[1], the McCarthys explain the idea of a team IQ, with each member of the team contributing to the overall IQ of a team. Pair programming relies on the same premise, and the team size is two for the coding task being developed.

I'm Not Sitting with Him!

I have been astounded and astonished more than once to hear fully grown adults utter these words: "I'm not sitting with him." It is almost as much as I can do sometimes to ask whether they think they are still in grade school. However, that would be unproductive.

The Professional Attitude

The reality of the modern workplace is that we might not connect with everyone as well as we might like. We will have to work with some folks who have bad breath, speak too loudly or too quietly, and so on. As professional software developers, we need to act in a professional manner and exhibit a professional attitude toward our colleagues.

Get With the Winning Approach

If we have a technique that enables us to deliver software that is better in some way (quicker to deliver, more robust and smaller), we should use it until we find a technique that creates more of what we want. In my opinion, this philosophy should be applied to more than just software development, but that's a topic for another book.

It's a Game

As the saying goes, "Time flies when you're having fun." I think this could easily be extended to "Time flies when you're having fun developing software." It always amazes me how quickly the day goes by when I am in programmer mode. I am sure that in part it is because I am enjoying what I am doing. I love writing code and developing software; to me it is like a puzzle game.

As a young kid learning to program, I had a good friend who was also keen to learn, and we would often sit together at my father's Commodore computer and type in lines of code, suggesting ideas as we went and improving on each other's code. It was a lot of fun, and we created some pretty cool little applications (at least, we thought they were).

Upon learning of pair programming, I realized that as kids, my friend and I had been pair programming, and that if it was fun then it should surely be a lot of fun now.

Exercise 2-1: Game to Teach Pair Programming

This game is based on another game called the Perfection Game, which can be found in *Software for Your Head*. You can play it with two or more people. To play this game, you need one PC with one keyboard, one mouse, .NET Framework development tools installed, enough chairs, and space for all developers to sit and see the screen. With more than two people, I suggest you use a projector so that all the participants can see what is going on.

There are two roles in this game: programmer and supporter. Each person takes turns to be the programmer, while everyone else takes the role of the supporter.

1. The programmer declares what the function he is going to write will do. He states his intention. I suggest something small that can be completed in less than 5 minutes.

2. When the programmer is finished, he declares he is done.

3. Each supporter in turn grades the function from 0 to 10, with 10 being the highest value and 0 being the lowest. For every point less than 10 that is given, the supporter must come up with a way of making it a 10.

   a. The supporter then follows his grading with a statement of what he likes about the code as written.

   b. The supporter then states what it would take to get a 10.

4. One of the supporters takes the role of the programmer, and the process begins again.

5. After everyone has had one turn at being the programmer, you can repeat the cycle, but this time the programmer starts with the code that he or she wrote before and tries to improve it for a couple of minutes to raise the grade.

Here is an example round between two of the programmers in our eXtreme .NET team, Deepak and Sue.

 Deepak: I'll go first. I'm going to write a function that increments a private variable until it reaches a certain number and then resets it.

Sue: Okay, go to it.

< Deepak types the following>

```
class PairGame
{
    int var;

    public void Increment()
    {
        var++;
        if (var > 500)
        {
            var = 0;
        }
    }
}
```

Deepak: Done!

Sue: Cool. I give the code 5 out of 10. What I like about it is that it is concise, the naming of the class and method is clear, and the code is easy to read. To get a 10, the integer variable should be named something meaningful; var doesn't mean much to me. The integer variable should be initialized somewhere. The limit and reset numbers, 500 and 0, should be in variables or constants to make them easier to change later. You should write a test to prove it works. If it had all that, I would give the function 10 out of 10.

Deepak: Thanks, Sue.

Sue: You're welcome—now it's my turn.

Pointers for the supporter:

- Keep the feedback positive. Say what you like and what it would take to get to 10. Do not say what you don't like.
- Don't be personal. Keep your comments focused on the product, not on the programmer. Phrasing the statements is important. It is better to say, "I like the way the function uses the increment operator" rather than "I like the way you used the increment operator."
- Remember you are scoring the product, not the programmer

Pointers for the programmer:

- Remember, it is not personal. The supporter is scoring the code, not you.
- Always remember to thank the supporter for the input. It is helping the product get better.

Exercise 2-2: Step-by-Step Exercise to Get a Feel for Pair Programming

In this exercise, you focus on the pair programming aspect and do not worry about the other practices. This exercise can be done without having read any of the other chapters in this book. The aim is to help the two of you get a feeling for writing code as a pair.

To do this exercise, you need one PC with one keyboard, one mouse, .NET Framework development tools installed, two chairs, enough space for both developers to sit in front of the PC and see the screen, and one copy of this exercise (i.e., this book).

Start off with one of you controlling the PC (the driver) and the other holding the exercise (the navigator). The navigator is going to guide the driver through developing the code. At certain points, you will swap roles. It is very important that you do swap at the specified times and no later. While you are in the role of navigator, try not to show your partner the code as it is written in the exercise. You should attempt to verbally communicate what needs to be done. You can draw diagrams and as a last resort read out the line of code to be typed. If at any point either of you feel unsure that you have done the correct thing, it is time to compile and test what you have done. You should be able to compile and run the program after nearly every step.

In keeping with the theme of pairing being fun, you are going to develop a screen saver together:

1. Start off by setting up a Windows Forms application to work as a screen saver. Create a new C# Windows Forms application project called Extreme Screen Saver.

2. Change the name of the created form class to **SaverForm**.

3. Edit the constructor to take an integer parameter and store it in a member variable of the class called ScreenID.

```
private int screenID;
public SaverForm(int screen)
{
    InitializeComponent();
    screenID = screen;
}
```

4. Edit the Main method to use parameters to determine how to run the application. This is how Windows launches a screen saver.

It might help if you can draw a table for your partner (on a white board or a scrap of paper).

Argument	Meaning
/c	Display the config/settings screen
/s	Launch the screen saver
/p	Preview the screen saver

```
static void Main(string[] args)
{
    if (args.Length > 0)
    {
        // config
        if (args[0].ToLower().Trim().Substring(0,2) == "/c")
        {       }
        // saver
        else if (args[0].ToLower() == "/s")
        {       }
        // preview
        else if (args[0].ToLower() == "/p")
```

```
        {           }
    }
    else
    {           }
}
```

5. Create a static protected method in the SaverForm class called **LaunchSaver**. In this LaunchSaver method, add code to iterate through all the screens connected to the PC and create a new form to run in that screen.

```
static protected void LaunchSaver()
{
    for (int i = Screen.AllScreens.GetLowerBound(0);
        i <= Screen.AllScreens.GetUpperBound(0); i++)
    {
        System.Windows.Forms.Application.Run(new SaverForm(i));
    }
}
```

6. Back in the Main method, call this static method from the launch and default argument cases.

```
static void Main(string[] args)
{
    if (args.Length > 0)
    {
        if (args[0].ToLower().Trim().Substring(0,2) == "/c")
        {   }
        else if (args[0].ToLower() == "/s")
        {
            SaverForm.LaunchSaver();
        }
        else if (args[0].ToLower() == "/p")
        {   }
    }
    else
    {
        SaverForm.LaunchSaver();
    }

}
```

7. Compile and run the program. Close it, and then try renaming the created EXE file from eXtreme Screen Saver.exe to **eXtreme Screen Saver.scr**. You should be able to install this and run it as a screen saver.

8. Swap roles.

9. We will now set up the form to occupy the entire screen and respond to mouse and keyboard events to close down. In the design view for the Saver-Form, set the FormBorderStyle property to None.

10. Create an event handler for the Load event on the form. This can be done by double-clicking the form in design view. In this method, we need to set the Bounds of the form to those of the screen, hide the cursor, and set the form to display on top of all the other forms.

```
private void SaverForm_Load(object sender,
    System.EventArgs e)
{
    Bounds = Screen.AllScreens[screenID].Bounds;
    Cursor.Hide();
    TopMost = true;
}
```

11. In this Load method, we can also add handler code for the mouse and key-board events. We want to handle these events and decide whether we are going to end running the screen saver. Start by adding an event handler for the MouseMove event. Call this method **SaverForm_MouseEvent**. In Visual Studio.NET, you can type **MouseMove +=** and then pressing the Tab key should generate the handler skeleton.

```
private void SaverForm_Load(object sender,
    System.EventArgs e)
{
    ...
    MouseMove +=new MouseEventHandler(SaverForm_MouseEvent);
}
```

When the application first runs, it will get the mouse location through a mouse move event, so the first time we get the event, we just need to trap the position of the mouse in a member variable. After that, if the mouse moves, we need to close the application.

```
private Point initialMousePt;
private void SaverForm_MouseEvent(object sender,
    MouseEventArgs e)
{
    if (!initialMousePt.IsEmpty)
    {
        if (initialMousePt != new Point(e.X, e.Y))
            Close();
    }
    initialMousePt = new Point(e.X, e.Y);
}
```

12. We can use this same event handler for the mouse down event that occurs when a user clicks a mouse button. Add the method to the event in the Load method. Then change the MouseEvent method to also close the form when a click has occurred.

```
private void SaverForm_Load(object sender,
    System.EventArgs e)
{
    ...
    MouseMove +=new MouseEventHandler(SaverForm_MouseEvent);
    MouseDown +=new MouseEventHandler(SaverForm_MouseEvent);
}

private void SaverForm_MouseEvent(object sender,
    MouseEventArgs e)
{
    if (!initialMousePt.IsEmpty)
    {
        if (initialMousePt != new Point(e.X, e.Y))
            Close();
        if (e.Clicks > 0)
            Close();
    }
    initialMousePt = new Point(e.X, e.Y);
}
```

13. Now let's do the same with a handler for the KeyDown event.

```
private void SaverForm_Load(object sender,
    System.EventArgs e)
{
    ...
```

```
        KeyDown +=new KeyEventHandler(SaverForm_KeyDown);
    }

    private void SaverForm_KeyDown(object sender,
        KeyEventArgs e)
    {
        Close();
    }
```

14. Compile and run the program. It is starting to work more like a screen saver. Rename the EXE file to an SCR file and test it. We now have a basic screen saver.

15. Swap roles.

16. The next thing to do is to add some drawing functionality so that the screen saver actually does something. We will start by adding a Paint event handler to the Form class. Again we can do this in the Form load method.

```
    private void SaverForm_Load(object sender,
        System.EventArgs e)
    {
        ...
        Paint +=new PaintEventHandler(SaverForm_Paint);
    }

    private void SaverForm_Paint(object sender,
        PaintEventArgs e)
    {
    }
```

17. In the Paint event method, we will add some code to draw the text eXtreme .NET in the center of the screen. We will use the TranslateTransform method to shift the drawn text to the center of the screen.

    You need to add the System.Drawing.Drawing2D namespace to this class file because we need to use the MatrixOrder enumerated type from there.

```
    private void SaverForm_Paint(object sender,
        PaintEventArgs e)
    {
        Graphics gc = e.Graphics;
```

```
Point screenCenter = new Point(
    (int)(gc.VisibleClipBounds.Width/2),
    (int)(gc.VisibleClipBounds.Height/2));

gc.TranslateTransform(screenCenter.X,
    screenCenter.Y,
    MatrixOrder.Append);

int fntSize = 12;
Font fnt = new Font(FontFamily.GenericSansSerif,fntSize);
Brush brsh = Brushes.Red;
StringFormat format = new
    StringFormat(StringFormat.GenericTypographic);
format.Alignment = StringAlignment.Center;
format.LineAlignment = StringAlignment.Center;

SizeF size = gc.MeasureString("eXtreme .NET", fnt);

RectangleF rect = new RectangleF(
    0 - size.Width/2,
    0 - size.Height/2,
    size.Width,
    size.Height);

gc.DrawString("eXtreme .NET", fnt, brsh, rect, format);
}
```

18. Add a timer control to the form and use the timer event to redraw the screen so that we can add some animation to the text. You do that in the design view. The timer control can be dragged from the toolbox onto the form and then double-clicked to generate the event handler method. Make sure you set the Enabled property of the timer to true so that it raises the events.

19. In the timer event handler, we will call **Invalidate**.

```
private void timer1_Tick(object sender,
    System.EventArgs e)
{
    Invalidate();
}
```

20. Next animate the text. We will make the text grow and shrink on the screen using the ScaleTransform method of the Graphics object. To do this, we need some class member variables to represent the current scale and the amount to change the scaling. We can manipulate these in the timer tick event.

```
private float scale = 1;
private float scaleChange = 0.1F;

private void SaverForm_Paint(object sender,
    PaintEventArgs e)
{
    Graphics gc = e.Graphics;
    Point screenCenter = new Point(
        (int)(gc.VisibleClipBounds.Width/2),
        (int)(gc.VisibleClipBounds.Height/2));

    gc.ScaleTransform(scale,
        scale, MatrixOrder.Append);
    gc.TranslateTransform(screenCenter.X,
        screenCenter.Y,
        MatrixOrder.Append);
    ...
}

private void timer1_Tick(object sender,
    System.EventArgs e)
{
    scale+= scaleChange;
    if (scale < 1)
    {
        scaleChange = 0.1F;
    }
    if (scale > 20)
    {
        scaleChange = -0.1F;
    }
    Invalidate();
}
```

21. Compile and run the program. You may want to decrease the Interval property on the timer to make the animation more viewable.

22. Swap roles.

23. We will use some of the built-in double buffering provided by the .NET Framework to remove the screen flicker. We will also add some more movement to the text animation. Before we add the double buffer in the constructor of our Form class, we need to set the style of the form to use WMPaint, the UserPaint style, and DoubleBuffer.

```
public SaverForm(int screen)
{
    InitializeComponent();
    screenID = screen;
    this.SetStyle(
        ControlStyles.AllPaintingInWmPaint|
        ControlStyles.UserPaint|
        ControlStyles.DoubleBuffer, true);
}
```

24. Now let's add rotation to the text animation so that it spins around as it grows and shrinks. We will use two class member variables to indicate the current angle of the text and the next amount by which to change the angle. We can vary this in our timer tick event method. In the Paint event method, we will use the RotateTransform method to rotate the text around the origin.

```
private float angle = 0;
private float angleChange = 5;

private void SaverForm_Paint(object sender,
    PaintEventArgs e)
{
    Graphics gc = e.Graphics;

    Point screenCenter = new Point(
        (int)(gc.VisibleClipBounds.Width/2),
        (int)(gc.VisibleClipBounds.Height/2));

    gc.RotateTransform(angle, MatrixOrder.Append);
    gc.ScaleTransform(scale,
        scale, MatrixOrder.Append);
    . . .
}

private void timer1_Tick(object sender,
    System.EventArgs e)
{
```

```
angle+=angleChange;
scale+= scaleChange;
if (scale < 1)
{
    scaleChange = 0.1F;
    angleChange = 5F;
}
if (scale > 20)
{
    scaleChange = -0.1F;
    angleChange = -5F;
}
Invalidate();
}
```

25. Compile and run the program. The animation should look much smoother. Try it as a screen saver by renaming the EXE file.

This exercise should have provided you with an understanding of how often you should swap roles and how important it is for both of you to be involved with the code being developed. Pairing is no fun if you are just watching someone else write code. It also has very little value if that is all that occurs during a pair-programming session.

Pair programming is about both developers being present and focused on the task at hand and both developers aiming to help make the code better.

Try It Together

You are now ready to try pairing on some code together. Remember, pair programming is a skill as much as learning to code is a skill. The more you do, the better at it you will become.

Exercise 2-3: Exercises for Two Developers to Work On Together

These following tasks are for you to work through together and try to develop the screen saver we developed further. During the exercise, make sure you swap roles often; I suggest that if you haven't swapped for ten minutes, you should stop and swap roles.

1. Extend the screen saver to display a preview.

   In the preceding exercise, you have created an entry point in the code that will get called when the program is run with the /p argument. Extend the code to draw the animation in the preview window provided.

   Hint: The second argument in the command-line arguments is a handle to a window (hWnd) in which to draw the screen saver preview.

2. Extend the screen saver to display a settings box.

   Carry on from the screen saver exercise again, and this time add functionality to display a configuration dialog box so that the user can alter the settings on the screen saver. The entry point is already created in the Main method when a /c parameter is passed to the application.

   The settings to be altered are the speed of the animation, the angle of rotation, the text color, and finally the ability to customize the text.

Conclusion

As mentioned throughout this chapter, pair programming is a skill that needs to be learned. Some practices covered in this chapter are intended to help you become a better partner when pairing. The perfection game can teach us how to help each other create a better product in a positive way. Keeping the conversation going during the pairing session is critical. The communication that occurs while pairing is what enables us to create something better than we would have done on our own.

As a closing thought, I want to share with you the fact that the more I pair program, the more I realize what I don't know. It is the best way I have found of learning new skills from another developer. Whenever I have an opportunity to pair program with a developer, I do so. I have learned as much from junior developers as I have from experts. With the combined intelligence and experience of two developers at work on the same code, this is the closest thing to having a genius write every line of code.

The next chapter explores another practice we can use to help us toward genius—a practice that helps us to solve big problems.

1 McCarthy, Jim. & Michele McCarthy. *Software For Your Head*. Upper Saddle River, New Jersey: Addison-Wesley Professional, 2001.

3

How to Solve Big Problems

THIS CHAPTER EXAMINES HOW TO BETTER solve programming problems. The aim is to get tasks to a level where we can have some functionality accomplished at the end of every day. Then we do not have to be so concerned with the bigger-picture stuff while we solve today's problems.

This chapter, like Chapter 1, is not specific to the .NET Framework. You can use these ideas in other development environments. We will be using the lessons learned from this chapter later on in this book. Be sure that you understand how to break down tasks and make time estimates before you jump ahead.

When mentoring development teams, I often encounter developers who do not (or cannot) break down a task into really small pieces of work that are achievable in a matter of a few hours or minutes. This is a skill that you need to learn. This chapter examines why it is important to have these small tasks, and shows how to break down some complex problems into simple easy-to-solve units of work. This chapter discusses XP practices that help us accomplish this task breakdown.

The Software Development Problem

When developing a piece of software, you are often dealing with many issues at the same time, some of which might detract your focus from the particular problem you are trying to solve. Issues you are dealing with will include the following:

- Adhering to the design of the system
- Making sure your new code doesn't break any existing functionality
- Ensuring you are following the coding conventions
- Worrying how this solution will impact future tasks that need to be completed

Wouldn't it be good if you could forget about those other issues? Then you could just code a solution today to the problem you have at hand. Problems are hardly ever so small and focused that you can actually accomplish them today, or even this week.

That is what we are going to attempt to achieve. First, we will explore what makes a good solution. Second, we will work through an exercise that demonstrates how we can carry out focused small tasks that lead us towards the completed solution.

The Genius Is in the Simplicity

A genius is a person who can take a complex problem and find a very simple solution that solves it. This solution is usually fairly trivial to implement *after* you know what it is. Most of us take the easy option, however, and create complex solutions to solve our complex problems. We do this for a number of reasons; the two main ones are as follows:

- We take on too much at one time.
- We look at how a similar complex problem has been solved before and try to copy that solution.

Our egos don't help in this matter. We want to show off how smart we are at implementing some complicated solution. We want to justify that we should be paid more and promoted. We don't feel comfortable going to our boss and saying, "That problem was solved in five lines of code, but it took me the whole of the past three days to write those five lines."

Big, Complex Solutions

The trouble with designing these big, complex solutions is that we often then get stuck when trying to actually implement them. They are just too hard and have too many points of failure. These solutions end up becoming the bane of our existence. We have to maintain them and fix bugs in them. Sure, we can be good citizens and use design patterns and well-documented architectures. Ultimately, however, we end up, time and time again, juggling big issues while trying to get a new piece of functionality into the system.

Among the XP practices are some techniques that will help us reduce the complexity of the problem.

The Genius Function

Ideally, we should find some way that we can all be geniuses. If we are all geniuses, we can always create simple solutions to all of our problems. Something we all know is that it is easy to create simple solutions to solve simple problems. So to become a genius, all we need to do is break down all of our problems into lots of smaller problems that are easy to solve.

Any problem that I estimate to take longer than four hours to solve is too big for me to feel comfortable with. I want to accomplish at least one thing in a day; if I accomplish more than that, I feel even better. This is a personal decision, but most people I have worked with aim for four hours or less. I have never worked with anyone[1] who was comfortable with tasks that lasted more than six hours. If I get a task that I estimate will take longer than my maximum four-hour period, I break it down into several smaller tasks. If any of those tasks will take longer than four hours, I break those down again. Something that I have found interesting is that the most effective developers I know break down the majority of their tasks so that they require less than an hour to complete.

Example of Problem Breakdown

Let's see how this works, beginning with a trivial example before I lead you through a more complex problem breakdown.

Suppose the customer has asked us to develop a piece of software that emulates a calculator on the desktop. So this is our problem: develop a .NET Framework calculator. Easy. So how long will the development take? Do you know immediately? I don't, but I bet it will take longer than four hours, so I need to break down the problem. Here's a list of smaller problems:

1. **Add function**—Add two numbers together
2. **Subtract function**—Subtract one number from another
3. **Divide function**—Divide one number by another
4. **Multiply function**—Multiply two numbers together

Can I give time estimates for each of these functions? I feel confident that I can, and I estimate between one and two hours for each function. Some people might ask, "Why so much?" After all, they know that I am an experienced developer and might think that I should be able to put a simple calculator together pretty quickly. I am estimating that this will take me up to a day to complete based on my experience. I am breaking the problem down into even smaller steps, and I will go through that process with you now for the add function.

Task	Time to Complete
Test for adding zeros	15 minutes
Test for adding negative numbers	15 minutes
Test for adding minimum numbers and maximum numbers (forcing overflows)	15 minutes
Test for adding positive numbers	15 minutes
User interface	15 minutes
Check code into source control and integrate with any existing solution	5 minutes
Total	1 hour 20 minutes

Notice that I emphasize writing tests. In the next chapter, you will learn why and how to write tests before the code. For now, it is important to understand that it gives me more focus on developing only what is required and nothing extra. These tests define the behavior expected of the object that will be developed.

Also notice that I am including the time it takes to write these tests, to develop the user interface, and integrate the code with a source control system. All these extra things take time that is often not accounted for by less-experienced developers and project managers. These extra things are often the reason so many software projects run late; developers too often fail to account for the "other stuff" that we need to do to write high-quality code.

With less-trivial problems, you will often find yourself asking some tricky questions, and this is where having contact with the customer becomes important. It is hard to break tasks down without being able to get answers to questions you have. Consider the preceding example. I have made an assumption that the calculator will deal with negative numbers. What if negative numbers are not permitted or required by the system? Having the customer present while doing this task breakdown will make this very apparent. The conversation in our eXtreme .NET team might go something like this:

Chris: Why are you testing for adding negative numbers? We don't want to add negative numbers!

Pete: Panic! What should happen if we get a negative number?

Chris: You should inform the user that negative numbers are not allowed.

Eddie: Okay, change that test to "Test for handling negative inputs, 10 minutes."

Remember one of the practices discussed in Chapter 1 was the whole team. Here is an example where having the customer as part of the team can make a difference. If you cannot get a customer to be present during a task breakdown session, try to get him or her on the phone or instant messenger. Failing that, try your manger or other developers. At least they may spot some mistakes or incorrect assumptions you have made before you actually commit them to code. You should e-mail your customer the results from each task breakdown session so that they can review them and change their minds or reset the direction.

We return to this scenario later on in this book to write code for some of these tasks.

Problem Breakdown Exercise

Hopefully you have a good idea of what we're aiming for now, so let's try to tackle a slightly more complex problem. This problem may still seem trivial in comparison to many real-world problems you will encounter, but we have to start somewhere, and this should give you at least introduce you to the concept of breaking down customer stories into tasks.

Exercise 3-1: Defining the Story

The first thing to happen is that the customer will provide the development team with a story. A *story* is a simple description of a piece of functionality that the system needs to perform. In a full XP environment, the team will play the planning game. This involves the customer writing a number of stories on cards (usually index cards). Then the development team will place rough time estimates on each story. The customer then decides which stories to do first. The planning game provides a long-term view of how the project could pan out eventually, but also includes short-term goals for the next few weeks. By repeating the planning game every few weeks, the accuracy of the estimates should get better and you enable the customer to choose the direction of the project on a smaller scale. Figure 3-1 shows a sample story card.

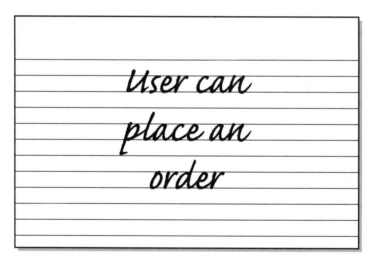

Figure 3-1 An XP story card.

A story can be considered similar (and are often compared) to a UML Use Case. The story should not explain all the details of the functionality. A story provides a rough idea of the scope. Stories are promises to hold conversations between the developers and the customer. This conversation occurs when the time comes to begin implementing the story. The conversation enables the developers to explore exactly what tasks will have to be carried out to satisfy the customer that the functionality described in the story is finished.

The best way to start this is to begin a conversation with your customer. Let's see how our team does it:

Eddie: What would you like this software to do?

Chris: I need to be able to display the time in different places in the world on my desktop.

Pete: You mean you want clocks, one for each place in the world?

Chris: Yes, but I want to be able to choose which places to display the time for, not just have a clock for every time zone that exists.

Eddie: Okay, how about we start with simply doing one clock for one time zone and then build the system from there.

Chris: Um… well, I want to choose the time zone and have multiple clocks.

Eddie: Yes, I understand that, but we want to get some core functionality for you to see as soon as possible, and then we can add to the software from there.

Chris: Okay, as long as you are aware that we will need more than one clock.

Eddie: Sure, so what shall we put down as the first story? How about "Select time zone to display?"

Chris: Sounds good. I also want to be able to put my own label next to the clock, so if I select GMT, I want to be able to label it as London.

Pete: Fine, so the second story could be "Add custom label to selected time zone?"

Chris: Yes that's right; so what next? I can select a time zone and associate a label with it, but I need to be able to see the clock. Do you need a story for displaying the clock?

Eddie: You're right; how do you want it displayed? I assume that just a digital text output is okay? Something like "Time in London is: 14:23." How does that sound?

Chris: No, no, no! You've misunderstood me! I need to see a *clock*. You know, with hands and a round face! Like this. (The customer grabs a scrap of paper and scribbles the picture shown in Figure 3-2.)

Figure 3-2   Customer drawing.

Pete: Panic! That wasn't what I was thinking.

Eddie: Sure, we can do that, but it will take a bit more work.

Chris: How much work? Doesn't sound that hard to me.

Eddie: Well let's break it down and I'll tell you how long it will take.

Chris: I don't have time for all this; I just want a clock on my screen for different places in the world!

Eddie: Okay, we'll get back to you soon with some estimates for timeframes.

Chris: Great, when?

Eddie: In the next hour.

Chris: Oh okay, that's not so bad.

Some of this conversation probably sounds familiar. It is not uncommon for customers (managers) to be short of time and want answers on the spot. As developers, we need to respect that they have other pressures and do what we can to help them. It is important not to let their stress get to us and force us to make on-the-spot decisions or provide time estimates based on nothing more than numbers plucked out of the air. Notice how Eddie, who has more experience, steers the conversation. Eddie is guiding both Pete and Chris through the process in a way that gives them the best chance of succeeding.

Exercise 3-2: Breaking Down the Stories into Small Subtasks

From the preceding conversation, Eddie and Pete can draw the following story cards:

1. Allow the user to select a time zone.
2. Allow the user to associate a custom label with the time zone selected.
3. Draw a clock for the time zone and a label for it.

From these stories, could you give reasonable time estimates? For the first two, you may be able to get reasonably close (apart from one issue). The third one is a little trickier because the clock has to show the correct time and be updated as the time changes. Let's see what Eddie and Pete come up with when they break these stories down.

Story 1: Allow User to Select a Time Zone

Task	Estimated Time
Get a list of time zones from the operating system	?
Test to check selected time zone is valid	15 minutes
Test to validate selected time zone is stored in memory	15 minutes
Test to validate correct behavior when invalid time zone selected	15 minutes
User interface to allow user to select a time zone from the list	10 minutes
Check code into source control	5 minutes

Eddie has put a question mark next to the first task because neither he nor Pete are sure what is involved in getting all the time zones from the operating system. They know the time zones must be there because when they set the Windows clock they can select from a list of available time zones. To find out where this list is stored, they need to carry out some investigation and experimentation.

In XP terminology, this is called *doing a spike* or *spiking*. This spike will be another task. Because they don't know how long the spike will take, they set an upper limit to the amount of time spent spiking before providing feedback to the customer. Eddie and Pete now have a list of tasks that looks like this:

Task	Estimated Time
Spike to discover how OS stores time zone information	4 hours
Get a list of time zones from the operating system	? (based on outcome of spike)
Test to check selected time zone is valid	10 minutes
Test to validate selected time zone is stored in memory	10 minutes
Test to test behavior when invalid time zone selected	10 minutes
User interface to allow user to select a time zone from the list	10 minutes
Check code into source control	5 minutes

They can now break down the next story.

Story 2: Allow User to Associate a Custom Label with the Time Zone Selected

Task	Estimated Time
Test to validate correct behavior when label is blank	10 minutes
Test to check label is stored and associated with time zone	10 minutes
Test to check label with non text characters is valid	10 minutes
User Interface to allow user to enter label for selected time zone	15 minutes
Check code into source control and integrate with existing code	5 minutes

Finally, they can tackle the third story: Draw a clock for the time zone and a label for it. Eddie thinks this story is too big, so he proposes they break it down into smaller stories:

3.1 Draw clock face

3.2 Draw label next to clock face

3.3 Draw clock hands

3.4 Update clock hands to reflect current time in selected time zone

3.5 As time changes, redraw clock hands to reflect current time in selected time zone

From these five stories, they can create a set of tasks for which it should be reasonably easy to provide time estimates. The tasks for each story are estimated as follows.

Story 3.1: Draw Clock Face

Task	Estimated Time
Code to draw circle	15 minutes
Code to draw 12 marks to indicate time intervals	15 minutes
Check code into source control and integrate with existing code	5 minutes

Story 3.2: Draw Label Next to Clock Face

Task	Estimated Time
Code to calculate offset from clock face to draw label	15 minutes
Code to draw label	10 minutes
Check code into source control and integrate with existing code	5 minutes

Story 3.3: Draw Clock Hands

Task	Estimated Time
Code to get time	10 minutes
Code to draw hour hand	15 minutes
Code to draw minute hand	10 minutes
Check code into source control and integrate with existing code	5 minutes

Story 3.4: Update Clock Hands to Reflect Current Time in Selected Time Zone

Task	Estimated Time
Test converting current time when time zone is in summer time savings	20 minutes
Test converting current time when time zone is in standard time	20 minutes
Code to draw clock hands based on converted time (dependent on story 3.3)	10 minutes
Check code into source control and integrate with existing code	5 minutes

Story 3.5: As Time Changes, Redraw Clock Hands to Reflect Current Time in Selected Time Zone

Task	Estimated Time
Thread function which updates clock hands based on current time (dependant on story 3.4)	20 minutes
Check code into source control and integrate with existing code	5 minutes

Based on this task breakdown, Eddie and Pete can get back to Chris, their customer, with some confidence in the estimated timeframes. The timeframes are still estimates, but the developers are happier that they have thought about the job and the tasks to complete. They can also explain that the first thing they need to do is spend half a day understanding how time zone information is stored in the operating system. When they know how the time zones are stored, they can use them in the program.

As you can see, the estimated times for each task are small; all of them except the spike are less than 30 minutes. This is a good indicator that they have got their tasks to the correct level of granularity. If you have several tasks that are four or five hours long, you should think harder about how to break them down. For me, the spike task is still cause for concern. After the customer has had time to review the task breakdowns and give the go ahead on the project, I would break down the spike task further. Let's see how Eddie and Pete go about doing this.

Exercise 3-3: Breaking Down the Subtasks Even Further

To break down the spike task, Eddie and Pete need to think about the approach to take to find the information they are after. There are some likely candidates to find out how they can access the time zone information:

1. .NET Framework support
2. Win32 API
3. Work out how the date and time Control Panel applet works
4. COM controls
5. Windows Registry

Based on the fact they have given themselves 4 hours to come up with some answers, Eddie suggests spending no longer than 45 minutes investigating each area. Because both he and Pete are working on the project, they could each take a different area to investigate. This gives Eddie and Pete a task list for the spiking tasks.

Spiking Tasks

Task	Estimated Time
Investigate .NET support for time zones	45 minutes
Investigate Win32 support for time zones	45 minutes
Work out how the date and time Control Panel applet gets it time zone data	45 minutes
Investigate whether there are any COM controls that provide access to time zone data	45 minutes
Explore the Registry for time zone data	45 minutes

If they come to a dead end before 45 minutes, they can stop and move on to the next area of investigation. Likewise, if they find a mechanism that provides access to the time zone data, they don't need to continue with any of the other spiking tasks.

Eddie and Pete are now ready to start this project with some very tightly defined tasks and outcomes at the end of each task. This tight definition of tasks enables them to move at a fast and furious pace during the working day.

Exercises to Help You Toward Genius

You now understand some of the reasoning behind breaking down stories into extremely focused tasks. This section contains some conversations between you and your customer. Read these conversations, and then try to work out the stories and break them down into tasks. At the end of the book (Appendix I), I provide some possible solutions to these exercises; however, they are not definitive answers. When carrying out the task breakdown, there is not *one right way* to do it, but there are certainly some wrong ways. Remember to keep each story adding one piece of functionality and each task doing just one thing. Each exercise should take you no more than an hour to complete.

Exercise 3-4: The Shopping Cart

Customer: I need a shopping cart for my Web site.

You: Okay, what do you need it to do?

Customer: You know, shopping cart stuff!

You: I guess you need to add items to the cart?

Customer: Of course! And take items out

You: Anything else?

Customer: Yes, I want to have a running total of the value of items in the user's cart.

You: So each user can see his or her own running total?

Customer: Yep.

You: Does the system need to remember what's in my cart the next time I log on?

Customer: No. I don't think so; they can start again.

You: Okay, give me an hour and I'll get you some timeframes and an idea of how we'd go about developing that.

Exercise 3-5: Derived Stock Market Data

 Stock trader (customer): I want to be able to see a set of derived data for my portfolio.

You: Where is your portfolio stored?

Stock trader: I don't know! It's in my software somewhere; I think it saves a file to my disk.

You: Okay, and what do you want calculated?

Stock trader: The open price for the day, the high for the day, the low for the day, the close price for the previous day, and how much I've made on that stock.

You: Hold on. That's too much for me to do at one time; let's go through those one by one, first the open price for the day.

Stock trader: Yes, that's the first price that the stock gets quoted at after the market opens at 9 a.m.

You: So, the high for the day is the highest price the stock is quoted at from the time the market opens till it closes?

Stock trader: Yes, the market closes at 5 p.m.

You: And the low is the lowest price between open and close?

Stock trader: Exactly.

You: The close for the previous day? Is that the price at 5 p.m.?

Stock trader: Pretty much. It's the last quoted price before the market closes.

You: And the last one was how much you've made on the stock?

Stock trader: Yes. My software tells me how much of a stock I've got and how much I paid for it, so you can use that information to work out how much I've made, or lost, on the stock.

You: Okay, I'll have to work out how to get that information from your software.

Stock trader: Great. Well, now you know what I want, tell me how long will it take and how much it will cost me.

You: Give me an hour and I'll get back to you with some estimates.

Exercise 3-6: What's the Weather Like?

Customer: I am running a hot air balloon race around the world and I need to have some way to know what the weather is like in the areas around where the balloons will be.

You: So you want me to write some software that does weather forecasting?

Customer: No! That would be a bit expensive, and the race would probably have finished before you get it right!

You: So what do you want?

Customer: Well, there's all this weather information on the Web, and I thought if we could somehow collate it, it would be really useful for me.

You: You want me to develop a portal site for weather information Web sites around the world?

Customer: Would that be like a Web page where I could click a map of the world and get a weather report for the location I click?

You: Yes, we could do that. Do you have a list of sites that we can use to get the weather from?

Customer: No. I thought you'd know what was best

You: I'll put together a list for you to look through. Is there anything else you need it to do?

Customer: Oh yes, I need to know if there are any severe weather conditions around the world that should be avoided.

You: So you need a list of typhoons, hurricanes, hailstorms, floods?

Customer: Yes. I need to be able to see that list at all times; it must be up-to-date.

You: Okay, let me take all this information away and get back to you with some estimates for delivery times

Customer: Great, I have to dash; I have a race to run. Call me in an hour with what you have.

Exercise 3-7: The Unfinished Solution

Manager (customer): Ah, there you are; I've been looking for you.

You: Why? What do you want?

Manager: Remember Bob was working on that Mailer program?

You: Sure, he seemed to be enjoying doing a .NET project.

Manager: Yes, well he's been pulled off because he knows everything about the C++ code in the TY project.

You: And…?

Manager: I need you to pick up where Bob left off and finish the Mailer program.

You: Okay, can I have a few days with Bob to hand over the project?

Manager: It's too late for that. Bob's already on a plane to HQ to work with the other guys on TY.

You: Oh… so did Bob have a spec or any Use Cases or stories he was working from?

Manager: I don't know. I never saw him write anything down in the entire time I've worked with him. That guy is just so smart he remembers everything you tell him.

You: Great, but I need to know what the software is supposed to do!

Manager: Okay, calm down. I'll go through it with you now. It is a program that enables you to collect a group of contacts together with their e-mail addresses and then send one e-mail that goes to all of them but with different bits being only for certain people on the list.

You: Okay, so do you know how far Bob got?

Manager: Yes, he had built a way of creating a contact, with an e-mail address and a collection of tags, and adding that contact to a collection of contacts. He said it was all stored in an XML file.

You: That's a good start; sounds like each contact has a profile?

Manager: That is the idea.

You: So the next thing to do would be to provide the user with a mechanism to enter an e-mail with tags in it?

Manager: Yes, and then send the e-mail to each person in the contact collection.

You: Only sending each person the tags that included contact details in their profile?

Manager: Yes. How long will that take you to do? Because we need you back on the other project shortly.

You: Let me get back to you on that.

Conclusion

Although this chapter has not focused on anything that is special to .NET, it has introduced you to a technique you should be able to use whenever you are developing software. From the ideas presented, you have hopefully gained an understanding of why XP is often quoted as being a methodology that requires a large dose of self-discipline. You should also have gained some insight as to the value of working closely with your customers to define exactly what they want.

A valuable input that I have received when running through these task breakdown exercises in the classroom is that developers often jump straight into breaking down the problem with the idea of coding the entire solution themselves. The more experienced developers tend to do a search on the Web for any existing tools or components that do some (or even all) of the work for them. Then they can think about how to break down the rest of the work.

I hope you can see the importance of some of the key values emerging from the content of this chapter, with *communication*, *feedback*, *simplicity*, and *respect* all being evident through the dialogues presented. Now you have to find the *courage* to do it yourself at work.

---

[1] I have worked with more than 100 developers in the past two years while consulting with software development teams.

4

Test-Driven Development

TEST-DRIVEN DEVELOPMENT (A.K.A. TEST-FIRST PROGRAMMING) represents an important change to the way most programmers think about writing code. The practice involves writing a test before each new piece of functionality is coded into the system. The preceding chapter hinted at this, with some of the tasks defined as tests.

The tests themselves become part of the software. They are written in the same language that the production code is being written in (in this case, C#). This is a new concept for many developers, and they find it hard to move into the mindset of writing test code before they write "production" code. This chapter emphasizes the need to develop high-quality code and guides you through exercises to reinforce the practices. To help you write the tests, you are going to use NUnit, a freely available testing framework for development with the .NET Framework. Before starting with the exercises and writing the tests, first take a step back and think about how doing so can help you with your job.

 What Is Your Job?

This is a question I often ask my students. Interestingly, nearly everyone responds in the same way: "programmer," "senior developer," "project manager," or "software engineer." I find this interesting because these are smart guys, and yet they are telling me the title of their job and not their job. So when I clarify and ask them, "Okay, so what do you do in this job," the answers I generally get are "develop software," "write code," and "manage projects."

Sometimes I get answers that pertain to the robustness or quality of the code, and occasionally I have a student answer with "to increase the value of the company I work for." When you are developing software or any IP (*intellectual property*) for a company, you are attempting to increase the value of company through your inventions. The IP is an asset for the company, and the reason they hire you is to build the assets. The value of the asset that you are developing depends in part on its quality.

Is It Possible to Write Bug-Free Code?

This is another question I like to ask, and the response is often "no, of course not" or "not with a serious piece of software." So my conclusion is that all these programmers who answer in this way write buggy software. With a belief that it is not possible to write bug-free code, they are setting themselves up for poor quality from day one.

As you learned in Chapter 1, one of the XP practices is playing to win. Playing to win is a mindset. If you play to win, you will believe that it is possible to write bug-free code and will aim for zero-defect solutions. This attitude gives you the edge, but attitude alone will not create bug-free code.

An interesting fact about bug-free code is that as the code is further developed, the bug count in it is less likely to increase than in code that is known to have bugs. Developers are more careful to ensure they do not introduce any errors to a solution that is bug free than they are when the solution is riddled with issues. It is what is known as "broken window syndrome."[1] If a building is in pristine condition, it tends to remain that way; people take better care of it. When one window is broken or a bit of graffiti goes up, however, the building falls into disrepair very rapidly. The same phenomenon exists with code. When code starts to fall into disrepair (has bugs), a typical belief follows that a few more bugs will not make any difference because the code is already broken. Therefore, it is important to keep the quality of the code high all the way through the process.

Increase the Quality of Your Code

To develop zero-defect software, you need some tools and the correct way of thinking about quality. XP champions several practices to increase quality. In my opinion, one of the most powerful tools is unit testing; and by developing the tests before writing the solution code, you are "turning the volume up."[2] Unit testing is not unique to XP, but the proliferation of agile methods, and especially XP, has raised the profile of unit testing in the past few years.

The Big Why

Our eXtreme .NET team is struggling to understand why the tests should be written first. The team turns to Eddie, the XP expert.

Eddie: Test-driven development is really important, so I want to make sure you know why we are writing code this way

Sue: Why do we need tests in our code at all?

Eddie: What is your job? Think hard enough about what we're being paid for here. As a developer, I believe that I should aim to write bug-free code. It is my job to test my code before shipping it, and I know that I can write code that tests my code.

Pete: Isn't that the job of the testers?

Eddie: This is my job, and if you write code, and have any pride in the work you do, then it is your job also. The testers should be there to validate we have written zero-defect code. Any time the testers do find a problem, it is our job to fix that problem and make sure it never happens again. If you don't believe your job is to ensure the work you do is of the highest possible quality, then I would seriously question your integrity and what you are actually doing here at work.

Pete: Panic!

Deepak: Why do we have to write test code?

Eddie: The best way for me as a programmer to validate that a function behaves as I expect is to write some code that tests that function. Writing tests in my code has many advantages for me:

I am less likely to have the code returned to me from the QA department with some negative comments attached.

I am more likely to get a good response from my customer.

With tests in my code, I am more confident that any changes I make don't cause side effects in other parts of the code.

The tests validate my beliefs in how a piece of code is working.

The tests document my theories and beliefs.

The tests give me confidence in the functionality I am providing.

I am happier to share my code with other developers, knowing that the tests will break if they do something that causes my code to fail.

Pete: Why not do manual testing?

Eddie: Manual tests introduce the possibility of human error entering the system, and, if like me, you occasionally get a little lazy you might be tempted to skip some (or all) of the manual tests. Manual tests are much harder to replicate. To replicate manual tests, we would require some documents with steps to take when carrying out the tests. The documents would quickly become out-of-date as the code changes, and that means more work to keep the documents up-to-date. Finally, manual testing is boring, although we can't use this as a good justification for our manager. Why do something manually when we can write some code to do it for us? We are programmers after all; let's use our skills for our own benefit!

Ultimately every piece of software has some aspect of manual testing applied to it in the form of visual checks and validations. Just don't rely on manual testing to provide anything of value for us on a regular basis.

Sue: Why write the test code before the "proper" code?

Eddie: I believe that one word answers most of this question: *focus*. Writing the test code first helps me to focus on writing the simplest code that will make the tests run. The tests define the pre- and post - conditions of a piece or unit of functionality, and this sets the boundaries for the code to be written.

Writing the tests first helps to keep the unit of code being written small and testable. It is an obvious side effect that if we write the tests first, the code we write must be testable because we've already written the tests for it! If we choose to write the tests afterward, we could easily find that we have units of functionality for which it is hard to write tests. We would then need to break the units down into testable units. This effort is wasted if we can avoid it by writing the tests first.

Chris: Why doesn't this whole process cost me more?

Eddie: In my experience, test-driven development has proven to be cheaper for the customer. The tests ensure a higher level of quality from day one. The biggest expense in software development has traditionally been in the maintenance and upgrade stages. The tests embedded in the code reduce each of these costs dramatically. Maintenance becomes easier. Defect diagnosis is aided by a suite of tests in the system. Fixing bugs is far less likely to cause any ill side effects if none of the tests in the system fail. Making an upgrade to a system that has tests will be easier because the whole system can be regression tested for changes in functionality.

This reduction in cost is so large that I believe as more systems get developed that have testing built in to them it will be very difficult for other systems to keep up with the pace of change.

Whole team: Thanks, Eddie.

 Beware The Cheap Customer

A customer who doesn't want to pay for testing is a customer who doesn't want to pay for quality. This doesn't mean they don't want it; it just means they don't want to pay for it! Unless your customer is asking you to knock up a prototype that you will then throw away, you have a customer who wants quality.

Many years ago, when I was far more naïve, I was running a software company. I had a customer who had a proposal for a very interesting project. They asked us to bid for the project, and we put in a proposal to carry out the work. They came back and negotiated the price down, saying they didn't want to pay for the testing; stupidly, we agreed. We put a clause in the contract saying we didn't assure any level of quality with the software produced. Over the course of the next six weeks, we knocked out huge quantities of code that basically did the job. We shipped the code to the customer, who promptly turned around and threatened to sue us because the quality was so poor. The software crashed every so often and wasn't consistently providing the data in a timely manner. We pointed the customer to the clause in the contract and said, "But you didn't want to pay for testing, so we didn't do any; of course it might crash!' After much wasted time and effort, we came to an arrangement where the customer agreed to pay some more for the software to be tested and any bugs fixed.

Needless to say, I learned my lesson (the hard way): I will *never again* allow a customer to drop the price and remove testing from the schedule. If they want to drop the price, a customer must drop functionality. I am not prepared to develop buggy code; it costs too much money, time, and effort in the long run.

Introducing NUnit

Now that you understand the role of test-driven development in producing high-quality code, it is time to get started and put some code together using test-driven development. NUnit is a .NET Framework class library that can locate unit tests that have been written in your project. NUnit comes with a GUI windows application and a console-based application that both enable you to run the tests and see the results. Tests either pass or fail, as indicated by a green or red progress bar, respectively.

Creating a New Project in C# Using NUnit

NUnit (version 2.2) has been written specifically for testing .NET-based applications and is the class library used in this example. To complete this example yourself, you need Visual Studio.Net and NUnit version 2.2 installed on your machine. NUnit is available from http://www.NUnit.org and is free to use.

The aim of the exercise is not to produce a fully functional product, but to demonstrate how to write tests first. The project built through this example is a very simple calculator application, one with the functionality to add, subtract, divide, and multiply positive integers. We started this project in Chapter 3 by breaking down the tasks. Now it is time to code some of those tasks, writing the tests first.

Exercise 4-1: Get NUnit Up and Running

1. Create a new Visual C# project called MiniCalc, using the Windows Application template, as shown in Figure 4-1.

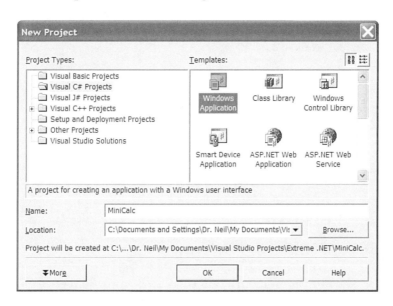

Figure 4-1   A new C# project.

2. In Solution Explorer, right-click References and select Add Reference.

3. Select Browse from the dialog box and go to where you have installed NUnit (the bin directory). Select nunit.framework.dll (see Figure 4-2). If you selected the default install directory for NUnit, it will be in the C:\Program Files\NUnit 2.2\bin folder.

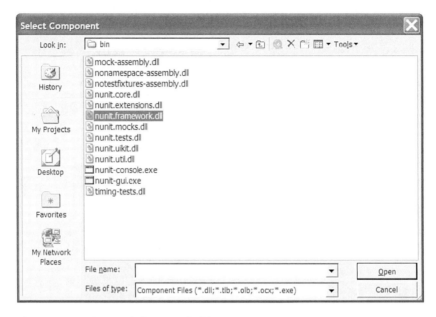

Figure 4-2   Select nunit.framework.dll.

4. Click OK. The nunit.framework will display in your References list (see Figure 4-3).

Figure 4-3   The nunit.framework in your References list.

5. Add a class called **CalcTests** to the project (see Figure 4-4), and place the following code in the class:

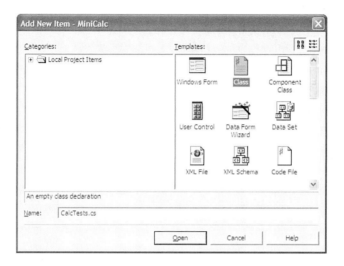

Figure 4-4   Add a class called Calctests.

```csharp
using System;
using NUnit.Framework;

namespace MiniCalc
{

    [TestFixture]
    public class CalcTests
    {
        [SetUp]
        public void SetUp()
        {
            Console.Out.WriteLine("SetUp called");
        }

        [TearDown]
        public void TearDown()
        {
            Console.Out.WriteLine("TearDown called");
        }

        [Test] public void TestThatFails()
        {
            Console.Out.WriteLine("TestThatFails called");
            Assert.Fail("This test is supposed to fail!");
        }

        [Test] public void TestThatSucceeds()
```

```
        {
            Console.Out.WriteLine("TestThatSucceeds called");
            Assert.IsTrue(true, "This test is supposed to succeed!");
        }
    }
}
```

6. Build the solution.

7. Open the NUnit GUI. Choose File > Open from the NUnit menu bar, and browse for the MiniCalc application EXE you just built. You will find it (called MiniCalc.exe) in the bin\debug folder in your project directory.

8. Click the Run button. Two tests will run, one of which will fail (see Figure 4-5).

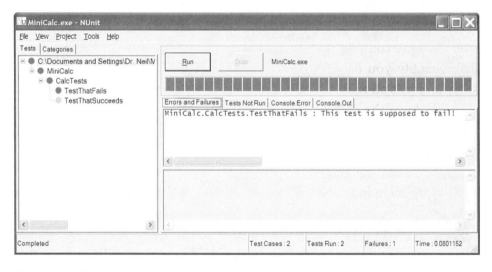

Figure 4-5   The NUnit GUI shows test results.

Consider what we have just done. First, we created a C# project and referenced the core NUnit assembly. This contains the definitions for classes and interfaces to support the NUnit testing framework.

Then we created a class called CalcTests and decorated this with the TestFixture attribute. A fixture usually consists of methods that are somehow related, often by their functionality or resource requirements. Usually, I write a test fixture for each class I am testing. Classes with the TestFixture attribute will be the building blocks of your testing infrastructure.

You can see two other important attributed methods, SetUp and TearDown; these methods will be called directly before and after (respectively) each test method is invoked. In the SetUp method, resources that are required for each of the test methods in the fixture can be initialized. In the TearDown method, they can be cleaned up. The TearDown method will always get called after a test even if the test fails or throws an exception. This is important because it enables us to clean up and make sure the test will not affect other tests even if it fails.

Then we actually get to create some test methods, albeit rather simple ones for now. The TestThatFails and TestThatSucceeds methods are tests to get us started, and give us something to prove that we have got the framework up and running. We'll start putting some real test code together in the next exercise. Notice these methods are decorated with the Test attribute, which identifies them to the NUnit framework as NUnit test methods.

After you have compiled this application, you can run the NUnit GUI and browse for the assembly you have just built (MiniCalc.exe). NUnit GUI then loads that assembly and lists all the types that support the TestFixture attribute. In this example, we only have the one CalcTests class. When you click the Run button, each method in the Fixture will be run, proceeded by the SetUp method and followed by the TearDown method. If you examine the output in the Console Out tab, you can see the order in which these methods are being called. You can also run tests individually by clicking them in the tree view on the left side of the window.

Exercise 4-2: Write a Test and Add Some Functionality

In this example, we start to add some functionality to the MiniCalc program, taking you through the process one step at a time so that you get the idea of how to write code, tests first.

We are going to build a very simple calculator application, with addition, subtraction, multiplication, and division functionality for positive integers. This example is fairly simple but provides some insight into how to go about building tests for your project.

1. We create a new method in our CalcTests class to test addition. As we write this method, we believe that we should encapsulate all our calculation methods in a class, so we create a Calculator class. Notice that we haven't actually created the class yet; we have just made some calls to use it. What we have done is defined the need for a Calculator class and required that it support the Add method. We have also defined how the Add method is expected to behave under a set of conditions, including an exception we would like to have thrown when the method is called illegally.

   This code will not compile because we have not defined the Calculator class or the exception. It is important to understand that when we write code the test-driven way, we do not define the classes or the methods we are going to need until after we have written a test that requires them. (Notice we have introduced a new type of assertion, the Assert.AreEqual method.)

```
[Test] public void TestAdd()
{
    Console.Out.WriteLine("TestAddition called");
    Calculator testCalc = new Calculator();
    //test for case of zeros'
    Assert.AreEqual(0, testCalc.Add(0, 0),
        "Adding 0 to 0 should produce 0");
    //test that param ordering isn't important
    Assert.AreEqual(1, testCalc.Add(1, 0),
        "Adding 1 to 0 should produce 1");
    Assert.AreEqual(1, testCalc.Add(0, 1),
        "Adding 0 to 1 should produce 1");
    //test for non zero case
    Assert.AreEqual(3, testCalc.Add(1, 2),
        "Adding 1 to 2 should produce 3");
    int nResult;
    try
    {
        nResult = testCalc.Add(int.MaxValue,
            int.MaxValue);
        Assert.Fail
            ("Should throw a ResultOutofRangeException");
    }
    catch (ResultOutOfRangeException)
    {
    }

    testCalc = null;
}
```

2. The next step is to build the skeleton code so that our program can compile. We need to define the Calculator class and the exception. First, we add a new class file called Calculator.cs. In this file, we then write the following code to define everything we need for the code to compile. Do not do anything other than make the code compile for now.

   Notice that I have also removed the constructor for the Calculator class. Code that does nothing is useless; so, we stick with the XP value of simplicity and just remove it.

```
using System;

namespace MiniCalc
{
    public class ResultOutOfRangeException:ApplicationException
    {
    }

    public class Calculator
    {
        public int Add(int a, int b)
        {
            return 0;
        }
    }
}
```

3. In the CalcTests class, we can now remove the TestThatFails and the TestThat-Succeeds methods.

4. You can now compile this program and run it through NUnit again. It compiles, but the test does not succeed. In fact, the first assertion in our TestAdd method does succeed! It is the second assertion that fails. After a test method has a failed assertion, NUnit doesn't carry on running any of the other code in that method. We are now in an excellent position to start writing our Add method; we need to work through the method, writing just enough code to make the test pass, and then we are done.

   Seeing the tests fail is part of the process. Sometimes you will find yourself in the fortunate position of writing a test and it passing before you have written any production code. I say "fortunate" because this teaches you that either the system is already doing something you want or that your test is not testing what you think it is testing. You are fortunate in that you have learned something.

5. First we do the simplest thing and add the parameters together and return the result. In the Add method we just created in the Calculator class, change the code as shown here.

```
public int Add(int a, int b)
{
    return a + b;
}
```

6. When we run this using the NUnit GUI, we see that it passes the first four assertions but fails in the try block.

We now have two choices: We can either change the test code to expect the .NET Framework exception or write some code to make sure we are throwing our own exception. I would lean toward the latter option. We have defined how we want to see the method behave, and there is a reason we defined the method to behave that way. We have defined a contract of behavior between the class and the consumer.

Therefore, we will change the Add method to reflect how we want it to behave.

```
public int Add(int a, int b)
{
    int result;
    result = a + b;

    if (result < 0)
    {
        ResultOutOfRangeException rangeEx =
            new ResultOutOfRangeException();
        throw rangeEx;
    }
    return result;
}
```

7. Now run the NUnit tests again, and you will see the bar go green. We have written the test and the code to pass the test. We're done (for this function).

We have built and tested one piece of functionality, the Add method. Now we want to actually call that method from the user interface.

Exercise 4-3: Plug the Business Logic into the User Interface

1. Add the user interface as shown in Figure 4-6 to the existing Windows Form in the project.

Figure 4-6 Add the user interface.

The controls I have added are as follows:

Two NumericUpDown controls called NumberA and NumberB

One label with the text +

One button called EqualsButton and the text =

One label called Result (showing the 3 in the figure)

2. Double-click the EqualsButton control to generate the event handler. In this click event, place the following code.

```
private void EqualsButton_Click(object sender,
    System.EventArgs e)
{
    try
    {
        Calculator calc  = new Calculator();
        Result.Text =
            (calc.Add((int)NumberA.Value,
            (int)NumberB.Value).ToString());
    }
    catch (ResultOutOfRangeException)
    {
        Result.Text = "Out of Range";
    }
}
```

Notice how none of the business logic resides inside this method; it just calls the Add method (which has been tested) and places the result on the GUI. Run it and see.

You may be asking a Why question now. Why do this? Why not just put the code in the button event handler? There are a couple of very good reasons: First, it is easier to test code that is detached from a user interface. Second, it is good programming practice to have a thin user interface layer. Suppose, for example, that we want to expose the functionality through a different kind of interface, such as the command line. It is now easy for us to reuse the business logic (addition) in a different interface. Test-driven development is helping us to write better object-oriented code. That has got to be a good thing.

Exercise 4-4: Plug the Business Logic into a Different User Interface

In this exercise, we expose our functionality through a command-line interface.

1. Change the code in the Main method of the MiniCalc form to read as follows:

```
static void Main()
{
    int nA, nB;
    string result;
    Console.Out.WriteLine("Welcome to Mini Calc");
    Console.Out.WriteLine("Please enter the first number to add");
    nA = Convert.ToInt32(Console.In.ReadLine());
    Console.Out.WriteLine("Please enter the second number to add");
    nB = Convert.ToInt32(Console.In.ReadLine());
    try
    {
        Calculator calc = new Calculator();
        result = (calc.Add(nA, nB)).ToString();
    }
    catch (ResultOutOfRangeException)
    {
        result = "Out of Range";
    }
    Console.Out.WriteLine(result);
}
```

2. Change the project properties. (Right-click the project in Solution Explorer.) Set the Output Type to be a Console Application.

3. Rebuild the project and run it from the command line. You have now reused the fully tested business logic of the Add method in a different user interface.

When developing software using tests, one of the rules is this: If you can think of a way of breaking it, write a test to prove that you can break it. Then write the code to make the test pass. At this stage, you can probably think of a few ways of breaking this code. However, the one that we explore here is the fact that we can add negative numbers in our Add method, even though the requirement was for a very simple calculator application with addition, subtraction, multiplication, and division functionality for *positive* integers. Let's now write a test that breaks it.

Exercise 4-5: Write a Test to Fix a Bug

1. In the CalcTests class, add a method called **TestAddNegatives**.

```
[Test] public void TestAddNegatives()
{
    Console.Out.WriteLine("TestAddNegatives called");
    Calculator testCalc = new Calculator();
    int nResult;

    try
    {
        nResult = testCalc.Add(-1, 0);
        Assert.Fail(
            "Should throw a NegativeParameterException");
    }
    catch (NegativeParameterException )
    {   }

    try
    {
        nResult = testCalc.Add(0, -1);
        Assert.Fail(
            "Should throw a NegativeParameterException");
    }
    catch (NegativeParameterException)
    {   }

    try
    {
        nResult =
```

```
        testCalc.Add(int.MinValue, int.MinValue);
      Assert.Fail(
        "Should throw a NegativeParameterException");
    }
    catch (NegativeParameterException)
    {   }

    testCalc = null;
  }
```

2. Notice that we have added a new exception type, so the code will not compile. Remember we must have a class or method used in a test before we define it. This keeps the code as simple as possible. To make the code compile, we need to create that exception type in the Calculator class file.

```
public class NegativeParameterException:ApplicationException
{
}
```

3. Now the code will compile, and you can run the tests in NUnit GUI again. The test should fail, as expected. (If you are following along with these exercises, make sure you do run the tests; it is good practice.) Now we can set about writing the code to fix it. Note: It's running the tests that is the good practice, not the tests themselves (well, the tests are part of it).

```
public int Add(int a, int b)
{
    int result;
    if (a < 0 || b < 0 )
    {
        NegativeParameterException npEx =
            new NegativeParameterException();
        throw npEx;
    }

    result = a + b;

    if (result < 0)
    {
        ResultOutOfRangeException rangeEx =
            new ResultOutOfRangeException();
```

```
        throw rangeEx;
    }
    return result;
}
```

4. Compile the program and run the tests again. When you see the bar go green, we're done. We spotted a way to break it, we wrote a test to prove we could break it, and then we fixed the code so that the tests all run.

Actually, however, we are not quite finished here yet; we now have some duplicate code in our tests. We can take out the creation of the Calculator object that is shared in both the tests and place it in the SetUp method. We can do the same with the freeing of the object in the TearDown method. After this small change, your CalcTests class should appear something like this.

```csharp
[TestFixture]
public class CalcTests
{
    private Calculator testCalc;
    private int nResult;

    [SetUp]
    public void SetUp()
    {
        Console.Out.WriteLine("SetUp called");
        testCalc = new Calculator();
    }

    [TearDown]
    public void TearDown()
    {
        Console.Out.WriteLine("TearDown called");
        testCalc = null;
    }

    [Test] public void TestAdd()
    {
        Console.Out.WriteLine("TestAddition called");
        //test for case of zeros'
        Assert.AreEqual(0, testCalc.Add(0, 0),
            "Adding 0 to 0 should produce 0");
        //test that param ordering isn't important
        Assert.AreEqual(1, testCalc.Add(1, 0),
            "Adding 1 to 0 should produce 1");
```

```
        Assert.AreEqual(1, testCalc.Add(0, 1),
            "Adding 0 to 1 should produce 1");
        //test for non zero case
        Assert.AreEqual(3, testCalc.Add(1, 2),
            "Adding 1 to 2 should produce 3");
        try
        {
            nResult = testCalc.Add(int.MaxValue,
                int.MaxValue);
            Assert.Fail
                ("Should throw a ResultOutofRangeException");
        }
        catch (ResultOutOfRangeException)
        {
        }
    }

    [Test] public void TestAddNegatives()
    {
        Console.Out.WriteLine("TestAddNegatives called");

        try
        {
            nResult = testCalc.Add(-1, 0);
            Assert.Fail(
                "Should throw a NegativeParameterException");
        }
        catch (NegativeParameterException )
        {    }

        try
        {
            nResult = testCalc.Add(0, -1);
            Assert.Fail(
                "Should throw a NegativeParameterException");
        }
        catch (NegativeParameterException)
        {    }

        try
        {
            nResult =
                testCalc.Add(int.MinValue, int.MinValue);
            Assert.Fail(
                "Should throw a NegativeParameterException");
        }
        catch (NegativeParameterException)
```

```
    {    }

  }
}
```

Now we are ready to expand the functionality and add subtraction to the system, so the first thing to write is, you guessed it, a test for the (as yet unwritten) Subtract method.

Exercise 4-6: Write a Test and Then Add Another Function

1. Add a new method to the CalcTests class called **TestSubtract**.

```
[Test] public void TestSubtract()
{
    Assert.AreEqual(0, testCalc.Subtract(0, 0),
        "Subtracting 0 from 0 should produce 0");
    Assert.AreEqual(1, testCalc.Subtract(0, 1),
                "Subtracting 0 from 1 should produce 1");

    try
    {
        nResult = testCalc.Subtract(1, 0);
        Assert.Fail(
    "Subtracting 1 from 0 should throw a ResultOutofRangeException");
    }
    catch (ResultOutOfRangeException)
    {    }

    Assert.AreEqual(0,
        testCalc.Subtract(int.MaxValue, int.MaxValue),
        "Subtracting max value from max value should produce 0");

    try
    {
        nResult = testCalc.Subtract(-1, 0);
        Assert.Fail(
            "Should throw a NegativeParameterException");
    }
    catch (NegativeParameterException)
    {    }

    try
    {
        nResult = testCalc.Subtract(0, -1);
```

```
        Assert.Fail(
            "Should throw a NegativeParameterException");
    }
    catch (NegativeParameterException)
    {    }

    try
    {
        nResult = testCalc.Subtract(int.MinValue,
            int.MinValue);
        Assert.Fail(
            "Should throw a NegativeParameterException");
    }
    catch (NegativeParameterException)
    {    }
}
```

2. Again we have written code that will not compile; we need to add a skeleton method to the Calculator class.

```
public int Subtract(int numberToSubtract,
        int subtractFrom )
{
    return 0;
}
```

3. Now we can compile the code and run the tests. As expected, the bar goes red, indicating that the TestSubtract method has failed. We are in the position of knowing that if we write just enough code to make this test pass, we can declare we're done.

```
public int Subtract(int numberToSubtract,
        int subtractFrom )
{
    int result;
    if (subtractFrom < 0 || numberToSubtract < 0 )
    {
        NegativeParameterException npEx =
            new NegativeParameterException();
        throw npEx;
    }

    result = subtractFrom - numberToSubtract;
    if (result < 0)
```

```
    {
        ResultOutOfRangeException rangeEx =
            new ResultOutOfRangeException();
        throw rangeEx;
    }
    return result;
}
```

4. Compile the program and run the tests through NUnit again. They should all pass.

If you are being observant, at this point you should notice there is some more duplicate code. The check for negative parameters occurs at the top of both the Add and Subtract methods. This can be extracted out into its own method.

Exercise 4-7: Write a Test and Then Extract the Method

1. Before we can just change the code, we should write a test so that we can validate that the functionality we have extracted does what we want it to do. Therefore, in the CalcTests class, add a method called **TestCheckForNegativeNumbers**.

```
[Test] public void TestCheckForNegativeNumbers()
{
    try
    {
        testCalc.CheckForNegativeNumbers(0, 0);
    }
    catch (NegativeParameterException)
    {
        Assert.Fail("Zeros are not negative numbers");
    }

    try
    {
        testCalc.CheckForNegativeNumbers(1, 1);
    }
    catch (NegativeParameterException)
    {
        Assert.Fail("1's are not negative numbers");
    }

    try
    {
```

```
        testCalc.CheckForNegativeNumbers(
            int.MaxValue, int.MaxValue);
    }
    catch (NegativeParameterException)
    {
        Assert.Fail("Max Vals are not negative numbers");
    }

    try
    {
        testCalc.CheckForNegativeNumbers(-1, -1);
        Assert.Fail("-1's are negative numbers");
    }
    catch (NegativeParameterException)
    {    }

    try
    {
        testCalc.CheckForNegativeNumbers(
        int.MinValue, int.MinValue);
        Assert.Fail("Min Vals are negative numbers");
    }
    catch (NegativeParameterException)
    {    }
}
```

2. Again we have defined a function name and declared its behavior before we have written a line of code for that function. So the next thing to do is write a skeleton for that function in the Calculator class.

```
public void CheckForNegativeNumbers (int a, int b)
{    }
```

3. Now you can compile and run the tests again. The test we just wrote should fail, as expected. So we need to fill in the CheckForNegativeNumbers method. We have the code for this already in the other two methods, so we should be able to copy and paste[3] it from the Add method into the new method.

```
public void CheckForNegativeNumbers (int a, int b)
{
    if (a < 0 || b < 0 )
    {
        NegativeParameterException npEx =
```

```
        new NegativeParameterException();
    throw npEx;
    }
}
```

4. Recompile the program and run the tests again; they should all pass this time. Now you can confidently replace the duplicated code in the Add and Subtract methods with a call to a method that you know has been tested. So the Add method will change from this:

```
public int Add(int a, int b)
{
    int result;

    if (a < 0 ||  b < 0 )
    {
        NegativeParameterException npEx =
            new NegativeParameterException();
        throw npEx;
    }
    .
    .
    . .
}
```

To this:

```
public int Add(int a, int b)
{
    int result;

    CheckForNegativeNumbers (a, b);
    .
    .
    .
}
```

5. After you have replaced the code with a call to the new CheckForNegative Numbers method, compile and run the tests again to ensure that we have not broken any of our tested functionality in the Add and Subtract methods.

Exercise 4-8: Add the UI for Subtraction

1. All that's left to do now is hook up the UI to the Subtract method. First, make sure the project settings are changed back to build a Windows application and the main method is changed back to call the Application.Run method with a new instance of the form. To allow both addition and subtraction, you can modify the form to include radio buttons to enable the user to choose what type of calculation to do (see Figure 4-7). Name the radio buttons **AddRButton** and **SubtractRButton**.

Figure 4-7 Add radio buttons.

2. You can then change the code in the Equals button click event to accommodate this.

```
private void EqualsButton_Click(object sender,
    System.EventArgs e)
{
    try
    {
        Calculator calc  = new Calculator();
        if (AddRButton.Checked)
        {
            Result.Text =
                (calc.Add((int)NumberA.Value,
                (int)NumberB.Value).ToString());
        }
        else
        {
            Result.Text =
                (calc.Subtract((int)NumberB.Value,
                (int)NumberA.Value).ToString());
        }
    }
    catch (ResultOutOfRangeException)
    {
        Result.Text = "Out of Range";
```

```
        }
        catch (NegativeParameterException)
        {
            Result.Text = "Negatives not allowed";
        }
    }
}
```

3. Compile the program and run it. You should be able to add and subtract positive integers. Remember that we have to put the project properties back to compile this as a Windows application, and you'll need to change the Main method back to create and run the form.

```
static void Main()
{
    Application.Run(new Form1());
}
```

Also note that because the minimum value of the NumericUpDown controls is zero, you cannot actually enter an invalid negative number. If you want to test this, you need to change the minimum value property of the controls.

We are not quite finished yet. The GUI layer is starting to get a bit "smelly[4]"; there is functionality that might break and that is not tested. This functionality can be taken out of the GUI layer and into the Calculator class.

Exercise 4-9: Extract Functionality Out of the UI Layer

1. Let's start by factoring out the decision of which type of calculation to perform. If we create a method in the Calculator to perform more than one type of calculation, we need to somehow define which calculation to do, addition or subtraction. This seems like a good case for introducing an enumerated type. We'll start by building the test for this new method.

```
[Test]
public void TestCalculate()
{
    Assert.AreEqual(2,
        testCalc.Calculate(1, CalcOperation.Add, 1),
```

```
            "Adding 1 to 1 failed");
        Assert.AreEqual(0,
            testCalc.Calculate(1, CalcOperation.Subtract, 1),
                "Subtracting 1 from 1 failed");
    }
```

2. Again, this won't compile. We need to put some skeleton code in the Calculator class file. Starting with the new enumerated type we have introduced, create this in the Calculator.s file but outside of the class.

```
public enum CalcOperation
{
    Add = 0,
    Subtract = 1,
}
```

Then add the framework for the Calculate function in the Calculator class.

```
public int Calculate(int a, CalcOperation op, int b)
{
    return 0;
}
```

3. Now we can compile and run the tests in NUnit. You can see the output provided by the Assert.AreEqual statement when it fails.

4. Next we can move the logic for the Calculate function from the GUI layer.

```
public int Calculate(int a, CalcOperation op, int b)
{
    int nResult = 0;
    if (CalcOperation.eAdd == op)
    {
        nResult = Add(a, b);
    }
    else if (CalcOperation.eSubtract == op)
    {
        nResult = Subtract(b, a);
    }
    return nResult;
}
```

5. Compile and run the tests. They should pass. Now we can call this method from the UI.

```
private void EqualsButton_Click(object sender,
        System.EventArgs e)
{
    try
    {
        Calculator calc  = new Calculator();
        CalcOperation op = new CalcOperation();
        if (AddRButton.Checked)
        {
            op = CalcOperation.Add;
        }
        else
        {
            op = CalcOperation.Subtract;
        }
        Result.Text = calc.Calculate((int)NumberA.Value,
            op, (int)NumberB.Value).ToString();
    }
    catch (ResultOutOfRangeException)
    {
        Result.Text = "Out of Range";
    }
    catch (NegativeParameterException)
    {
        Result.Text = "Negatives not allowed";
    }
}
```

6. You can simplify this further by changing the operation to be performed in the radio button handlers. To do this, you must make the local CalcOperation type a member of the Form class.

```
private CalcOperation op = CalcOperation.Add;
```

Then you must add new methods to handle the radio buttons being clicked.

```
private void AddRButton_CheckedChanged(object sender,
    System.EventArgs e)
{
    if (AddRButton.Checked)
```

```
    {
        op = CalcOperation.Add;
    }
}

private void SubtractRButton_CheckedChanged(object sender,
    System.EventArgs e)
{
    if (SubtractRButton.Checked)
    {
        op = CalcOperation.Subtract;
    }
}
```

Finally, you can further simplify the handler method for the Equals button.

```
private void EqualsButton_Click(object sender,
      System.EventArgs e)
{
    try
    {
        Calculator calc  = new Calculator();
        Result.Text = calc.Calculate((int)NumberA.Value,
            op, (int)NumberB.Value).ToString();
    }
    catch (ResultOutOfRangeException)
    {
        Result.Text = "Out of Range";
    }
    catch (NegativeParameterException)
    {
        Result.Text = "Negatives not allowed";
    }
}
```

In this set of exercises, we have started from scratch building a project using test-driven development principles. By now, you should understand that there is a cycle to this kind of development:

1. Decide what unit of functionality you are going to build (design); this could also be fixing a bug.

2. Write some test code.

3. Write skeleton code to allow a compile.

4. Compile and run the tests. (They should fail.)

5. Fill in the skeleton with enough code to pass the tests.

6. Compile and run the tests. If the tests fail, go back to Step 5.

7. Simplify the code where possible; this may involve Steps 1 through 6 again.

8. You're done. Take a break and start again!

Each step in the cycle is simple to do, and at the end of the cycle you should have added one unit of functionality (or fixed one bug) that has tests that pass. You can then move on with programming other units of functionality with more confidence.

How Do You Feel About TDD?

For the next exercise, we are going to build the same program twice. First, we are going to build the program without doing any tests, and then we are going to build the same program writing the tests first. We will then see how we feel about each program.

We are going to write some code to calculate some derived data from stock price data that is passed to our code. We are going to write a class library to encapsulate the calculations for other developers to use.

The library has to take a collection of prices and timestamps for a stock price and return the high and low prices for a given date. The collection is in the form of a HashTable containing DateTime objects mapping to double values to represent time-stamps mapping to prices.

Exercise 4-10: Without Tests

I provide the skeleton for you, and then you can finish the exercise. This exercise should not take more than 30 minutes to complete.

1. Start by creating a new C# project using the class library template called **NoTests**.

2. Change the name of the class that is created for you from Class1.cs to **Calc-Class.cs**.

3. In the CalcClass.cs file, change the code to read as follows.

```
using System;
using System.Collections.Specialized;
```

```
namespace NoTests
{
    public class CalcClass
    {
        public void CalcHighLow(Hashtable DatePriceList,
            DateTime day, ref decimal high, ref decimal low)
        {
        }
    }
}
```

4. Now write the code to calculate the high and low values, but do not write any tests! Good luck.

Exercise 4-11: With Tests

We are now going to do the same project again, this time by writing tests first. I will get you started, and then you can finish the exercise yourself. This exercise should not take you more than 30 minutes to complete.

1. Create a new C# project using the class library template called **WithTests**.
2. Rename the generated class file from Class1.cs to **CalcClass.cs.**
3. Change the code in the CalcClass.cs file to read as follows.

```
using System;

namespace CsWithTests
{
    public class CalcClass
    {
    }
}
```

4. Add a reference to the Nunit.Framework.dll file.
5. Add a new class called **CalcTests**.
6. In the CalcTests class, enter the following code.

```
using System;
using System.Collections;
using NUnit.Framework;
```

```
namespace CsWithTests
{
    [TestFixture]
    public class CalcTests
    {
        [Test]
        public void TestCalcHighLow()
        {
            Hashtable datePriceList;
            DateTime day;
            Decimal high;
            Decimal low;
            CalcClass calc;

            //calc.CalcHighLow(datePriceList, day, high, low);
        }
    }
}
```

7. Now you can fill in the test code yourself and then build the CalcHighLow function in the CalcClass function to make sure the tests pass. Good luck!

Confidence Test

How do you feel after completing the last two exercises? Which class library are you more confident is correct?

If you have built meaningful tests, you should feel very confident with the second library. Even if you do not believe you have put much effort into the tests in the second exercise, the very fact that you have some means of validating your code should give you some extra level of certainty.

Visual Studio.NET 2005 Team System

The next version of Visual Studio.NET will be available in several flavors. A group of these flavors is called Visual Studio.NET 2005 Team System. This group is aimed at the enterprise development community. Two of the products in this group will include an integrated unit-testing framework. This framework will be similar to NUnit. The two products that include the unit testing will be Visual Studio Team Developer and Visual Studio Team Tester.

The beta of Visual Studio 2005 Team System indicates that the attributes you have learned in NUnit will differ slightly:

- TestFixture is called TestClass.

- Test is called TestMethod.

- SetUp is called TestInitialize.

- TearDown is called TestCleanup.

The lessons you have learned in this chapter will all still hold true. It will be easy to move from NUnit to the unit-testing system in Visual Studio.NET Team System.

The current plans indicate that the unit-testing tools will not be shipped with other versions of Visual Studio.NET 2005. Testing is a cornerstone of the XP practices. Testing is important to all the practices in this book. Is Microsoft making a mistake by not shipping unit-testing tools with all the versions of Visual Studio?

Conclusion

This chapter has introduced you to test-driven development, which is without a doubt one of the most important practices of XP. These tests underpin many of the practices in XP, such as refactoring, short releases, continuous integration, pair programming, and collective ownership.

The tests were intended to increase your confidence in the code you are writing. If you follow the test-driven development methodology and are a member of a team of developers who are all writing tests, you will have more confidence in their code, and they will have more confidence in your code. The outcome of this is that you can now move forward more quickly and tackle problems more aggressively.

You should now see the reason this practice is called test-driven development. The tests are driving the development process. By writing the tests first, you should find your focus on the code you are writing changes substantially. Your goal now is to define how the class will be used with a test method and then to get the tests to pass. You will learn about more testing techniques later in the book.

This chapter simplified the code in several places. The next chapter explores the practice of refactoring. Refactoring provides techniques for simplifying code.

[1] Gladwell, Malcolm. *The Tipping Point*. Boston, Massachusetts: Back Bay Books, 2002.

[2] "Turning the volume up" means taking something that works well and making it work even better.

[3] Copy and paste is often referred to as *editor inheritance* by parts of the developer community.

[4] A code smell is a term used in XP to define code that has something amiss. XP teams will call code smelly when it can be improved.

■ 5 ■
Refactoring

L IKE TEST-DRIVEN DEVELOPMENT, refactoring is a mindset that can be best achieved by doing it and understanding what has been gained from the process. Martin Fowler's book, *Refactoring: Improving the Design of Existing Code* (Addison-Wesley, 1999), is the most complete resource to date, and I have no interest in competing with it. This chapter instead presents scenarios in which refactoring the code leads to a dramatic improvement in the readability, lowers the cost of change, and increases the quality of the code produced. These scenarios take the form of step-by-step exercises.

What Is Refactoring

Refactoring is changing the structure of existing code without changing the behavior of that code. A refactoring (noun) is one particular (usually small) well-defined change that is made to the structure of the code. When developers are refactoring (verb) code, they are applying one or more refactorings (noun) to their code; they are making one or more changes to the code's structure.

The changes are made to the code to improve the design, with the aim of making the code easier to read, simpler to understand, and cheaper to change. In Chapter 4, we simplified the code and removed code duplication several times. We were refactoring the code.

Do It As You Go

In XP, refactoring is done after each new piece of functionality is added to the system. The aim is to write the tests, write the code to get the tests running, and then simplify the code by refactoring. This cycle of activities is then repeated over and over again for each new function added to the system. By carrying out this constant refactoring, the changes made each time will be small and few, and so they should also be easy to do.

The Importance of Tests

If you are not working in an XP environment, you can still reap some benefits from using refactoring, but I strongly recommend you do this only if you have tests in place. The tests will validate that when you carry out refactorings you have not changed the behavior of the software. The tests are your safety net.

The Benefits

It is important to understand the benefits that you should expect to see from performing refactoring on your code as you develop it. Refactoring is certainly no "silver bullet," but Martin Fowler describes refactoring as "a pair of silver pliers that helps you get a good grip on your code."

Refactoring is an important tool for all programmers to have in their toolboxes. There will always be certain points in any software project where the structure of the code needs to be changed, and the refactoring tool can be used for this.

By continually refactoring and using the test-code-refactor approach to developing code, you will see patterns[1] emerge in the code. This enables you (the developer) to work with these emerging patterns and further improve the structure of your code.

Always being on the look out for changes that will improve the structure of your code will force you to be reviewing the code. By constantly reviewing the code, you will be getting a deeper understanding of how the code works and what it is doing. Without knowing the code, it is much harder to refactor it.

Let's look at how refactoring works with the XP values we discussed in Chapter 1.

Feedback

The ability to refactor your code takes the pressure off the design phase of software development. Formal methods (such as waterfall) advocate developing a perfect design before any code is written. In the real world, perfect design upfront is impossible because during the implementation of the code you will learn lessons that affect the design.

Refactoring enables you to change the design of the code at a later stage. This means that you do not have to get the design absolutely right before you write any code. You can get a rough design worked out, code it up, and then if (when) you spot a better design you can refactor your code toward the better design.

Refactoring enables you to get started on the coding earlier than you might have been able to otherwise. Getting started earlier enables you to get feedback on the progress from other coders and even customers at an earlier time. This feedback is valuable because it might force you to rethink the original design. The earlier you rethink designs, the higher your chances are of getting the final result that the customer wants.

Communication

Some of the refactorings we will do in this chapter do nothing more than improve the readability of the code. The benefit in the short term is that other programmers will find it easier to work with the code. In the medium to long term, more-readable code is easier to understand and therefore easier to maintain.

Simplicity

By simplifying your code through refactoring, you get the immediate benefit to the development team of having less to understand. This in turn improves the quality of the code. Bugs often result because of misunderstanding existing code and writing code that causes existing code to break.

Some More Big "Why" Questions

Our eXtreme .NET team has gathered together again to question Eddie about refactoring.

Sue: Why not just get it right the first time?

Eddie: It is very rare for any piece of software to be developed "right the first time." I should qualify that by adding that every programmer I have ever spoken to has said that if given a second opportunity to code a solution they would do it differently. I have met a few arrogant individuals who claim they are so smart they always code the correct solution the first time. Personally, I don't believe they can always be right, and even if they are, they are in a very small minority. Most of us need all the help we can get to ensure we get a good piece of software written. Refactoring is some of that help; it allows us to admit that we are less than perfect and provides us with a tool to enable us to work toward perfection over time.

Deepak: Why not just start again if you know it's wrong?

Pete: Yeah! If we know we will always do a better job the second time around, why don't we build a throwaway prototype and then start again when we have learned the lessons to be gained from this?

Eddie: There are development methods that use this approach, and they appear to work well because the developers can make mistakes in the first version and learn from these mistakes. The problem in my mind is this: Where is the cutoff point? At what stage should we stop prototyping and start building the real application? There are always lessons to be learned as we develop a system.

Chris: If you have the time to build the entire system first and then throw it away and start again, then you are in an enviable position. We are not in that position!

Eddie: Right, most of us developers are working under tight time constraints, and we need some way to incorporate the lessons we are learning back into the code being developed. Refactoring is a mechanism that allows this constant learning to be fed back into improving the software. The prototyping approach doesn't scale when adding new feature to an existing system; it is not feasible to recode the entire solution every time a new feature has to be added. Refactoring allows existing software to be scaled and enhanced over time.

Pete: Why can't I just refactor at the end of the project?

Eddie: So, we can do bigger code "tidy ups" at the end of the project or large periods of coding, but we will lose the benefits to be gained by constantly refactoring. I am not sure I would call this refactoring either. Refactoring is making small changes through the project. By constantly refactoring, we are making the next piece of work we do potentially easier. We will also see patterns emerge more rapidly, and we can then work with those patterns to make the code easier to understand.

Deepak: Why does this help me develop more robust code?

Eddie: Refactoring forces us to review the code we have written and look for ways to simplify it. The very fact that we are reviewing the code is a good starting point for increasing the quality of our software. It has been shown time and time again that code reviews are valuable for improving the code quality. Many of the refactoring techniques that you will learn have been developed because they do enforce robustness in the code. For example, one refactoring replaces an enumerated type with an object hierarchy. This introduces a level of type safety not previously present in the code.

Time to Tidy Your Code

In the early 1990s, I was working on a software project in C; at the end of each deliverable (usually every month), I would spend a few days "tidying up my code." My boss was not overjoyed by this, but I was so insistent about it being important that he let me carry on; he was a smart boss! The tidying up meant that I could get the code into better shape for building the next deliverable, and I have no doubt that helped the project succeed. This tidying up was really a big refactoring exercise. I could see patterns in the software that needed to be improved so the next stage would be easier to develop. Although I insisted on spending three or four days doing this refactoring, I actually didn't like it much. It is boring to spend four days moving code around and not get any new functionality into the system. I did it because, like cleaning the car windows, I wanted to see where I was going more clearly. By doing constant refactoring at the end of each test-code cycle, I was spreading the boredom out into smaller chunks of refactoring throughout the development process.

Why Should I Do It When No One Else Does?

This is not a question that has much to do with refactoring but more to do with team dynamics; however, with refactoring, the question comes up more often than other techniques because developers believe they are spending time refactoring "other peoples' code," and see this as unfair. A common cry I hear is this: "Why can't they refactor their own code?"

My opinion is that when you are working as part of a team, the goal is for the team to succeed, not individuals. If this means I spend more of my time refactoring "other people's code" than they do and that refactoring is making the system easier to develop and maintain, then I am adding value to the team. If I ignore code that would be better refactored, I am doing damage to the team. Ideally, the whole team will be refactoring their code. If they are not, however, I still want to add as much value to the team as I possibly can, so I refactor code even when those around me don't.

Why Do Something That Doesn't Add Any New Features to the Code?

All the answers I have given to the previous questions contribute to answer this one question. Refactoring does not add any new features to the code, but it is very valuable to the longevity of the code. If I had finished working on a piece of software, it was tested and ready to ship, and I knew there was no more work to do on the code; I would not refactor it. A metaphor I like to use is that refactoring is like doing exercises for your code. To function well and get a sense of well being, humans need to exercise and stretch their bodies. Code is similar; if you want your code to live for a long time, it's good to exercise it, and refactoring is a workout for your code. After refactoring your code, it is in better shape and ready to take on the challenges presented in the future.

Let's Start Refactoring

Hopefully by now you can see there are some benefits to giving your code the refactoring workout. So how do you go about doing it? Let's get started with an exercise to introduce some basic ideas about refactoring.

Exercise 5-1: Currency Converter Refactoring

For this exercise to be both achievable and printable within the size constraints of this book, the example is reasonably small. If this were the entire piece of software, it is highly unlikely you would refactor it. It is also unlikely you would get paid anything for building it! The application is a simple currency converter that works with conversion rates that are purely the wishes of an Englishman who spends much of his time in Australia and the United States. We will start with the existing Currency Converter application and take some steps to refactor the code. You can download the source code for this application from http://eXtreme.NET.Roodyn.com/Book Exercises.aspx.

After we have done the refactoring, the code will be in better shape for us to add new functionality, such as increasing the number of currencies. The refactoring steps each contain one or two well-defined refactoring techniques. The names of these techniques have come from Martin Fowler's *Refactoring* book.

Step One: Extract Method

1. Open the Currency Converter solution in Visual Studio.

2. Examine the code and the form. Notice that it is a very simple program with a basic form. Things to notice include the following:

    a. All the functionality occurs in the form code.

    b. There are no tests.

    c. There is not much else to it!

3. First we need some tests. We cannot refactor without validating we have not changed behavior. This presents a dilemma: There are no tests to start with, so how do we know we are not refactoring a bug? Also all the code is tightly tied into the GUI; this makes it hard to test and write tests for. Should we move the code away from the GUI first, or should we attempt to write some clever tests to test the code in the GUI layer? As with many real-world scenarios, we are going to compromise. We will write tests for the code we are going to extract from the GUI layer. Then we will get the tests to pass as we move the code. First we need to add a reference to NUnit in the References section, so right-click References, select Add Reference, and browse for the Nunit.Framework.dll file.

4. We will create a test fixture class to hold our tests. Right-click the project and select Add / Add Class from the pop-up menu. We will name this class **ConvertTests.cs**.

5. Edit the class code so that it uses the Nunit.Framework namespace, and add the TestFixture attribute to the class.

```
using System;
using NUnit.Framework;

namespace CurrencyConverterCS
{
    [TestFixture]
    public class ConvertTests
    {
    }
}
```

6. Now we can start writing some tests. The first test will be a breadth test that enables us to start refactoring some functionality with the confidence that we haven't broken anything.

```
[Test]
public void ConversionBreadth()
{
    decimal result;
    decimal amount;
    CurrencyType fromCur;
    CurrencyType toCur;

    amount = 100.0M;
    fromCur = CurrencyType.US;
    toCur = CurrencyType.US;
    result = MainForm.CurrencyConvert(amount,
        fromCur, toCur);
    Assert.AreEqual(100.0M, result,
        "US to US should be no change");

    fromCur = CurrencyType.UK;
    toCur = CurrencyType.UK;
    result = MainForm.CurrencyConvert(amount,
        fromCur, toCur);
    Assert.AreEqual(100.0M, result,
        "UK to UK should be no change");
```

```
    fromCur = CurrencyType.AUS;
    toCur = CurrencyType.AUS;
    result = MainForm.CurrencyConvert(amount,
        fromCur, toCur);
    Assert.AreEqual(100.0M, result,
        "AUS to AUS should be no change");

    decimal expected;
    fromCur = CurrencyType.US;
    toCur = CurrencyType.AUS;
    result = MainForm.CurrencyConvert(amount,
        fromCur, toCur);
    expected = amount * 2;
    Assert.AreEqual(expected, result,
        "US to AUS is incorrect");

    fromCur = CurrencyType.UK;
    toCur = CurrencyType.AUS;
    result = MainForm.CurrencyConvert(amount,
        fromCur, toCur);
    expected = amount / 0.5M * 2;
    Assert.AreEqual(expected, result,
        "UK to AUS is incorrect");
}
```

7. As you have probably worked out, this won't compile. We have added a new enumerated type called CurrencyType and are calling a method on the Main-Form that doesn't exist. We need to go back to the MainForm and create these. In the MainForm above the class, we add the CurrencyType enum.

```
public enum CurrencyType
{
    US,
    AUS,
    UK,
}
```

8. Next we add the CurrencyConvert method to the MainForm code. We need to make it static or shared so that it can be accessed from the test code. This isn't ideal, but we can work on refactoring away from that later.

```
public static decimal CurrencyConvert(decimal amount,
    CurrencyType fromCur, CurrencyType toCur)
```

```
{
    return 0;
}
```

9. Now you can compile and run the test. It will fail because the method has no body. We need to move the body from the button click.

```
public static decimal CurrencyConvert(decimal amount,
                CurrencyType fromCur, CurrencyType toCur)
{
    decimal converted = 0.0M;
    decimal initial = 0.0M;

    initial = amount;
    converted = initial;

    if (fromCur == CurrencyType.UK)
    {
        converted = initial / UKInUS;
    }
    else if(fromCur == CurrencyType.AUS)
    {
        converted = initial / AusInUS;
    }

    if (toCur == CurrencyType.UK)
    {
        converted = converted * UKInUS;
    }
    else if(toCur == CurrencyType.AUS)
    {
        converted = converted * AusInUS;
    }

    return converted;
}
```

10. This will not compile because the UKInUS and AusInUS variables are not static, so we need to change the declaration of these, too.

```
private static decimal AusInUS = 2;
private static decimal UKInUS = 0.5M;
```

11. Now compile and run the test in the NUnit GUI (or console if you prefer); the test should pass.

12. We can now call this new method from the button click event.

```
private void ConvertButton_Click
    (object sender, System.EventArgs e)
{
    decimal converted = 0.0M;
    decimal initial = 0.0M;

    CurrencyType fromCur = CurrencyType.US;
    CurrencyType toCur = CurrencyType.US;

    initial = Convert.ToDecimal(Amount.Text);

    if (FromUK.Checked)
    {
        fromCur = CurrencyType.UK;
    }
    else if (FromAUS.Checked)
    {
        fromCur = CurrencyType.AUS;
    }

    if (ToUK.Checked)
    {
        toCur = CurrencyType.UK;
    }
    else if (ToAus.Checked)
    {
        toCur = CurrencyType.AUS;
    }

    converted = CurrencyConvert(initial, fromCur, toCur);

    Result.Text = converted.ToString();

}
```

You can see that we now have more code than before, and in fact it appears less obvious. This often happens in the early stages of a refactoring session. Don't be afraid of this. If you have an idea of where you want to go, you think at first that you are going in the wrong direction. Have the courage that you are going to get somewhere that is much better in the end, however, and you will find you can get there most of the time. Occasionally, you will be wrong, and then you need to have the courage to admit defeat and throw your changes away. Just do it.

Step Two: Extract Class

At this point, I am looking at the code and thinking that the CurrencyType should be encapsulated in a class that has the conversion routines as methods. To move in this direction, we must create a new class called ConvertibleCurrency. Do this from the right-click pop-up menu in Solution Explorer, as we did before.

1. Before we get started on the code in the new class, we will define some behaviors of the class in a test. This documents what we are expecting the class to do. Back in the ConvertTests class, we add a new method:

```
[Test]
public void ConvertTo()
{
    ConvertibleCurrency currency;
    decimal result;
    decimal expected;

    currency = new ConvertibleCurrency(
        CurrencyType.US, 100.0M);

    result = currency.ConvertTo(CurrencyType.US);
    Assert.AreEqual(100.0M, result,
            "US to US should be no change");

    currency = new ConvertibleCurrency(
        CurrencyType.AUS, 100.0M);
    result = currency.ConvertTo(CurrencyType.UK);
    expected = 100.0M / 2 * 0.5M;
    Assert.AreEqual(expected, result,
        "AUS to UK incorrect result");
}
```

2. We have now defined the constructor of the new class and one method, so let's add those to the class.

```
public ConvertibleCurrency(CurrencyType type, decimal val)
{
}
```

```
public decimal ConvertTo(CurrencyType type)
{
    decimal converted = 0.0M;
    return converted;
}
```

3. Compile and run the tests; the latest test will (as expected) fail. We need to implement the constructor and move the code from the MainForm static method into the class.

```
public class ConvertibleCurrency
{
    private decimal amount;
    private CurrencyType currency;

    public ConvertibleCurrency(CurrencyType type, decimal val)
    {
        currency = type;
        amount = val;
    }

    public decimal ConvertTo(CurrencyType type)
    {
        decimal converted = amount;

        if (currency == CurrencyType.UK)
        {
            converted = converted / UKInUS;
        }
        else if(currency == CurrencyType.AUS)
        {
            converted = converted / AusInUS;
        }

        if (type == CurrencyType.UK)
        {
            converted = converted * UKInUS;
        }
        else if(type == CurrencyType.AUS)
        {
            converted = converted * AusInUS;
        }

        return converted;
    }
}
```

4. The code will not compile yet because the UKInUS and AusInUS variables cannot be reached from this class; they need to be moved into the class, but they no longer need to be static.

```
private decimal AusInUS = 2;
private decimal UKInUS = 0.5M;
```

5. Now compile and run the tests; they should pass. We are now ready to use this class from the MainForm code.

6. Change the CurrencyConvert method in the MainForm as follows.

```
public static decimal CurrencyConvert(decimal amount,
                CurrencyType fromCur, CurrencyType toCur)
{
    decimal converted = 0.0M;

    ConvertibleCurrency currency =
        new ConvertibleCurrency(fromCur, amount);
    converted = currency.ConvertTo(toCur);

    return converted;
}
```

7. You can also delete the UKInUS and AusInUS variables from the MainForm code. These variables are now declared and used in the ConvertibleCurrency class.

8. Now would also be a good time to move the CurrencyType enum declaration into the ConvertibleCurrency class file.

9. Compile the project and run the tests. The tests should pass, and the program should still function as before. We have encapsulated the behavior of the currency converter into a class and reduced the functionality in the GUI. This helps with testing and with porting the program to another user interface such as the Web.

Step Three: Move Method and Extract Method

Before we finish with the GUI layer, we can move the static CurrencyConvert method from the MainForm to the ConvertibleCurrency class. This is a more sensible place for this method because it deals with the ConvertibleCurrency class.

Cut and paste the method into the class and compile the project. You should get some build errors—six to be precise. Five are in the test class for calls to the Main-Form method we just moved, and the sixth one is in MainForm where the call to the method was made.

The method we moved is still static, so we need to prefix it with the class name ConvertibleCurrency in these six places.

I often use the compiler in this way to detect the places I have broken code when I move a method or change a name. The compiler is far better at finding all the places the change has effected than I am!

1. Now compile and run the tests again; they should pass. The program should still function as before.

2. We can now turn our attention to the code in the ConvertibleCurrency class. The if-else blocks of code that convert the amount to U.S. dollars and then to the currency requested look like good candidates for extraction. We'll start by taking the block that converts the amount to U.S. dollars and create a method called **ConvertToUS**.

```
private decimal ConvertToUS()
{
    decimal converted = 0.0M;
    converted = amount;

    if (currency == CurrencyType.UK)
    {
        converted = converted / UKInUS;
    }
    else if (currency == CurrencyType.AUS)
    {
        converted = converted / AusInUS;
    }

    return converted;
}
```

Then replace the code in the ConvertTo function so it looks like this:

```
public decimal ConvertTo(CurrencyType type)
{
    decimal converted = ConvertToUS();
```

```
        if (type == CurrencyType.UK)
        {
            converted = converted * UKInUS;
        }
        else if(type == CurrencyType.AUS)
        {
            converted = converted * AusInUS;
        }

        return converted;
    }
```

Compile and run the tests to validate we haven't broken anything.

3. We can do the same with the second if-else block by creating a function called **ConvertFromUS**.

```
    private decimal ConvertFromUS(CurrencyType type,
            decimal USAmount)
    {
        decimal converted = 0.0M;

        converted = USAmount;

        if (type == CurrencyType.UK)
        {
            converted = converted * UKInUS;
        }
        else if (type == CurrencyType.AUS)
        {
            converted = converted * AusInUS;
        }

        return converted;
    }
```

4. Again we need to change the code in the ConvertTo method so that it calls this new method.

```
    public decimal ConvertTo(CurrencyType type)
    {
        decimal converted = ConvertToUS();

        converted = ConvertFromUS(type, converted);
```

```
        return converted;
    }
}
```

5. Compile and run the tests. The fact they work shows us we haven't made any changes to the functionality, even though we have changed the structure of the code in a fairly big way.

Step Four: Replace Type Code with State/Strategy and Replace Conditional with Polymorphism

We are now in a far stronger position to change the structure of the code further and remove some more "bad smells"[2] from the code. There are two areas of the code that are smelly: the enumerated type and the if-else blocks. Interestingly, the enumerated type and if-else code are related. The fact they are related makes the smell even fouler!

1. We will start by using Replace Type Code with State/Strategy. The CurrencyType enumerated type can be replaced with a simple object hierarchy. We'll start by coding the hierarchy.

```
public abstract class BaseCurrency
{
    public abstract decimal InUS
    {
        get;
    }
}

public class USCurrency : BaseCurrency
{
    public override decimal InUS
    {
        get{ return 1; }
    }
}

public class UKCurrency : BaseCurrency
{
    public override decimal InUS
    {
        get{ return 0.5M; }
    }
}
```

```
public class AUSCurrency : BaseCurrency
{
    public override decimal InUS
    {
        get{ return 2; }
    }
}
```

2. Check it compiles and the tests still run. They should because we haven't yet touched any of the code being called. We will do this now by replacing the use of the enumerated type in the CovertibleCurrency class with the class types we have just created.

```
public class ConvertibleCurrency
{
    private decimal amount;
    private BaseCurrency currency;

    public static decimal CurrencyConvert(decimal amount,
        BaseCurrency fromCur, BaseCurrency toCur)
    {
        decimal converted = 0.0M;

        ConvertibleCurrency currency =
            new ConvertibleCurrency(fromCur, amount);
        converted = currency.ConvertTo(toCur);

        return converted;
    }


    public ConvertibleCurrency(BaseCurrency type, decimal val)
    {
        currency = type;
        amount = val;
    }

    public decimal ConvertTo(BaseCurrency type)
    {
        decimal converted = ConvertToUS();

        converted = ConvertFromUS(type, converted);

        return converted;
    }
```

```
    private decimal ConvertToUS()
    {
        decimal converted = 0.0M;

        converted = amount / currency.InUS;

        return converted;
    }

    private decimal ConvertFromUS(BaseCurrency type,
        decimal USAmount)
    {
        decimal converted = 0.0M;

        converted = USAmount * type.InUS;

        return converted;
    }
}
```

3. Pay careful attention to what has changed in the ConvertibleCurrency class. The if-else statements have disappeared through the use of the hierarchy. The replacement of the enumerated type with a hierarchy has enforced a better code base. The two member variables AusInUS and UKInUS are no longer needed; they have also been deleted.

If we now compile this project, we should find all the places that call the class that also need to be changed; this will be in the MainForm and in the tests. The tests are an area of the code where we need to tread especially carefully. Changing the test code could cause us to inadvertently break one of the tests. The methods in the test code should now read as follows.

```
    [Test]
    public void ConversionBreadth()
    {
        decimal result;
        decimal amount;
        BaseCurrency fromCur;
        BaseCurrency toCur;

        amount = 100.0M;
        fromCur = new USCurrency();
        toCur = new USCurrency();
        result = ConvertibleCurrency.CurrencyConvert(amount,
```

```
            fromCur, toCur);
        Assert.AreEqual(100.0M, result,
            "US to US should be no change");

        fromCur = new UKCurrency();
        toCur = new UKCurrency();
        result = ConvertibleCurrency.CurrencyConvert(amount,
            fromCur, toCur);
        Assert.AreEqual(100.0M, result,
            "UK to UK should be no change");

        fromCur = new AUSCurrency();
        toCur = new AUSCurrency();
        result = ConvertibleCurrency.CurrencyConvert(amount,
            fromCur, toCur);
        Assert.AreEqual(100.0M, result,
            "AUS to AUS should be no change");

        decimal expected;
        fromCur = new USCurrency();
        toCur = new AUSCurrency();
        result = ConvertibleCurrency.CurrencyConvert(amount,
            fromCur, toCur);
        expected = amount * 2;
        Assert.AreEqual(expected, result,
            "US to AUS is incorrect");

        fromCur = new UKCurrency();
        toCur = new AUSCurrency();
        result = ConvertibleCurrency.CurrencyConvert(amount,
            fromCur, toCur);
        expected = amount / 0.5M * 2;
        Assert.AreEqual(expected, result,
            "UK to AUS is incorrect");
    }

    [Test]
    public void ConvertTo()
    {
        ConvertibleCurrency currency;
        decimal result;
        decimal expected;

        currency = new ConvertibleCurrency(
            new USCurrency(), 100.0M);

        result = currency.ConvertTo(new USCurrency());
        Assert.AreEqual(100.0M, result,
```

```
                  "US to US should be no change");

      currency = new ConvertibleCurrency(
          new AUSCurrency(), 100.0M);
      result = currency.ConvertTo(new UKCurrency());
      expected = 100.0M / 2 * 0.5M;
      Assert.AreEqual(expected, result,
          "AUS to UK incorrect result");
}
```

4. In the MainForm code, the button click code should now look like this.

```
private void ConvertButton_Click
    (object sender, System.EventArgs e)
{
    decimal converted = 0.0M;
    decimal initial = 0.0M;

    BaseCurrency fromCur;
    BaseCurrency toCur;

    initial = Convert.ToDecimal(Amount.Text);

    if (FromUK.Checked)
    {
        fromCur = new UKCurrency();
    }
    else if (FromAUS.Checked)
    {
        fromCur = new AUSCurrency();
    }
    else
    {
        fromCur = new USCurrency();
    }

    if (ToUK.Checked)
    {
        toCur = new UKCurrency();
    }
    else if (ToAus.Checked)
    {
        toCur = new AUSCurrency();
    }
    else
    {
        toCur = new USCurrency();
```

```
            }

    converted = ConvertibleCurrency.CurrencyConvert(
        initial, fromCur, toCur);

    Result.Text = converted.ToString();

    }
```

5. Notice that we have actually added an extra else condition to the if-else block. The fact that we have replaced the enum with a hierarchy means we no longer can have a default value; this is forcing our code to be more type safe. This lack of type safety might have been the cause of a bug in a later stage, but we have prevented this bug from being born.

6. Compile and run the tests. We should be back to a working state and ready to move forward to the last step.

Step Five: Replace Conditional with Polymorphism

1. Because we are now confident that we do not need the enumerated type anymore, we can delete it from the code. However, there is still a small whiff in the MainForm code. Although we've eliminated the if-else blocks of code in the ConvertibleCurrency class, they still linger in the button click method. To remove them, we can use the same hierarchy we have already created. We can also take advantage of a feature of the .NET Framework; if you bind a list of objects to a list box or a combo box, the box will display each object using its ToString method. We will therefore override the ToString method in our concrete currency type classes.

```
public class USCurrency : BaseCurrency
{
    public override decimal InUS
    {
        get{ return 1; }
    }
    public override string ToString()
    {
        return "US$";
    }
}
```

```
public class UKCurrency : BaseCurrency
{
    public override decimal InUS
    {
        get{ return 0.5M; }
    }
    public override string ToString()
    {
        return "UK£";
    }
}

public class AUSCurrency : BaseCurrency
{
    public override decimal InUS
    {
        get{ return 2; }
    }
    public override string ToString()
    {
        return "AU$";
    }
}
```

2. Return to the MainForm in the design view and replace the From and To radio button groups with combo boxes (called fromCombo and toCombo), as shown in Figure 5-1.

Figure 5-1   Replace radio buttons with combo boxes.

3. Double-click the form to generate the MainForm_Load method. In here we will create a list of the concrete currency types and bind them to the combo boxes.

```
private void MainForm_Load(object sender, System.EventArgs e)
{
    ArrayList currencyList = new ArrayList();
```

```
        currencyList.Add(new UKCurrency());
        currencyList.Add(new USCurrency());
        currencyList.Add(new AUSCurrency());

        fromCombo.DataSource = currencyList;
        toCombo.DataSource = currencyList.Clone();
    }
```

4. In the button click event, we now need to get the selected object from the combo boxes.

```
    private void ConvertButton_Click
        (object sender, System.EventArgs e)
    {
        decimal converted = 0.0M;
        decimal initial = 0.0M;

        BaseCurrency fromCur;
        BaseCurrency toCur;

        initial = Convert.ToDecimal(Amount.Text);

        fromCur = fromCombo.SelectedItem as BaseCurrency;
        toCur = toCombo.SelectedItem as BaseCurrency;

        converted = ConvertibleCurrency.CurrencyConvert(initial,
            fromCur, toCur);

        Result.Text = converted.ToString();
    }
```

5. Compile and run the tests, and then do some manual testing to verify you have now created a working piece of software.

Step Six: Customize

I leave it to you to now explore what else you can do with this code. Some ideas for you are as follows:

- Create an ASP.NET Web interface for the code.
- Add another set of currencies to the application.
- Collect the currency exchange rates from an XML file.

When Not to Refactor

Now that you are all excited about refactoring, you probably want to go and look at some other code and start doing some refactoring. First some words of warning:

1. Do not refactor code that is not going to change. You will be wasting your time. If you know the code is working and doesn't need a bug fix or enhancement, leave it alone.

2. Learn when to stop refactoring. It takes practice, but be aware you only want to refactor enough to make the code easy to understand and maintainable. The code doesn't have to be a thing of beauty; it is far better if it works and you can deliver your solution quickly.

3. Refactoring is not an excuse to hide the fact that you think someone else's code is rubbish and so you need to rewrite it. I have seen people who rewrite other people's code because they don't like it and call this "refactoring." It is not refactoring. The fact this is happening indicates you have a bigger problem with your development team that needs to be addressed. Don't hide behind refactoring.

Tools for Refactoring

You have manually done the refactoring in this chapter. You have had to cut and paste code, create new methods, and change structures. You can download tools that will help you to achieve this. Refactory from Xtreme Simplicity (http://www.xtreme-simplicity.net/) is the best one I have tried. Refactory plugs into Visual Studio and provides a menu item with a selection of refactorings.

Visual Studio .NET 2005 is going to include refactoring tools within the IDE. You will be able to highlight code from a method and then click an Extract Method menu item. The extract method refactor will be done for you. The refactors supported in the Visual Studio.NET 2005 beta are as follows:

- Extract Method

- Rename

- Encapsulate Field

- Extract Interface

- Promote Local Variable to Parameter

- Remove Parameters

- Reorder Parameters

- Generate Method Stub

- Add Using Unbound Type

You will find two aspects of the Visual Studio.NET 2005 refactoring tool extremely innovative. First, each time you perform a refactor, the tool brings up a preview window that shows you the changes about to be made in the code. Second, the refactoring tool enables you to perform a refactor across multiple projects in the same solution.

Like all good developer tools, this will make our lives as developers better. We will be able to refactor code more easily. And like all good developer tools, it will work best when you understand exactly what the tool is doing. I suggest you learn to refactor your code manually to start with. After you have learned the skill of refactoring, the tools will become very powerful in your hands.

Conclusion

This chapter provided you with some hands-on experience with refactoring and explained how you can develop your code using the test-code-refactor cycle. I strongly recommend reading *Refactoring* by Martin Fowler; though the examples are in Java, don't let that scare you from seeing how they would apply to C#.

If you are the only one on your team doing refactoring, it will be hard at first, but don't try to force others to see the wisdom of your ways; instead, let them learn by seeing the results you produce. If they think you are wasting your time, that is fine, too. Many people think I am wasting my time going to the gym three days a week or getting up early for a run on the beach. I know I am doing some good for myself and for the good of my team, and that is enough. They will see that the code that has been refactored has more flexibility and is easier to work with. Your code will be fitter than code that has not been refactored.

[1]   Gamma, Erich, Richard Helm, Ralph Johnson, & John Vlissides. *Design Patterns*. Reading, Massachusetts: Addison-Wesley Professional, 1995.

[2]   Fowler, Martin. *Refactoring*. Reading, Massachusetts: Addison-Wesley Professional, 1999. In this book, Fowler describes code that has something amiss as having a bad smell.

▪6▪

Spiking

E XPERIMENTATION IS A FUNDAMENTAL PART of research. To understand and validate how something works, we experiment with it. *Spiking* is the XP term given to research and experimentation. Spiking provides a way to discover more information about a specific part of the project.

This chapter guides you through carrying out some spikes (research) on technologies that you have not encountered. After you have spiked an area of technology, you have a much better understanding of what it will take to develop software using that technology. This understanding will enable you to more effectively break down stories into tasks and make more accurate time estimates for those tasks.

You Can't Know Everything

The vast amount of information available about even something as focused as just the .NET Framework means that it is nearly impossible to know everything about it. Most of us don't just concentrate on one area of work. XP development environments do much to discourage specialization.

If you specialize in a particular field, you are potentially damaging both your career and the business you are working with. The specialization takes your focus away from seeing the bigger picture, which is harmful to both you and your business. There is no point in knowing everything about how to optimize databases if the core business needs of the software are not being met. If the data is stored in a way that does not provide easy access to valuable information for people in the company, it matters not how well its storage is optimized.

What is important is knowing how to get that information when you need it. Spiking is the tool that will help you get that information when you need it.

Raise Your Confidence

By having a rough understanding of how a technology works, you can boost your confidence in that area by doing some experimentation. You don't want to build the entire system or develop a fully working prototype. It is more important to drive a thin vertical wedge of understanding through the area of concern. This is where the term *spike* comes from; it is a thin vertical slice of information.

When you are experimenting, focus on understanding one specific thing, not a whole host of things. That way you can focus on solving one problem and not become distracted. Set a goal that is achievable in a relatively short time period. If you are trying to understand a complex technology, use your task breakdown skills. Break down the problem into a collection of smaller problems. As mentioned in Chapter 3, I like to aim for something that I believe is achievable within a four-hour timeframe. If a problem takes longer than this to solve, I realize I have bitten off more than I can chew. I need to take a step back and break down the problem.

In each spiking session, I attempt to build a prototype that I will be happy to throw away. The point is not to build a piece of software from these sessions, but to gain an understanding that I can apply to the software system being developed.

Let's Discover Something

Let's rejoin our eXtreme .NET team to see how they are learning about spiking.

 Sue: What are we going to do about the task to get a list of time zones from the operating system?

Deepak: Yes, I was hoping to find a component that did that for us. I searched on Google for something to help us.

Pete: Cool idea! What did you find?

Deepak: Nothing.

Pete: Panic!

Eddie: Looks like we'll have to work this one out for ourselves. Time for a spike; anyone really want to do this?

Deepak: Hold on. First we need to know what operating system we want the information for.

Sue: Windows!

Pete: Yeah, Windows. Doh!

Deepak: You are assuming every version of Windows works the same way? I know that is not true from previous problems I've solved that are like this one.

Pete: Panic!

Eddie: Wow! Okay. Chris? What version of Windows does this need to run on?

Chris: Ninety percent of our customers are running Windows XP.

Eddie: Okay, let's change the spike task to get a list of time zones from Windows XP.

Deepak: That makes me happy.

Eddie: Good; who wants to do this spike?

Dr. Neil and you: We'll do it!

Exercise 6-1: Spiking How Time Zone Data Works in Windows

In this exercise, we are going to investigate how we can use time zone information in our application. In Chapter 3 we encountered this as a task we couldn't accurately estimate. We didn't know enough about how time zones are stored to give an accurate estimate. We need to understand how to access the time zone data from the operating system. Then we need to work out how to use this information to get the time in different places in the world. With this knowledge, we can go back to our team with some firmer estimates about how long this task will take to develop.

The first place to look is the classes that ship as part of the .NET Framework. If there is support for time zone data there, our lives will be made much simpler.

1. Open up the help file and look up the .NET Framework DateTime structure.

   Unfortunately the only time zone–related functionality provided is to convert local times to time in UTC (formally GMT; don't ask me why this was changed!) and back again. This just works using the local time zone that the machine is currently running in. As the documentation states:

This method assumes that the current DateTime holds the local time value, and not a UTC time. Therefore, each time it is run, the current method performs the necessary modifications on the DateTime to derive the UTC time, whether the current Date-Time holds the local time or not.

This method always uses the local time zone when making calculations. (Source: MSDN library)

2. Within the System namespace, there is a TimeZone class; let's see whether that is useful for us.

All the documentation has to say about it is this:

A time zone is a geographical region in which the same standard time is used. (Source: MSDN library)

Not very verbose, but it sounds as though it might be promising.

If you examine the methods, you will discover that the constructor is protected, and the only way to create an instance of this class is to use the static property CurrentTimeZone. This is not very useful if we want to get the time zone information for different time zones.

(As another exercise, you can try to build a test application using the Time-Zone type and see whether you can get time zone for some other part of the world.)

3. Our next stop is to see what the Win32 API provides in terms of time zone functionality. A couple of functions look interesting: GetTimeZoneInformation and SetTimeZoneInformation. They both work with a TIME_ZONE_INFORMATION structure, which contains all the data that we need to build our application; for a given time zone, the fields in the structure are as shown in the following table.

Time Zone Fields

Field	Description
Bias	The offset from UTC in minutes
Standard Name	The name of standard time on this machine in this time zone
Standard Date	The date and time that daylight savings moves over to standard time
Standard Bias	The additional difference from UTC during standard time (usually zero)
DaylightName	The name of daylight savings time on this machine in this time zone
DaylightDate	The date and time of the transition from standard time to daylight savings time
DaylightBias	The additional difference from UTC during daylight savings time (usually –60)

This looks promising, but the methods only enable you to get or set the time zone on the local machine and retrieve time zone information about the time zone set on the local machine.

We are still stumped. We want to get time zone information for all the available time zones in the world. We figure it must be possible because the Control Panel extension that you use to set the Date and Time does it in the Time Zone tab.

4. That is the next place for us to look. If we could work out how the timedate.cpl (basically a DLL) worked, we could emulate that and get all the time zone information for around the world. So, first, we can look to see whether it exposes any form of interface (COM or .NET). You can try to open it using OLE View or ildasm, but no luck there; it supports neither a COM interface nor does it contain CLR header information.

5. Back to basics, open the CPL in Visual Studio as a resource to examine whether there are any clues in there. Maybe the time zone information might have been stored in the DLL (maybe in a string table).

Nope.

The only thing left we can think of is to open up the timedate.cpl file in a hex editor. (Yuck, I haven't poked around inside Windows system files for a while; surely there's a good reason for that!)

We begin this stage of the investigation by examining the DLLs that the code uses, all the usual suspects: KERNEL32, NTDLL.DLL, USER32.dll, COMCTL32.dll, ole32.dll, SHELL32.dll, GDI32.dll, ADVAPI32.dll, IMM32.dll and SHLWAPI.dll. Nothing of use here.

So carry on looking through the file for any other obvious clues; maybe the time zone data is hard coded in the DLL. Again no.

So where did the time zone information get stored? How about the Registry? Look for any references to Registry paths in the CPL file; you should find a few. The first ones lead to information about time synchronization via a time-server and then some Registry entries for storing the current time zone settings for the local machine. Then about halfway down the file you can find a reference to the Registry key: Software\Microsoft\Windows NT\CurrentVersion\Time Zones.

Eureka!

6. This key contains a subkey for each time zone that is listed in the combo box in the second tab of the timedate.cpl. The data in each of the subkeys has to provide all the data required to build a TIME_ZONE_INFORMATION structure so that the application can set the time zone for the system. Now we just have work out how the data is formatted.

Registry Information for Each Time Zone

Value	Meaning
Display	Extra information about the time zone for display purposes
Dlt	DaylightName; the name of daylight savings time on this machine
Index	Unknown
MapID	Presumably used for placing on the bitmap of the world in the CPL
Std	StandardName; the name of standard time on this machine
TZI	All the other data we need to fill a TIME_ZONE_INFORMATION structure

7. The string data is reasonably clear, as shown in the preceding table; we just need to work out how the byte data in the TZI (Time Zone Information) is stored. We start off by going back to the documentation on the structure, from which we can draw up the following table. So adding up the numbers, we are looking for 44 bytes of information, and the TZI value in the Registry is exactly 44 bytes long. Therefore, we must assume that we have all the data we need in the byte array. All we need to do is figure out which byte means what!

Break Down of Time Zone Information

Data Type	Name	Description	Bytes
LONG	Bias	In minutes	4
SYSTEMTIME	StandardDate	Month, day of week and day only	16
LONG	StandardBias	Mostly o (minutes)	4
SYSTEMTIME	DaylightDate	Month, day of week and day only	16
LONG	DaylightBias	Mostly –6o (minutes)	4

8. On your own, write a program that decodes the byte data in the TZI fields in the Registry, and try to work out how the time zone information data is stored in the TZI field. The best thing to do would be to write some tests that validate how we believe the time zone data is stored. We can run those tests when the OS changes and check whether the way time zone data is stored has changed.

    You should have deduced the data was stored in the following order: Bias, Standard Bias, Daylight Bias, Standard Date, and Daylight Date. Okay, now we are ready to put together some code to use this information.

    Below are some functions written in C# that use the time zone information from the Registry.

9. To populate a list with the available time zones, a static method on a class is shown first. It is static because it requires no instance data to be functional.

```
public static string[] GetTimeZones()
{
    RegistryKey regKey = Registry.LocalMachine;
    regKey = regKey.OpenSubKey(
```

```
        @"SOFTWARE\Microsoft\Windows NT\CurrentVersion\Time Zones\");
    return regKey.GetSubKeyNames();
}
```

GetTimeZones Function

After a time zone has been selected, you must get the time zone information for the place selected. The next set of code demonstrates this.

1. Open the Registry key for the time zone provided.

2. Read in the TZI value to a byte array.

3. Use some helper functions to extract the data out of the byte array and into the member variables of the PlaceTime object.

The helper functions MakeUShort and MakeInt are equivalent to the traditional Windows MAKEWORD and MAKELONG macros. Remember that a Long in .NET world is 64 bits and not 32 bits as it was in the old Win32 world. GetValueFromBytes builds a 32-bit integer value from an array of bytes, using an offset from the beginning of the array at which to start "stripping" the bytes.

```
protected void GetTimeZoneInfo(string strTimeZone)
{
    RegistryKey regKey = Registry.LocalMachine;
    regKey = regKey.OpenSubKey(
        @"SOFTWARE\Microsoft\Windows NT\CurrentVersion\Time Zones\" +
            strTimeZone);
    System.Byte[] tziData = (Byte[])regKey.GetValue("TZI");

    m_nBias =  GetValueFromBytes(tziData, 0);
    m_nStandardBias = GetValueFromBytes(tziData, 4);
    m_nDaylightBias = GetValueFromBytes(tziData, 8);

    m_StandardDate = GetDateTimeFromBytes(tziData, 12);
    m_DaylightDate = GetDateTimeFromBytes(tziData, 28);
}


private static ushort MakeUShort(byte low, byte high)
{
    return (ushort) (low | (high<< 8));
}

private static int MakeInt(ushort low, ushort high)
{
```

```
    return (int) (low | (high<< 16));
}


private static int GetValueFromBytes(byte[] data, int offset)
{
    int nResult = 0;
    ushort lowWord = MakeUShort(data[offset],data[offset+1]);
    ushort highWord = MakeUShort(data[offset+2],data[offset+3]);
    nResult = MakeInt( lowWord, highWord );
    return nResult;
}

private static DateTime GetDateTimeFromBytes(byte[] data, int offset)
{
    DateTime dateTime = DateTime.UtcNow;

    int Year = MakeUShort(data[offset],data[offset+1]);
    int Month = MakeUShort(data[offset+2],data[offset+3]);
    DayOfWeek DayofWeek =
         (DayOfWeek)MakeUShort(data[offset+4],data[offset+5]);
    int Day = MakeUShort(data[offset+6],data[offset+7]);
    int Hour = MakeUShort(data[offset+8],data[offset+9]);
    int Minute = MakeUShort(data[offset+10],data[offset+11]);
    int Second = MakeUShort(data[offset+12],data[offset+13]);
    int Milliseconds = MakeUShort(data[offset+14],data[offset+15]);

    dateTime = dateTime.AddMonths(Month - dateTime.Month);
    dateTime = dateTime.AddDays(1-dateTime.Day);
    dateTime = dateTime.AddHours(Hour - dateTime.Hour);
    dateTime = dateTime.AddMinutes(Minute - dateTime.Minute);
    dateTime = dateTime.AddSeconds(Second - dateTime.Second );
    dateTime = dateTime.AddMilliseconds(Milliseconds -
        dateTime.Millisecond );
    bool bFoundDay = false;
    int nCoveredRequiredDay = 0;
    while (dateTime.Month == Month)
    {
        if (dateTime.DayOfWeek == DayofWeek)
        {
            nCoveredRequiredDay +=1;
            if (nCoveredRequiredDay == Day)
            {
                bFoundDay = true;
                break;
            }
        }
        dateTime = dateTime.AddDays(1);
```

```
    }
    while(!bFoundDay)
    {
        dateTime = dateTime.AddDays(-1);
        if (dateTime.DayOfWeek == DayofWeek)
        {
            bFoundDay = true;
        }
    }
    return dateTime;
}
```

GetTimeZoneInfo and Related Functions

The final helper function, GetDateTimeFromBytes, builds a .NET Framework Date-Time structure from the byte array passed in, starting at the offset provided. This is the more complicated of the methods here and requires some extra explanation.

The TZI byte array contains 2 sets of 16 bytes, which correspond to a Win32 SYS-TEMTIME structure. These SYSTEMTIMEs contain the data for the Standard Date and Daylight Date in the TIME_ZONE_INFORMATION structure. The standard and daylight dates represent the date and time at which the transition occurs from daylight savings to standard time and back again.

The TIME_ZONE_INFORMATION structures contain the month, the day of the week (for example, Sunday), the day on which the transition occurs, along with the time. The day can be a value between 1 and 5. If the month is 4, the day is 1, and the day of the week is 0 (Sunday), that would represent the first Sunday in April. If the day value is 5, that always means the last of that day in the month. If the month is 9, the day is 5, and the day of the week is 6, which represents the last Saturday in September.

The GetDateTimeFromBytes function sets the DateTime structure to the first day of the month given and walks through the month until it finds the correct day of the transition. If the method fails to do this, it assumes (dangerous, I know) that we want the last occurrence of that day of the week in the month and starts walking backward through the month until it finds that day. I have no doubt this could be greatly optimized, but I leave that as another exercise for you!

Encode the Knowledge in Tests

As previously mentioned, putting your newly found knowledge into tests is a great way to capture the knowledge you have gained. The tests not only document your findings for other developers to read, they also ensure the knowledge is still valid and not out-of-date. It is sometimes hard to write the tests when you do not know what you are testing, so spiking is often carried out without tests being written first. This is not always the case, as Ron Jeffries shows us in his book *Extreme Programming Adventures in C#* (Microsoft Press, 2004). In the book, Ron carries out spikes purely with tests.

It is not a hard-and-fast rule, and I personally find I can be more playful and creative if I can muck around with ideas in code without the concern of testing. I can write the tests after I understand the technology being researched.

Let's put our newly gained knowledge of how the time zones are stored into a test fixture. Notice that we are testing the helper methods that build the values out of the byte arrays. These helper methods will likely be extracted into a real class when we come to use the time zone information in our project. Having tests for them means that the refactoring exercise that will happen when we need those methods can be done with much more confidence.

```
using System;
using Microsoft.Win32;
using NUnit.Framework;

[TestFixture]
public class TimeZoneTests
{
    [Test]
    public void TestRegistryKey()
    {
        RegistryKey regKey = Registry.LocalMachine;
        regKey = regKey.OpenSubKey(@"SOFTWARE\Microsoft\Windows NT\CurrentVer-
sion\Time Zones\");
        Assert.IsNotNull(regKey, "Invalid registry key");
    }

    [Test]
    public void TestMakeUShort()
    {
        ushort testVal = MakeUShort(0, 0);
        Assert.AreEqual(0,testVal);
```

```csharp
    testVal = MakeUShort(1, 0);
    Assert.AreEqual(1,testVal);

    testVal = MakeUShort(byte.MaxValue, 0);
    Assert.AreEqual(byte.MaxValue,testVal);

    testVal = MakeUShort(0, 1);
    Assert.AreEqual(byte.MaxValue+1,testVal);

    testVal = MakeUShort(byte.MaxValue, byte.MaxValue);
    Assert.AreEqual(ushort.MaxValue,testVal);
}

[Test]
public void TestMakeInt()
{
    int testVal = MakeInt(0, 0);
    Assert.AreEqual(0,testVal);

    testVal = MakeInt(1, 0);
    Assert.AreEqual(1,testVal);

    testVal = MakeInt(ushort.MaxValue, 0);
    Assert.AreEqual(ushort.MaxValue,testVal);

    testVal = MakeInt(0, 1);
    Assert.AreEqual(ushort.MaxValue+1,testVal);

    testVal = MakeInt(ushort.MaxValue, ushort.MaxValue);
    Assert.AreEqual(-1,testVal);
}

[Test]
public void TestGetValueFromBytes()
{
    byte[] testBytes = {0,0,0,0,0,0,0,0};
    int testVal = GetValueFromBytes(testBytes,0);
    Assert.AreEqual(0, testVal);

    testVal = GetValueFromBytes(testBytes,4);
    Assert.AreEqual(0, testVal);
    testBytes[0] = byte.MaxValue;
    testBytes[1] = byte.MaxValue;

    testVal = GetValueFromBytes(testBytes,0);
    Assert.AreEqual(ushort.MaxValue, testVal);

    testBytes[2] = byte.MaxValue;
```

```
        testBytes[3] = byte.MaxValue;

        testVal = GetValueFromBytes(testBytes,0);
        Assert.AreEqual(-1, testVal);

        testBytes[0] = 0;
        testBytes[1] = 0;

        testVal = GetValueFromBytes(testBytes,0);
        Assert.AreEqual(-1-ushort.MaxValue, testVal);
    }

    private ushort MakeUShort(byte low, byte high)
    {
        return (ushort) (low | (high<< 8));
    }

    private int MakeInt(ushort low, ushort high)
    {
        return (int) (low | (high<< 16));
    }

    private int GetValueFromBytes(byte[] data, int offset)
    {
        int nResult = 0;

        ushort lowWord = MakeUShort(data[offset],data[offset+1]);
        ushort highWord = MakeUShort(data[offset+2],data[offset+3]);
        nResult = MakeInt( lowWord, highWord );

        return nResult;
    }


    [Test]
    public void TestTimeZoneInfoForGMT()
    {
        RegistryKey regKey = Registry.LocalMachine;
        regKey = regKey.OpenSubKey(
            @"SOFTWARE\Microsoft\Windows NT\CurrentVersion\Time Zones\GMT Stan-
dard Time");
        Assert.IsNotNull(regKey, "Invalid registry key");
        System.Byte[] tziData = (Byte[])regKey.GetValue("TZI");

        int bias = GetValueFromBytes(tziData, 0);
        Assert.AreEqual(0, bias, "Bias was incorrect");
        int standardBias = GetValueFromBytes(tziData, 4);
        Assert.AreEqual(0, standardBias,
            "Standard Bias was incorrect");
```

```
int daylightBias = GetValueFromBytes(tziData, 8);
Assert.AreEqual(-60, daylightBias,
    "Daylight Bias was incorrect");

int month = MakeUShort(tziData[14],tziData[15]);
Assert.AreEqual(10, month,
    "Month for change to standard time should be Oct");
DayOfWeek dayofWeek = (DayOfWeek)
    MakeUShort(tziData[16],tziData[17]);
Assert.AreEqual(DayOfWeek.Sunday, dayofWeek,
    "Time should change on a Sun");
int day = MakeUShort(tziData[18],tziData[19]);
Assert.AreEqual(5, day,
    "Time should change on 5th or last Sunday of month");
int hour = MakeUShort(tziData[20],tziData[21]);
Assert.AreEqual(2, hour,
    "Time should change at 2am");
int minute= MakeUShort(tziData[22],tziData[23]);
Assert.AreEqual(0, minute,
    "Time should change at 2am - zero minutes");

month = MakeUShort(tziData[30],tziData[31]);
Assert.AreEqual(3, month,
    "Month for change to daylight savings should be Mar");
dayofWeek = (DayOfWeek)
    MakeUShort(tziData[32],tziData[33]);
Assert.AreEqual(DayOfWeek.Sunday, dayofWeek,
    "Time should change to daylight on a Sun");
day = MakeUShort(tziData[34],tziData[35]);
Assert.AreEqual(5, day,
    "Time should change on 5th or last Sunday of month");
hour = MakeUShort(tziData[36],tziData[37]);
Assert.AreEqual(1, hour,
    "Time should change at 1am");
minute= MakeUShort(tziData[38],tziData[39]);
Assert.AreEqual(0, minute,
    "Time should change at 1am - zero minutes");
    }
}
```

Go Where No Man Has Gone Before

Spiking is a skill, one that must be learned. And one thing you must learn is to relax and open your mind to the different possible solutions to your problem. Often, obvious solutions will not solve your problem; you have to look deeper. That's why we get paid as software developers to solve such problems!

The following exercises reinforce what you have learned in this chapter and require that you consider spiking in a bit more detail. As you work through the exercises, remember to encode your learned knowledge into tests. If you get stuck at any point, look for some clues on my Web site at http://eXtreme.NET.Roodyn.com.

Exercise 6-2: Spike Web Services Without a Web Server

The client wants to build an application that can be run on many machines in his company (laptops, desktops, and servers). He wants each machine to provide some status information via a Web service that can be queried on that particular machine. The machines might not necessarily be running IIS. The question is whether can we build a .NET Web service without the need for that machine to host a Web server.

Exercise 6-3: Spike Session State Across Service Calls

Our customer wants to amalgamate a number of Web service functions through a Web site. We propose to build the Web site in ASP.NET. The issue is that some of the Web services need to maintain state. Is it possible to do this?

Exercise 6-4: Spike Drag and Drop Documents in a Rich Text Control

The application we are building requires that it interact with other documents by allowing the user to drag a document from Explorer and drop it onto a Rich Text box. As with Outlook when you send an e-mail, the user wants to see the document as an icon and not the contents of the document. Is this something we can easily achieve?

Conclusion

Spiking is about experimentation and about being prepared to throw away the code you have written while retaining the knowledge gained from it. It is a fundamental skill that many developers start with but lose when under pressure to deliver business-value functionality under strict deadlines. The discipline to take a step back and experiment in a structured way will prove very valuable in the long run, enabling you to better understand new technologies and validate theories about various systems.

7

Automating the Build Process

I F YOU CAN AUTOMATE A STEP IN THE development process, you should do so. By doing this, you make the process simpler to carry out repeatedly in a consistent way. Remember, simplicity is a core value of XP. This chapter examines the tools that are available to aid automating the compilation and testing of your code.

This chapter includes some ideas about how to set up machines to carry out integration and build tasks. This chapter also covers some of the command-line tools available in the .NET Framework SDK. The exercises show how these tools enable you to automate steps of the build process. This chapter also introduces NAnt, a tool that carries out tasks defined in an XML file.

What is the Build Process?

The build process consists of a number of steps that you should carry out every time you have finished a task. As discussed in Chapter 3, the tasks are generally small; this means you will be carrying out these steps a number of times a day. Here is a list of the typical steps you need to complete:

1. Get the latest version of the code for the entire solutions from the source control software.
2. Build the latest version, including the changes made to complete the task.
3. Run all the tests.
4. If the tests all pass, add new changes to the source control system.

5. Rebuild the solution to a central location.

6. Build the installer to a central location.

A few readers might now be asking, "What is source control software?" If you are one of those readers, please read this carefully. *Source control software* provides a central location for the entire team to store the code that has been developed. Think of it as a database for your code. It will let you look at the changes made over time and roll back to examine how the code looked at a given time. Microsoft currently supplies Visual SourceSafe with Visual Studio.NET as a source control software solution. Visual SourceSafe integrates with Visual Studio.Net and works well enough for the examples in this book. If you are developing software without using source control, stop reading this book and go and deploy source control software for your team *now*!

XP teams often carry out these tasks on another computer called an *integration machine*. Having a separate machine for carrying out integration tasks proves valuable on several levels.

- An integration machine prevents more than one set of code changes from being integrated into the system at the same time. This helps to prevent conflicts from occurring. This works best in small teams of less than 15. With a large team, the bottleneck caused by having only one integration machine can be detrimental.

- Using an integration machine increases the visibility, to the entire development team, of the current state of the project. The feedback from this machine provides a continual reminder of the importance of having a working build and ensuring the tests run. As you will discover in the first exercise in this chapter, I like to set the entire screen of the machine to be either green for a good system state or red to indicate there is something broken in the system. Remember, feedback is one of the XP values, and this can help promote that feedback to the team.

- Having a separate machine to test your code before checking it in to the source control software helps to prevent the "it works fine on my machine" chant that I often hear from development teams. By testing the code on at least more than one machine, you reduce the chances of hearing these frustrating words again.

What's Wrong with F5?

If you are a regular user of Visual Studio, you are sure to know that the F5 function key compiles and runs your application. You can extend the functions carried out in this process by adding pre- and post- build steps to your projects. This is good for a certain number of things, such as copying all the compiled assemblies to a common folder. The trouble is, it doesn't go far enough or provide clear enough feedback.

Larger software solutions consist of multiple Visual Studio solutions. Each solution might contain multiple projects. When we want to check whether we have broken anything through the changes we have just made, we need to run all the tests exposed by these components of the system. This involves getting the latest version of the source for these projects, compiling all the projects from the different solutions, and then running all the tests they expose. This calls for more than the support provided by an F5 compile and run. You could extend Visual Studio to do this, but it would not be the simplest thing you could do, and therefore it would break one of the XP tenets: Do the simplest thing that could possibly work.

I'm Just Too Lazy

One of the reasons I have a fascination with computers and software is the belief that they should make our lives easier. I am lazy; I don't want to have to type up letters, print them out, and mail them to someone. I love e-mail; it is the lazy person's answer to staying in touch. Instant messenger is even better! The same goes for spreadsheets; they save me having to do loads of calculations on a calculator or, worse yet, on paper. Computers can do lots of things to make my life easier and give me more time to do the things I enjoy doing. So when I see a task that I am having to repeat on a regular basis, such as building my application or running the tests, the Mr. Lazy in me says, "Hey, let's automate this so you can stop wasting your time and get on with something more fun."

I Make Mistakes

A good reason to automate steps in a process is that the automation helps to reduce the likelihood of human error creeping in. This is even more important when those steps have to be repeated many times. The more you do something, the less careful you are. This is true with many areas of life, and when you have to carry out a build and test process hundreds of times a week, it gets pretty damn boring. I tend to go into a trance when I do those tasks; I might forget to get the latest version from the source control or to run the tests on the components being developed in the other office or to build the installer. I need some way to remove the chance of my mistakes entering the system. Having a repeatable set of steps encoded into a program seems the most obvious way for a programmer to solve this problem.

If a Computer Can Do It, Then It Should

I believe as programmers we should use the tools we have at hand for our own advantage, and the computer is an ideal tool for carrying out many of these repetitive steps. When the team I am working with starts a new project, I always insist on setting up a build procedure as one of the first steps in the development process. I also like to ensure that we have an installer program ready from day one. This makes shipping the software easier at the end of the project, because we dealt with it at the beginning.

Let's see how our eXtreme .NET team is dealing with automating the build process.

Sue: I understand that setting up the build process is going to be more work for us to do. I don't see the point. I just hit F5, and Visual Studio builds and runs the code.

Eddie: F5 doesn't do everything we need. It doesn't run our tests for a start. It doesn't get the latest version of the code from SourceSafe, and it probably shouldn't.

Deepak: Okay, so we're doing something different here than just building and running our app. I think I get that. So what else should we be doing in our build process?

Eddie: Well, there are a lot of things we could do in our automated build. In the last project I worked on, we got the latest version from the code control, compiled the code, ran all the tests, and sent out an e-mail to all the team members indicating the status of the build and the results from the test.

Deepak: We could get the automated build to look through all our code for any issues!

Sue: What do you mean?

Deepak: Well, there's some software that sniffs the code for potential issues. Microsoft has a package called FxCop. It will tell us where the code doesn't comply with our coding standards

Pete: Panic!

Eddie: That would be cool!

Deepak: When the code has compiled and run all the tests successfully, we should get the automated build to create our install package. Then it will be easy for Chris to get the latest good build whenever he wants to play with it.

Chris: That would be great, but I'm not just playing, you know? This is serious; I love the idea of being able to get the latest version on a regular basis. Then I might be able to spot any issues more quickly than I could before

Pete: Panic!

Sue: Could we store the results from these builds in a database?

Eddie: Sure, that is a good idea. Then we can see how the build has been going over a period of time. We can chart our progress and see if there are any patterns to failing builds. That could be really useful.

Pete: Hey, we could also obfuscate the assembly in this process. That would be worth doing; I always forget to do that.

Sue: Okay, I can see there is more to this than I realized. Let's do it!

Do It the Old Way

You can automate builds, run tests, and deploy packages from the command line. This requires a little work and is often the simplest way to get started. In the following exercises, we set up some projects in Visual Studio and create a batch file that builds the files, runs the tests, and provides visible feedback as to whether anything failed.

A *batch file* is just a text file that executes a set of commands from the command prompt. To run the batch file, you need to have the correct command prompt environment variables set up. The simplest way to ensure this is to run the Visual Studio Command Prompt from the Visual Studio Tools folder in the Start menu.

Exercise 7-1: Creating an Integration Build Batch File

In this exercise, we create a simple batch file that gets a solution from Visual Source-Safe, builds it, and runs the tests.

1. Create a new blank solution called **MySolution**. I have created it in a directory on my C: drive called Work; you can create it where you want, but make sure you replace anywhere I have C:\Work\ with the directory you have used.

2. Right-click the solution and add a new C# Library project called **MyLibrary**.

3. Right-click the solution again and create a new Visual Basic Windows application called **MyWindowsApplication**.

4. Right-click the solution again and select Add Solution to Source Control from the pop-up menu (see Figure 7-1). I am adding the solution to a database I have created for this exercise called MySolution; if you use another database, remember what it is called.

Figure 7-1   Add solution to source control.

5. We are now ready to create a batch file to get the latest version of the source from the database and build the solution. The batch file I created is shown below, and yours should look something like it. I used my favorite batch file editor, Notepad, but you can use any text editor, including Visual Studio.

Remember to change the names of the directories depending on where you have created the solution and where your Visual SourceSafe database is. Notice how easy it is with the devenv command to build a Visual Studio Solution; we don't have to worry about the fact that it contains a C# project and a VB.NET project.

```
@echo off

rem: set the source safe database
set SSDIR=C:\Work\SSDB\MySolution

rem: set the working directory for the source safe database root project
ss Workfold $/ C:\Work

rem:change to the directory where all the projects work is
C:
cd Work

rem: get the latest version of the source files from source safe
ss get $/ -R -I-

rem: check that it worked
if errorlevel 1    goto DisplayResult

rem: use the Visual studio cmd line to rebuild the entire solution
devenv /rebuild Debug "C:\Work\MySolution\MySolution.sln"

rem: check that it worked
if errorlevel 1    goto DisplayResult

:DisplayResult
if errorlevel 1 goto failed

echo Success!! :-)
goto end

:failed
echo FAILURE :-(

:end
```

6. Save the file as **Build.bat** and don't forget to save the solution. Then run the batch file to make sure it compiles. Remember, this needs to run in a command prompt with the correct environment variables (such as paths to the

Visual Studio folders) set correctly. As mentioned previously, Visual Studio provides a Visual Studio command prompt that has this set up already.

7. We can now add some unit test code to the library and get the batch file to run the tests as well. Back in Visual Studio, check out the My Library Project using the right-click pop-up menu.

8. Add a reference to the NUnit.Framework.Dll, as you learned in Chapter 4.

9. Add a new class called **LibraryTests** to the Library project.

10. In this class, we will create two tests, one that always passes and one that always fails, as shown in the following code.

```
using System;
using NUnit.Framework;

namespace MyLibrary
{
    [TestFixture]
    public class LibraryTests
    {
        [Test]
        public void AlwaysPasses()
        {
        }

        [Test]
        public void AlwaysFails()
        {
            Assert.Fail("This test should fail");
        }
    }
}
```

11. Make sure it compiles in Visual Studio, and then save the file and the project. Check it back into SourceSafe, and then run the batch file to make sure it still compiles.

12. We can now add two lines to the batch file to run the tests.

```
@echo off

rem: set the source safe database
set SSDIR=C:\Work\SSDB\MySolution
```

```
rem: set the working directory for the source safe database root project
ss Workfold $/ C:\Work

rem:change to the directory where all the projects work is
d:
cd Work

rem: get the latest version of the source files from source safe
ss get $/ -R -I-

rem: check that it worked
if errorlevel 1     goto DisplayResult

rem: use the Visual studio cmd line to rebuild the entire solution
devenv /rebuild Debug "C:\Work\MySolution\MySolution.sln"

rem: check that it worked
if errorlevel 1     goto DisplayResult

rem: run the tests
nunit-console C:\Work\MySolution\MyLibrary\bin\Debug\MyLibrary.dll

rem: check that they passed
if errorlevel 1     goto DisplayResult

:DisplayResult
if errorlevel 1 goto failed
echo Success!! :-)
goto end
:failed
echo FAILURE :-(

:end
```

13. Run the batch file again. It should run the tests and report a failure. You can play with commenting out the test that fails, and the tests should pass.

14. You can use this batch file for an integration machine in an XP environment. As I mentioned earlier, I like to be able to see the state of a build on the integration machine from the other side of the room so that I know where we are. Therefore, I have added a couple of lines in the batch file to change the color of the screen based on the result (red for failed and green for succeeded).

```
@echo off

rem: set the source safe database
```

```
set SSDIR=C:\Work\SSDB\MySolution

rem: set the working directory for the source safe database root project
ss Workfold $/ C:\Work

rem:change to the directory where all the projects work is
d:
cd Work

rem: get the latest version of the source files from source safe
ss get $/ -R -I-

rem: check that it worked
if errorlevel 1     goto DisplayResult

rem: use the Visual studio cmd line to rebuild the entire solution
devenv /rebuild Debug "C:\Work\MySolution\MySolution.sln"

rem: check that it worked
if errorlevel 1     goto DisplayResult

rem: run the tests
nunit-console C:\Work\MySolution\MyLibrary\bin\Debug\MyLibrary.dll

rem: check that they passed
if errorlevel 1     goto DisplayResult


:DisplayResult
if errorlevel 1 goto failed
color A1
echo Success!! :-)
goto end
:failed
echo FAILURE :-(
color C1

:end
rem: for continuous builds the line below
call C:\work\Build.bat
```

I have also added a line at the bottom of the file to run the batch file again when it has finished. If I now set this up on an integration machine, it will continuously be getting the latest version from Visual SourceSafe, building it, and running the tests. This is useful because the integration machine can now give the development team feedback as to the state of the system. For this reason, I always recommend putting the integration machine somewhere highly visible. As soon as something breaks, the whole team can do something about getting it fixed.

Introduction to NAnt

The following exercise introduces NAnt, a build tool based on ANT, which is an XML-based Java build tool. NAnt enables us to define how we are going to build and test our .NET projects by using an XML file. The advantage this has over the batch file we just created is that it can be more configurable. We can define different build targets within the NAnt build file.

At the time of this writing, NAnt is still in early stages of development, with version 0.84 being the latest release. So we are dealing with a piece of software that is not yet at version 1.0. Saying that, NAnt does have much of what is needed to build and test your project. You can download the latest version from http://nant.source-forge.net/, and then we can get started and create a NAnt build file.

To use NAnt, you need to have configured the path environment variable to include the Nant\bin directory. NAnt is a command-line tool; therefore, you also need to have the Visual Studio .NET (or .NET Framework if you are working without Visual Studio) environment variables registered in your command-line environment. There is a batch file called vsvars32.bat in the Microsoft Visual Studio .NET\Common7\Tools directory, which will most likely be in your Program Files directory. This batch file will set up your environment variables for you.

Exercise 7-2: Using NAnt to Automate the Build Process

We will start by building a simple C# Windows application project and setting up the NAnt build file for it.

1. Create a new C# Windows application project called NAntTest.

2. In Solution Explorer, right-click the NAntTest project and select Add/Add New Item from the pop-up menu. Then select XML file and call it **NAntTest.build** (see Figure 7-2). The standard practice for NAnt build files is to call them the project name and use the extension .build. NAnt build files are XML files.

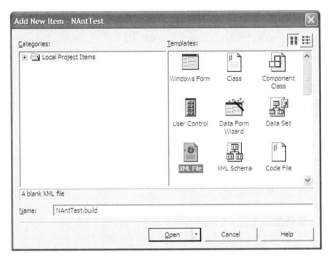

Figure 7-2   Add a new NAntTest.build file.

3. Now we can work on adding the tags to this XML file that we need to be able to build the project using NAnt. We'll start by defining the project in the build file, as shown. The project element is attributed with name and basedir; these represent the project name and the base directory for the build process, respectively.

> **Note**
>
> You can get the Visual Studio.NET IDE to display your build file as syntax-highlighted XML by right-clicking the file, selecting Open With, and then selecting the HTML/XML Editor.

```xml
<?xml version="1.0" encoding="utf-8" ?>
<project name="NAntTest" basedir=".">

</project>
```

4. Next we will add some properties to the project; these will be used by the other sections in the build file.

```xml
<project name="NAntTest" basedir=".">
    <property name="basename" value="NAntTest"/>
    <property name="debug" value="true"/>
    <property name="build.dir" value="build"/>
</project>
```

5. We can now define a target, nested within the project, for the build, as shown here.

```xml
<?xml version="1.0" encoding="utf-8" ?>
<project name="NAntTest" basedir=".">
    <property name="basename" value="NAntTest"/>
    <property name="debug" value="true"/>
    <property name="build.dir" value="build"/>
    <target name="build">
        <mkdir dir="${build.dir}"/>
        <csc target="exe" output="${build.dir}\${basename}.exe"
            debug="${debug}"
            imports="System,System.Collections,
                System.Data,System.Diagnostics,
                System.Drawing,System.Windows.Forms"
            rootnamespace="NAntTest" >
            <sources>
                <includes name="*.cs"/>
            </sources>
            <references>
                <absolute file="System.dll"/>
                <absolute file="System.Data.dll"/>
                <absolute file="System.Drawing.dll"/>
                <absolute file="System.Windows.Forms.dll"/>
                <absolute file="System.XML.dll"/>
            </references>
            <arg value="/main:NAntTest.Form1"/>
        </csc>
    </target>
</project>
```

Build File Components

Let's examine what this file consists of:

- The target element has a name; we will use this later when we define more than one target.

- Then we use the mkdir element to make the build directory for the build output to go in. Notice we use the build.dir property we just defined in the previous step.

- The next element is csc for C# compiler options. We use the target attribute to state we are building an EXE rather than a DLL assembly. The output attribute defines the location and name of the output from the compilation. Again, notice we are using properties we defined earlier.

  - The debug attribute uses the debug property we defined to indicate whether we are building the project for debug.

  - Then the imports attribute defines all the assemblies to import into the project.

  - The final attribute we use here is the rootnamespace attribute to define the root namespace of the code being compiled. For us that's the NAntTest project namespace.

- The sources element, which is a child of the csc element, defines the source files to compile for this target. Notice here we are including all C# files.

- The references element enables us to define all the assemblies we need to reference for the build of this target to work.

- The final child element of the csc element is arg; this enables us to define free-form text arguments to pass to the compiler. Here we are defining the main assembly entry point.

6. After saving the build file, go to the command line and call NAnt to build the project (see Figure 7-3).

Figure 7-3 Our first NAnt build.

7. We can now define some more targets within the project. This enables us to carry out more than one type of build from the same file. Let's start by defining a target that actually doesn't build at all but instead deletes all the build output. We create a new target called **clean**, as shown here.

```
<target name="clean"
    description="deletes the build directory">
    <delete dir="${build.dir}" verbose="true"
        failonerror="false"/>
</target>
```

Notice that we have added a description attribute to the target element. We then add the child delete element to the target. The dir attribute defines the directory to delete. The verbose attribute indicates whether the output should be explicit. The failonerror attribute indicates whether NAnt should consider it has failed if there is an error. Here we set this to false; we do so because if NAnt fails to delete the directory, we don't want to consider this an error because it might happen often when the directory is not there.

8. Save the file and run NAnt from the command line, passing clean as a parameter (see Figure 7-4).

```
Visual Studio .NET 2003 Command Prompt                          _ □ ×

C:\Work\NAntTest>nant clean
NAnt 0.84 (Build 0.84.1455.0; net-1.0.win32; release; 26/12/2003)
Copyright (C) 2001-2003 Gerry Shaw
http://nant.sourceforge.net

Buildfile: file:///C:/Work/NAntTest/NAntTest.build
Target(s) specified: clean

clean:

    [delete] Deleting directory C:\Work\NAntTest\build.
    [delete] Deleting file C:\Work\NAntTest\build\NAntTest.exe.
    [delete] Deleting file C:\Work\NAntTest\build\NAntTest.pdb.
    [delete] Deleting directory C:\Work\NAntTest\build.

BUILD SUCCEEDED

Total time: 0.1 seconds.


C:\Work\NAntTest>_
```

Figure 7-4   Run NAnt using the clean target.

9. We can go back to the outermost project element and add an attribute to indicate the default target, as shown; this will set the default target to our build target. You can test this by just calling NAnt from the command line without specifying a target to build.

```
<project name="NAntTest" default="build" basedir=".">
```

10. Now we can define how to make release and debug builds by changing the debug property. Notice how these targets have a depends attribute; this defines the other targets on which they depend. When NAnt encounters this, it will build the other target first. So before building either for release or debug, NAnt will now build the clean target, which deletes any files previously built.

```
<target name="debug" depends="clean">
    <property name="debug" value="true"/>
</target>
```

```
<target name="release" depends="clean">
    <property name="debug" value="false"/>
</target>
```

11. We can get a debug and release build from this file by calling NAnt with the correct parameters, as shown in Figure 7-5.

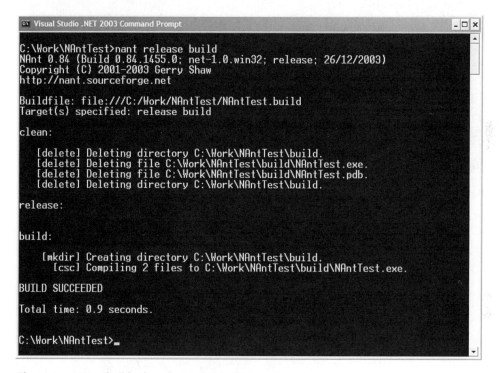

Figure 7-5   NAnt builds the release and build targets.

12. Finally, we are going to add a target that will execute the program that we have built. The exec element contains the program attribute to define the program to execute and the basedir attribute to define where to execute the program.

```
<target name="run" depends="build">
    <exec program="${build.dir}/${basename}.exe" />
</target>
```

13. We can now build and run the program using NAnt (see Figure 7-6).

Figure 7-6   Build and run the project from NAnt.

14. You can also choose whether to build and run the debug or the release version, as shown in Figure 7-7.

15. With the knowledge you have gained from this exercise, you should be able to add some NUnit tests to the project and then create a target that builds the project and runs the tests.

You now have the knowledge you need to automate your build using batch files and NAnt, and should be able to choose which would suit you best and set up an automated build and test process for your projects. If you can get access to another machine, I strongly recommend setting up an integration machine to carry out continuous build and test cycles.

To exercise your newly gained skills, take the project you are working on at the moment and set up an automated build for it. Even if it is not a .NET project, you can do this in a batch file or use the Windows Scripting Host.

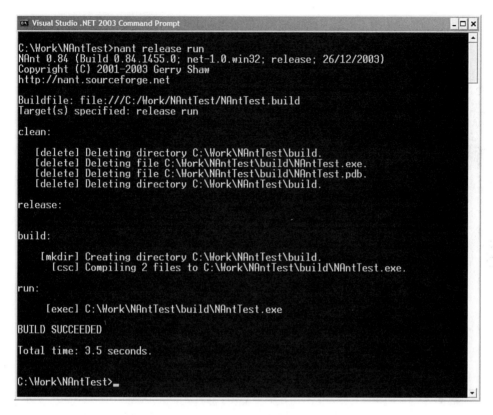

```
Visual Studio .NET 2003 Command Prompt                          - □ ×

C:\Work\NAntTest>nant release run
NAnt 0.84 (Build 0.84.1455.0; net-1.0.win32; release; 26/12/2003)
Copyright (C) 2001-2003 Gerry Shaw
http://nant.sourceforge.net

Buildfile: file:///C:/Work/NAntTest/NAntTest.build
Target(s) specified: release run

clean:

    [delete] Deleting directory C:\Work\NAntTest\build.
    [delete] Deleting file C:\Work\NAntTest\build\NAntTest.exe.
    [delete] Deleting file C:\Work\NAntTest\build\NAntTest.pdb.
    [delete] Deleting directory C:\Work\NAntTest\build.

release:

build:

    [mkdir] Creating directory C:\Work\NAntTest\build.
      [csc] Compiling 2 files to C:\Work\NAntTest\build\NAntTest.exe.

run:

    [exec] C:\Work\NAntTest\build\NAntTest.exe

BUILD SUCCEEDED

Total time: 3.5 seconds.

C:\Work\NAntTest>_
```

Figure 7-7   Use NAnt to do a release build and run the application.

MSBuild

MSBuild is a new build tool from Microsoft. MSBuild is Microsoft's version of NAnt. MSBuild files are XML scripts similar to the NAnt script we used in Exercise 7-2. Visual Studio.NET 2005 will automatically generate this script for each project you create from the IDE. What's more, the IDE will use this MSBuild script to compile and build the project. When you press F5, the MSBuild script will run.

You can edit the script the same way you edit a NAnt script. You can add steps to the build process, and then when you press F5 from the IDE those steps will be executed. This means that getting started with setting up automated builds will become much easier.

MSBuild has an extensible architecture through the use of a new ITask interface in the .NET Framework. If you build a class that supports the ITask interface, MSBuild can execute functionality in that class as part of your build process.

The .NET Framework version 2.0 will include MSBuild. Let me say that again: MSBuild will ship with the .NET Framework, not just future versions of Visual Studio.NET. The fact it ships with the framework is important. It means you can build your product without having Visual Studio.NET installed. Making the build process rely only on having the .NET Framework means that you can use any managed language or development environment of your choice and still have the same build process.

Conclusion

When working as part of a software-project team, it is very important to have a repeatable process for building and testing the system. Every member of the team should be able to build the software and run all the tests. By automating, you can reduce the amount of friction that occurs when you are ready to ship the product. You will also have a lot less difficulty integrating work done by different members of the team if the timeframe between code check-ins is kept small. Make it easy to run the automated build by putting an icon on the desktop that runs the script. Or even better, have a continuous build and test process running on a separate machine.

After reading this chapter and doing the exercises, you should see the benefits from having a one-step process to build and test your software.

8

More Testing

THIS CHAPTER FOCUSES AGAIN on testing. Testing is one of the cornerstones of XP development. We have seen how the tasks we created in Chapter 3 drive the tests. These tests *communicate* the tasks being carried out. We learned how the tests support the refactoring techniques we learned in Chapter 5. The refactoring aims to *simplify* the code. In Chapter 6, we discovered how we can encode new knowledge into tests. These tests validate whether this knowledge is still correct each time they are run. The tests *communicate* the learned knowledge. In Chapter 7, we discovered how the tests running repeatedly on a build or integration machine provide the team with visible *feedback* as to the state of the system. The tests support three values we learned were important in Chapter 1: communication, simplicity, and feedback. Because testing is so important, this chapter returns to it again to explain some extra techniques we can use for developing our tests.

User-Interface Testing

An excuse I often hear in my line of work is this: "It is not possible to use the practices because we build user-interface code." This chapter dispels that myth by introducing you to techniques to develop better user-interface code. These techniques enable you to test your user-interface code. I include additional ideas about test-driven development as well as cover some refactoring techniques.

It's Not Possible!

It seems like a human trait to find an excuse why something is not possible and therefore cannot be applied. This seems especially true when people do not see the reasoning behind doing something. Many of the XP techniques at first don't seem to add up to a sensible option for developing software. I have found the only way to prove whether something makes sense is to try it. After I have tried something, I can make a judgment as to its validity for the software I am developing. Reserve your belief that it is not possible until you have tried some of the exercises in this chapter. Then see whether you can see how to apply these ideas to your everyday project.

"We Are a Special Case"

"We are a special case" is another of the common cries I hear as an excuse as to why it is not possible to develop testable user-interface code. In my experience, most development teams are doing something reasonably special and different; that's why they are getting paid. If most teams are doing something different, does that mean they are all special cases?

The trick is to work out how to use a best practice to your advantage in the "special case" code you are developing. Let's examine some of the issues with user interfaces and then try some exercises. Then this chapter shows you how to write software with user interfaces that is more testable and therefore gives you more confidence in its correctness.

An Issue of Architecture

One of the things that make user-interface code hard to test is that many tools encourage the developer to create code in a place that is hard to get to from a testing framework. An example is Visual Basic. From version 1, Visual Basic has encouraged you to design the user interface and then add the code in the event handling methods that get created for the user-interface components. This is not good object-oriented code; it is, in fact, what is known as *event-oriented code*. Event-oriented code is notoriously hard to maintain, enhance, and test. On the plus side, it is very intuitive to develop and is often used in rapid application development tools.

So does this mean we cannot use tools such as Visual Basic and now C# seeing as Visual Studio.NET enables you to easily develop GUI applications using the event-driven model? Not in the slightest. These tools are very powerful and increase our development capabilities. We need to learn how to use them better and then develop our software in such a way that makes it easy to enhance, maintain, and test.

Ideally, you want to have a very thin user-interface layer on your application. The user interface should have a small amount of code. This has several advantages, including the following:

- It is easier to port your application to use a different user interface. Being able to support more than one interface is becoming more important as we move to developing applications that support mobile devices as well as desktop PCs and Web interfaces.

- It is easier to test code that is detached from the user interface. You can simulate inputs in code.

- The code is less dependent on the user interface and therefore easier to make cultural or language independent.

- Code that easier to test is more maintainable.

- If you need to change the behavior without changing the interface, this is easier to do.

If you develop your code test first, it forces you to build a thinner GUI layer. This GUI layer is not necessarily as thin as it could be, however, as shown in the following exercises.

Exercise 8-1: Building a Thin GUI Layer to Make Testing Easier

In the following exercise, we build a C# application that draws (stamps) shapes (circles and squares) in an area of the screen. The user can pick a shape to stamp and a color. This will emulate some children's toys that do a similar thing. The purpose of the exercise is not to create this application, but to discover how we can best write such an application to enable testing. Once again, I want us to try to do this by writing the tests first; let's see whether this is possible.

1. Create a new C# Windows application called **Stamper**.
2. Add a reference to the NUnit.Framework.dll.
3. Add a new class called **StampTests**.
4. In the StampTests.cs file, import the Nunit.Framework namespace and set the class up as a test fixture.

```
using System;
using NUnit.Framework;

namespace Stamper
{
    [TestFixture]
    public class StampTests
    {
    }
}
```

Now we are ready to think about adding our first piece of functionality test first. We will start by adding the ability to draw a black square. We need a method to test that the square has been drawn.

5. Create a function called **TestDrawSquare** in the StampTests class.

```
using System.Drawing;
using System.Drawing.Imaging;
    .
    .
    .
        [Test]
        public void TestDrawSquare()
        {
            Bitmap bmp = new Bitmap(50, 50,
                PixelFormat.Format24bppRgb);
            Graphics grph = Graphics.FromImage(bmp);
            grph.Clear(Color.White);

            Stamper stamp = new Stamper();
            stamp.DrawSquare(new Point(10, 10), 10, grph);

            Color col;
            Color expectedCol;


            int i;
```

```
expectedCol = Color.FromArgb(255, 0, 0, 0);
for (i = 10; i<20; i++)
{
    //check top and bottom
    col = bmp.GetPixel(i, 10);
    Assert.AreEqual(expectedCol, col,
        "Top Color incorrect");
    col = bmp.GetPixel(i, 20);
    Assert.AreEqual(expectedCol, col,
        "Bottom Color incorrect");
    //check sides
    col = bmp.GetPixel(10, i);
    Assert.AreEqual(expectedCol, col,
        "Left Color incorrect");
    col = bmp.GetPixel(20, i);
    Assert.AreEqual(expectedCol, col,
        "Right Color incorrect");
}
//check outsides
expectedCol = Color.FromArgb(255, 255, 255, 255);
for (i=9; i<21; i++)
{
    col = bmp.GetPixel(9, i);
    Assert.AreEqual(expectedCol, col,
        "Left Outside Color incorrect");
    col = bmp.GetPixel(21, i);
    Assert.AreEqual(expectedCol, col,
        "Right Outside  Color incorrect");
    col = bmp.GetPixel(i, 9);
    Assert.AreEqual(expectedCol, col,
        "Top Outside Color incorrect");
    col = bmp.GetPixel(i, 21);
    Assert.AreEqual(expectedCol, col,
        "Bottom Outside Color incorrect");
}
}
```

Many developers claim I'm crazy when they see this function! What are you doing? Testing that you've drawn a square? Well, yes, that is what I'm doing, and my level of craziness depends entirely on your point of view. If it is critical that your application draws perfect shapes, this technique could be useful for you.

Hint: Use a different algorithm to test the drawing than you use for doing the drawing.

6. Now we can write a class that lets us draw a square. Create a new C# class called **Stamper**.

7. In the Stamper.cs file, add a method to the class called **DrawSquare** that does nothing, so we can get the project to compile. Then compile and run the test; it will fail because we haven't drawn anything yet!

```
using System;
using System.Drawing;

namespace Stamper
{
    public class Stamper
    {
      public void DrawSquare(Point pt, int sideLength,
          Graphics grph)
        {
        }
      }
}
```

8. Add the following two lines of code to the method and then compile and run the test again. This time the test should pass.

```
public void DrawSquare(Point pt, int sideLength,
    Graphics grph)
{
    Rectangle rect = new Rectangle(pt,
        new Size(sideLength, sideLength));
    grph.DrawRectangle(new Pen(Color.Black), rect);
}
```

We have built a class that can draw a square and have tested that it draws the edges of the square. We haven't tested that it hasn't drawn inside the square or somewhere else away from the edges. How far you want to take this level of testing depends on the nature of your application.

In the next steps of the exercise, we add the capability of drawing a circle. We only test that the outside edges do not overlap and that four points of the circle all touch the edge of a square that the circle is drawn inside. This is far less rigorous than the test for the square and, in fact, the DrawSquare method would pass the test for drawing a circle, but not the other way around!

9. Back in the StampTests TestFixture class, add a method to test the circle drawing functionality called TestDrawCircle.

```
[Test]
public void TestDrawCircle()
{
    Bitmap bmp = new Bitmap(50, 50,
        PixelFormat.Format24bppRgb);
    Graphics grph = Graphics.FromImage(bmp);
    grph.Clear(Color.White);

    Stamper stamp = new Stamper();
    stamp.DrawCircle(new Point(10, 10), 10, grph);
    Color col;
    Color expectedCol;

    //check top and bottom
    int i;
    expectedCol = Color.FromArgb(255, 0, 0, 0);
    i = 15;
    col = bmp.GetPixel(i, 10);
    Assert.AreEqual(expectedCol, col,
        "Top Color incorrect");
    col = bmp.GetPixel(i, 20);
    Assert.AreEqual(expectedCol, col,
        "Bottom Color incorrect");
    //check sides
    col = bmp.GetPixel(10, i);
    Assert.AreEqual(expectedCol, col,
        "Left Color incorrect");
    col = bmp.GetPixel(20, i);
    Assert.AreEqual(expectedCol, col,
        "Right Color incorrect");
    //check outsides
    expectedCol = Color.FromArgb(255, 255, 255, 255);
    for(i=9; i<21; i++)
    {
        col = bmp.GetPixel(9, i);
        Assert.AreEqual(expectedCol, col,
            "Left Outside Color incorrect");
        col = bmp.GetPixel(21, i);
        Assert.AreEqual(expectedCol, col,
            "Right Outside  Color incorrect");
        col = bmp.GetPixel(i, 9);
        Assert.AreEqual(expectedCol, col,
            "Top Outside Color incorrect");
        col = bmp.GetPixel(i, 21);
        Assert.AreEqual(expectedCol, col,
```

```
                    "Bottom Outside Color incorrect");
            }
    }
```

10. This won't compile yet because we need to add the DrawCircle method, so let's add the stub for that and then compile and run the tests.

```
public void DrawCircle(Point pt ,int diameter,
    Graphics grph)
{
}
```

11. The TestDrawCircle failed, so let's put the code in to make it pass.

```
public void DrawCircle(Point pt ,int diameter,
    Graphics grph)
{
    Rectangle rect = new Rectangle(pt,
    new Size(diameter, diameter));
    grph.DrawEllipse(new Pen(Color.Black), rect);
}
```

12. The next thing to do is add the color functionality; we need to be able to draw squares or circles in red or black. So far our tests have just assumed they would be black. We can modify our tests to be more explicit about the fact they test for the black shapes, by changing the method names and setting a (yet to be created) color property on the Stamper object to black.

```
[Test]
public void TestDrawBlackSquare()
{
    Bitmap bmp = new Bitmap(50, 50,
        PixelFormat.Format24bppRgb);
    Graphics grph = Graphics.FromImage(bmp);
    grph.Clear(Color.White);

    Stamper stamp = new Stamper();
    stamp.Color = Color.Black;
    stamp.DrawSquare(new Point(10, 10), 10, grph);

    Color col;
    Color expectedCol;
    .
    .
```

```
        .
}

[Test]
public void TestDrawBlackCircle()
{
    Bitmap bmp = new Bitmap(50, 50,
        PixelFormat.Format24bppRgb);
    Graphics grph = Graphics.FromImage(bmp);
    grph.Clear(Color.White);

    Stamper stamp = new Stamper();
    stamp.Color = Color.Black;
    stamp.DrawCircle(new Point(10, 10), 10, grph);
    Color col;
    Color expectedCol;
        .
        .
        .
}
```

13. We must now add this new color property to the Stamper class. Notice we have hard coded the property to Black, and we are ignoring the set method. This is the simplest thing to do that will make all the tests run and not break any existing functionality. We know this will change in the next few steps when we add the capability for the shapes to be drawn in red.

```
public Color Color
{
    get{return Color.Black;}
    set{    }
}
```

14. Compile and run the tests.

15. We now can add the functionality for drawing the shapes in red. We start by adding a new test called **TestDrawRedSquare**. This is very similar to the test for the black square, so you can copy and paste that method and then make the following changes:

```
[Test]
public void TestDrawRedSquare()
{
    Bitmap bmp = new Bitmap(50, 50,
```

```
        PixelFormat.Format24bppRgb);
    Graphics grph = Graphics.FromImage(bmp);
    grph.Clear(Color.White);

    Stamper stamp = new Stamper();
    stamp.Color = Color.Red;
    stamp.DrawSquare(new Point(10, 10), 10, grph);

    Color col;
    Color expectedCol;


    int i;
    expectedCol = Color.FromArgb(255, 255, 0, 0);
    for (i = 10; i<20; i++)
    {
        .
        .
        .
```

16. The project should compile, and the test will fail. To make the test pass, we need to do some work in the Stamper class to actually use the color that is exposed as a property. First we create a member variable of the class of type Pen and use it to store (and set) the color property that is exposed from the class.

```
private Pen _pen = new Pen(Color.Black);
public Color Color
{
    get{return _pen.Color;}
    set{ _pen.Color= value; }
}
```

17. We can now use this _pen object in our Draw methods.

```
public void DrawSquare(Point pt, int sideLength,
    Graphics grph)
{
    Rectangle rect = new Rectangle(pt,
        new Size(sideLength, sideLength));
    grph.DrawRectangle(_pen, rect);
}

public void DrawCircle(Point pt ,int diameter,
    Graphics grph)
```

```
    {
        Rectangle rect = new Rectangle(pt,
            new Size(diameter, diameter));
        grph.DrawEllipse(_pen, rect);
    }
```

18. Compile and run the tests; they should pass. You should now add a test for drawing red circles as well.

19. So far we have not added a single thing to the real user interface. If you run the program, you will see a blank form that doesn't do much. We should now think about connecting the Stamper class we have built to some form of user interface. Open the form in design view and add a Picture Box control (leave it as PictureBox1), two labels (called Square and Circle), and two panels (called Red and Black). Set the background color property on the panels to the same color as the names; you can change the background color of the label controls and set the text to the same as their names (see Figure 8-1).

Figure 8-1 The user interface.

20. In the code file for the form, add a private member variable called **stamp** to hold an instance of the Stamper class.

```
public class Form1 : System.Windows.Forms.Form
{
    private Stamper stamp = new Stamper();
```

21. Create an event handler for the form load event; you can do this by double-clicking the form in the design view. Edit the code to set the stamper color to black by default.

```
using System.Drawing.Imaging;
.
.
.
        private void Form1_Load(object sender, System.EventArgs e)
        {
            stamp.Color = Color.Black;
            pictureBox1.Image = new Bitmap(pictureBox1.Width,
                pictureBox1.Height,
                PixelFormat.Format24bppRgb);
            Graphics grph = Graphics.FromImage(pictureBox1.Image);
            grph.Clear(Color.White);
        }
```

22. Next we want to add code to draw a square in the PictureBox when the user clicks the mouse button while the cursor is over the PictureBox. To add an event handler for the MouseDown event, go back to the design view and select the PictureBox. Then from the Properties window, select Events and double-click the MouseDown event. This will create the event handler function for us. We can now fill in the skeleton provided with code to call the Stamper and place a square in the picture box.

```
private void pictureBox1_MouseDown(object sender,
            System.Windows.Forms.MouseEventArgs e)
{
    Point pt = new Point(e.X, e.Y);
    Bitmap bmp = pictureBox1.Image as Bitmap;
    Graphics grph = Graphics.FromImage(bmp);
    stamp.DrawSquare(pt, 10, grph);
    pictureBox1.Refresh();
}
```

23. You can compile and run the program; you can draw squares in the picture box!

24. We will now add color functionality to the program. Back in the design view, select the Red panel and then in the Properties window double-click the Click event to create an event handler for the Mouse Click on the Red Panel. Edit the code to change the color of the Stamper to red.

```
private void Red_Click(object sender, System.EventArgs e)
{
    Red.BorderStyle = BorderStyle.Fixed3D;
    Black.BorderStyle = BorderStyle.None;
    stamp.Color = Color.Red;
}
```

25. You can do the same for the black panel on the click event, setting the color to black and changing the border style to reflect which color is selected. Then compile and run the program. You should now be able to draw red or black squares.

26. The last thing to do is add the capability to draw either squares or circles. We start by defining a new type to represent the shape we want to draw. In the Form1 class, add a new enum and a member of the class to store the shape.

```
enum Shape
{
    Square,
    Circle
}
private Shape stampShape = Shape.Square;
```

27. Add event handler methods for the Square and Circle Click events.

```
private void Square_Click(object sender, System.EventArgs e)
{
    Square.BorderStyle = BorderStyle.Fixed3D;
    Circle.BorderStyle = BorderStyle.None;
    stampShape = Shape.Square;
}

private void Circle_Click(object sender, System.EventArgs e)
{
    Circle.BorderStyle = BorderStyle.Fixed3D;
    Square.BorderStyle = BorderStyle.None;
    stampShape = Shape.Circle;
}
```

28. Finally, we need to use the shape in the PictureBox MouseDown event handler method.

```
private void pictureBox1_MouseDown(object sender,
        System.Windows.Forms.MouseEventArgs e)
{
```

```
    Point pt = new Point(e.X, e.Y);
    Bitmap bmp = pictureBox1.Image as Bitmap;
    Graphics grph = Graphics.FromImage(bmp);
    if (stampShape == Shape.Circle )
        stamp.DrawCircle(pt, 10, grph);
    else
        stamp.DrawSquare(pt, 10, grph);
    pictureBox1.Refresh();
}
```

29. Compile and run the program. You can draw circles or squares in red or black, how wonderful.

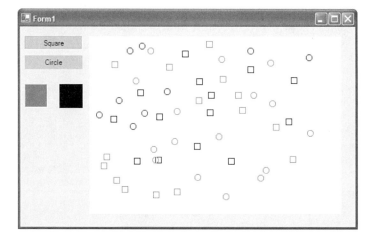

Figure 8-2   Stamping circles and squares in red and black.

I hope you can see that the use of tests to drive the development forced us to develop the core functionality before we connected it through to the GUI layer. This program is far from perfect, and there is some obvious refactoring that can be done to make the GUI layer even thinner.

Stamper Part Two

In this exercise, we need to add the functionality to stamp out triangles as well as the circles and squares that the program already does. Use your knowledge of refactoring to refactor the Stamper program and add the triangle functionality.

Stamper Part Three

Carrying on with the Stamper program, another software team now needs to use the Stamper functionality in their application. Take what you have worked on in Exercise 8-1 and build a Windows control with the Stamper functionality. If your refactoring of the Stamper was done well, this exercise should be fairly easy. (Hint: This control should expose the color and shape of the stamps as properties.)

Exercise 8-2: Using Reflection to Test the GUI

The preceding section discussed architecting the application to make the GUI layer thinner and therefore easier to test. We didn't actually test the GUI controls such as the buttons or panels. In the following exercise, we develop a Windows Forms application by writing the tests first. This exercise shows you how to use reflection to test the user-interface components on a Windows form. The application we will develop will itself use reflection to display the methods, properties, and fields (variables) of classes in an assembly.

Let's start off with creating the form.

1. Create a new C# Windows Application project called **GUITest**.

2. Add a reference to the NUnit.Framework.dll in the Project. (Right-click the References folder in Solution Explorer and select Add Reference.)

3. Add a new C# class to the project called **GUITests.cs** and edit the code in the class file to look like this.

```
using System;
using NUnit.Framework;
using System.Windows.Forms;
using System.Reflection;

namespace GUITest
{
    [TestFixture]
    public class GUITests
    {
    }
}
```

Notice we have added a using reference to System.Windows.Forms and System.Reflection; you will see why shortly.

4. The next thing to do is put some tests into the TestFixture we have just created. "Hold on," I can hear you thinking, "we haven't even added anything to the form!" Please bear with me and add the following code, and then let's see what we have done.

```
[TestFixture]
public class GUITests
{
    Form1 testForm;
    BindingFlags flags = BindingFlags.NonPublic|
        BindingFlags.Public|BindingFlags.Static|
        BindingFlags.Instance;
    Type tForm = typeof(Form1);

    [SetUp]
    public void SetupForm()
    {
        testForm = new Form1();
        testForm.Show();
    }

    [TearDown]
    public void TearDownForm()
    {
        testForm.Close();
        testForm.Dispose();
    }

    [Test]
    public void TestLoadAssembly()
    {
        FieldInfo textBoxInfo =
            tForm.GetField("AssemblyEntered",flags);
        TextBox textBox =
            (TextBox)textBoxInfo.GetValue(testForm);
        textBox.Text =
            @"C:\Work\GUITest\bin\Debug\GUITest.exe";

        MethodInfo clickMethod =
            tForm.GetMethod("LoadAssembly_Click",flags);
        Object[] args = new Object[2];
        args[0] = this;
        args[1] = new EventArgs();
        clickMethod.Invoke(testForm, args);

        FieldInfo labelInfo =
```

```
        tForm.GetField("LoadedAssembly",flags);
    Label label = (Label)labelInfo.GetValue(testForm);
    string strText = label.Text;
    Assert.AreEqual(
        @"file:///C:/Work/GUITest/bin/Debug/GUITest.EXE",
        strText,
        "Assembly Name Incorrect");
    }
}
```

We have added a setup and a teardown method. These methods run before and after each test method is run. They create and show the form, and then close and dispose of the form, respectively.

In our first test, we are getting down to business. We are using reflection to first get a FieldInfo class for a TextBox member variable of the form called AssemblyName. We then set the value in the text box to the path of this application. Next we get information about a method called LoadAssembly_Click (which I plan to be fired when a button is clicked) and invoke that method. Finally, we get details of a Label control that is a member of the form and assert that the text on the label is equal to GUITest.

We have done all this without adding any controls to our form, and yet this application will compile and run. If you run the test now in Nunit, you will notice the form flash up, although the test fails, obviously.

Deepak and Eddie from our eXtreme .NET team had a conversation about the test-first approach to develop GUI applications.

Deepak: Why do we use this test-driven development approach for GUI development? Surely it would be quicker to drag the controls onto the form and then add the tests for them?

Eddie: I have found that by developing the tests first in this way, I am forced to think more about the GUI and what it will contain. I am also forced to think of more sensible names for the controls, rather than Label1 or TextBox2. This makes the application code more readable.

Deepak: Is that all? We can rename our controls if we have a coding standard.

> **Eddie**: Another outcome I have found, unexpectedly, from developing user interfaces this way is that they tend to provide more feedback to the end user. A UI that has feedback built in it is easier to test.

Let's get the test running and hopefully you will see what Eddie is talking about.

5. In the design view for the form, add a button, label, and text box called **LoadAssembly**, **LoadedAssembly**, and **AssemblyEntered**, respectively (see Figure 8-3).

Figure 8-3   Add a button, label, and text box.

6. Double-click the LoadAssembly button to create the LoadAssembly_Click method that we invoked from the test code. At the top of the Form1.cs file, add the System.Reflection reference to the using list.

```
using System.Reflection;
```

7. Edit the code for the LoadAssembly_Click method as shown here.

```
private void LoadAssembly_Click(object sender, System.EventArgs e)
{
    try
    {
        string strApplication = AssemblyEntered.Text;
        AssemblyName aName =
            AssemblyName.GetAssemblyName(strApplication);
        Assembly assembly = Assembly.Load(aName);
```

```
        LoadedAssembly.Text = assembly.CodeBase;
    }
    catch(Exception)
    {
        LoadedAssembly.Text = "Error Loading Assembly";
    }
}
```

8. Compile the program and run the test. It should pass. If you are quick (or have a slow machine), you will notice the form load up briefly on the screen. You have now built a user interface and tested it without even having to run the program! You can run the program if you want and load up an assembly, but it doesn't do much yet.

   To add the rest of the functionality, we will add some radio buttons to select what we want to display and a TreeView control in which to display the methods, properties, and fields for each of the classes in the assembly.

9. We'll start by writing a test to validate that the TreeView (that we haven't created yet) is correctly displaying the classes for the assembly that is loaded. We know about the classes in this assembly we are building. We will use these classes to test the TreeView. In the GUITests class, add a new method called **ValidateClassesInTreeView**.

```
[Test]
public void ValidateClassesInTreeView()
{
    FieldInfo textBoxInfo =
        tForm.GetField("AssemblyEntered",flags);
    TextBox textBox =
        (TextBox)textBoxInfo.GetValue(testForm);
    textBox.Text =
        @"C:\Work\GUITest\bin\Debug\GUITest.exe";

    MethodInfo clickMethod =
        tForm.GetMethod("LoadAssembly_Click",flags);
    Object[] args = new Object[2];
    args[0] = this;
    args[1] = new EventArgs();
    clickMethod.Invoke(testForm, args);

    FieldInfo treeViewInfo =
        tForm.GetField("AssemblyTypesTree",flags);
    TreeView treeView =
```

```
                (TreeView)treeViewInfo.GetValue(testForm);
        Assert.AreEqual("Form1", treeView.Nodes[0].Text,
            "Incorrect Node(0) in Tree");
        Assert.AreEqual("GUITests", treeView.Nodes[1].Text,
            "Incorrect Node(1) in Tree");
    }
```

10. Compile and run the tests; this one should fail. Note: We have some duplicate code in the two tests. We'll come back and refactor that code soon.

11. We need to add the TreeView to the form and fill in the code necessary to make the tests pass. In the design view of the form, drag a TreeView control onto the form and rename it **AssemblyTypesTree** (as specified in the test above). In the LoadAssembly_Click method, add the following code to display the loaded assembly's types.

```
private void LoadAssembly_Click(object sender, System.EventArgs e)
{
    try
    {
        string strApplication = AssemblyEntered.Text;
        AssemblyName aName =
            AssemblyName.GetAssemblyName(strApplication);
        Assembly assembly = Assembly.Load(aName);
        LoadedAssembly.Text = assembly.CodeBase;

        Type[] aTypes = assembly.GetTypes();
        AssemblyTypesTree.Nodes.Clear();

        foreach(Type aType in aTypes)
        {
            AssemblyTypesTree.Nodes.Add(aType.Name);
        }

    }
    catch(Exception)
    {
        LoadedAssembly.Text = "Error Loading Assembly";
    }
}
```

12. Compile and run the tests. They should pass and once again we haven't yet run the application. Now run the application to check that the TreeView is displaying the classes. You will need to enter the path for the assembly in the

text box and click the LoadAssembly button. You should then see the classes for that assembly shown (see Figure 8-4).

Figure 8-4　See the types in an assembly.

13. Now we can refactor some of the test code that we spotted was duplicated earlier. We will use Extract method (discussed in Chapter 5) to place the duplicate code into a single method that both the other methods can call. These methods in the GUITest class should then look like this.

```
public void LoadGUITestAssembly()
{
    FieldInfo textBoxInfo =
        tForm.GetField("AssemblyEntered",flags);
    TextBox textBox =
        (TextBox)textBoxInfo.GetValue(testForm);
    textBox.Text =
        @"C:\Work\GUITest\bin\Debug\GUITest.exe";

    MethodInfo clickMethod =
        tForm.GetMethod("LoadAssembly_Click",flags);
    Object[] args = new Object[2];
    args[0] = this;
    args[1] = new EventArgs();
    clickMethod.Invoke(testForm, args);
}

[Test]
public void TestLoadAssembly()
{
    LoadGUITestAssembly();
```

```
        FieldInfo labelInfo =
            tForm.GetField("LoadedAssembly",flags);
        Label label = (Label)labelInfo.GetValue(testForm);
        string strText = label.Text;
        Assert.AreEqual(
            @"file:///C:/Work/GUITest/bin/Debug/GUITest.EXE",
            strText,
            "Assembly Name Incorrect");
    }

    [Test]
    public void ValidateClassesInTreeView()
    {
        LoadGUITestAssembly();

        FieldInfo treeViewInfo =
            tForm.GetField("AssemblyTypesTree",flags);
        TreeView treeView =
            (TreeView)treeViewInfo.GetValue(testForm);
        Assert.AreEqual("Form1", treeView.Nodes[0].Text,
            "Incorrect Node(0) in Tree");
        Assert.AreEqual("GUITests", treeView.Nodes[1].Text,
            "Incorrect Node(1) in Tree");
    }
```

14. Make sure the code still compiles and the tests run and pass as before.

15. Now let's add the radio buttons to select whether to show the methods, properties, or fields of the classes. Staying with the GUITest class, we'll add a method to test each of the button selections.

```
        [Test]
        public void ValidateMethodsInTreeView()
        {
            LoadGUITestAssembly();

            FieldInfo treeViewInfo =
                tForm.GetField("AssemblyTypesTree",flags);
            TreeView treeView =
                (TreeView)treeViewInfo.GetValue(testForm);

            MethodInfo clickMethod =
                tForm.GetMethod("Methods_Click",flags);
            Object[] args = new Object[2];
            args[0] = this;
            args[1] = new EventArgs();
            clickMethod.Invoke(testForm, args);
```

```
        TreeNodeCollection classMethods =
            treeView.Nodes[0].Nodes;
        Assert.AreEqual("OnMenuComplete",
            classMethods[1].Text,
            "Incorrect Method in Tree");
    }

    [Test]
    public void ValidatePropertiesInTreeView()
    {
        LoadGUITestAssembly();

        FieldInfo treeViewInfo =
            tForm.GetField("AssemblyTypesTree",flags);
        TreeView treeView =
            (TreeView)treeViewInfo.GetValue(testForm);

        MethodInfo clickMethod =
            tForm.GetMethod("Properties_Click",flags);
        Object[] args = new Object[2];
        args[0] = this;
        args[1] = new EventArgs();
        clickMethod.Invoke(testForm, args);

        TreeNodeCollection classProps =
            treeView.Nodes[0].Nodes;
        Assert.AreEqual("ActiveMdiChild",
            classProps[1].Text,
            "Incorrect Properties in in Tree");
    }

    [Test]
    public void ValidateFieldsInTreeView()
    {
        LoadGUITestAssembly();

        FieldInfo treeViewInfo =
            tForm.GetField("AssemblyTypesTree",flags);
        TreeView treeView =
            (TreeView)treeViewInfo.GetValue(testForm);

        MethodInfo clickMethod =
            tForm.GetMethod("Fields_Click",flags);
        Object[] args = new Object[2];
        args[0] = this;
        args[1] = new EventArgs();
        clickMethod.Invoke(testForm, args);
```

```
            TreeNodeCollection classFields =
                treeView.Nodes[0].Nodes;
            Assert.AreEqual("AssemblyEntered",
                classFields[1].Text,
                "Incorrect Field in in Tree");
    }
```

16. Run the tests in NUnit; these new ones should all fail.

17. We can now add the radio buttons and the code to make the tests pass. In the design view for the form, add three radio buttons next to the TreeView control. Name them Methods, Properties and Fields. Change the text on the radio buttons to also reflect the names. Then for each radio button generate a method for the click event. You can do this in the Properties window; just click the Events button and double-click the Click event. The methods should be named (automatically) Methods_Click, Properties_Click and Fields_Click.

18. To fill in the code for the radio button click events, we need access to the assembly that is loaded. To have this access, we need to extract the Assembly variable out of the LoadAssembly_Click method and make it a variable scoped by the class.

```
private Assembly assembly;
private BindingFlags flags =
    BindingFlags.NonPublic|BindingFlags.Public|
    BindingFlags.Static|BindingFlags.Instance;

private void LoadAssembly_Click(object sender, System.EventArgs e)
{
    try
    {
        string strApplication = AssemblyEntered.Text;
        AssemblyName aName =
            AssemblyName.GetAssemblyName(strApplication);
        assembly = Assembly.Load(aName);
        LoadedAssembly.Text = assembly.CodeBase;

        Type[] aTypes = assembly.GetTypes();
        AssemblyTypesTree.Nodes.Clear();

        foreach(Type aType in aTypes)
        {
            AssemblyTypesTree.Nodes.Add(aType.Name);
        }
```

```
        }
    catch(Exception)
    {
        LoadedAssembly.Text = "Error Loading Assembly";
    }
}

private void Methods_Click(object sender, System.EventArgs e)
{
    Type[] aTypes = assembly.GetTypes();
    AssemblyTypesTree.Nodes.Clear();

    foreach(Type aType in aTypes)
    {
        TreeNode node =
            AssemblyTypesTree.Nodes.Add(aType.Name);
        MethodInfo[] methods = aType.GetMethods(flags);

        foreach(MethodInfo method in methods)
        {
            node.Nodes.Add(method.Name);
        }
    }
}

private void Properties_Click(object sender, System.EventArgs e)
{
    Type[] aTypes = assembly.GetTypes();
    AssemblyTypesTree.Nodes.Clear();

    foreach(Type aType in aTypes)
    {
        TreeNode node =
            AssemblyTypesTree.Nodes.Add(aType.Name);
        PropertyInfo[] props = aType.GetProperties(flags);
        foreach(PropertyInfo prop in props)
        {
            node.Nodes.Add(prop.Name);
        }
    }
}

private void Fields_Click(object sender, System.EventArgs e)
{
    Type[] aTypes = assembly.GetTypes();
    AssemblyTypesTree.Nodes.Clear();

    foreach(Type aType in aTypes)
```

```
    {
        TreeNode node =
            AssemblyTypesTree.Nodes.Add(aType.Name);
        FieldInfo[] fields = aType.GetFields(flags);
        foreach(FieldInfo field in fields)
        {
            node.Nodes.Add(field.Name);
        }
    }
}
```

19. Note the tests are testing the value of the fields, methods, and properties of the Form1 class in this application. The order of declaration will be important. Compile the program and run the tests; they should all pass. If they don't, check that the order of your declarations matches what we are testing. For example, in the test ValidateFieldsInTreeView, we are testing that AssemblyEntered is the second field declared in the class. If this is not the case, the test will fail. To ensure it passes, change the order of declaration in your Form1 class file.

20. Now run the program and see whether you can break it. There is one obvious way. Load the application, and then, without loading an assembly, click one of the radio buttons. This causes an issue because the assembly variable has not yet been set. Let's fix this "test first."

21. Create a new method in the GUITests class called **TestMethodsInTreeWithInvalidAssembly**. This method will call the click method in the form before loading an assembly.

```
[Test]
public void TestMethodsInTreeWithInvalidAssembly()
{
    FieldInfo treeViewInfo =
        tForm.GetField("AssemblyTypesTree",flags);
    TreeView treeView =
        (TreeView)treeViewInfo.GetValue(testForm);

    MethodInfo clickMethod =
        tForm.GetMethod("Methods_Click",flags);
    Object[] args = new Object[2];
    args[0] = this;
    args[1] = new EventArgs();
    clickMethod.Invoke(testForm, args);
```

```
        Assert.AreEqual(0, treeView.Nodes.Count,
            "Tree contains nodes when no assembly is loaded");
}
```

22. Compile the program and run the test. It will fail, throwing an exception. We must now fix the code.

23. In the Methods_Click method, add the following highlighted lines to return when the assembly is not valid.

```
private void Methods_Click(object sender, System.EventArgs e)
{
    if (null == assembly)
    {
        Methods.Checked = false;
        return;
    }

    Type[] aTypes = assembly.GetTypes();
    AssemblyTypesTree.Nodes.Clear();

    foreach(Type aType in aTypes)
    {
        TreeNode node =
            AssemblyTypesTree.Nodes.Add(aType.Name);
        MethodInfo[] methods = aType.GetMethods(flags);
        foreach(MethodInfo method in methods)
        {
            node.Nodes.Add(method.Name);
        }
    }
}
```

24. Compile and run the tests again. They should all pass. I leave it for you to do the same for each of the other radio button click methods.

25. A lot of duplicate code is scattered around this little application. It should be refactored to remove duplication. This you can do on your own to test your refactoring skills. Remember to run the tests after every change to validate you have not broken anything.

This exercise has shown you how it is possible to develop user-interface code using the principles of test-driven design. By developing your code in a test-first manner, you need to think more about what you are going to call the controls before you drag them from the toolbox onto the form. I believe this is a good thing because you will be more likely to give meaningful names to the controls and their methods.

Exercises on Your Own

The following two exercises are for you to carry out on your own (or with a friend); they will help you to reinforce the techniques you have learned in this chapter.

Exercise 8-3: Building a Small System

Build a Windows application that, as in Exercise 8-2, uses reflection to show the methods, properties, and fields of classes in an assembly. But use a thinner GUI layer. Try to encapsulate as much of the functionality as possible into separate classes. Of course, use the test-driven development ideas you have learned along with refactoring.

This exercise should take you no more than an hour.

Exercise 8-4: Changing the GUI with Confidence

Now change the user interface on the Windows application you just built to operate from the command line.

(Optional extra) Output the results into an XML file.

This exercise should take no longer than 30 minutes.

Testing Third-Party Libraries

Many developers are now using third-party libraries. The .NET Framework development environment encourages this by promoting the development of component-based solutions across the enterprise. When using third-party libraries, there are approaches that can be taken to maximize the quality of the code produced and reduce the cost of change through the lifetime of the system. In the following exercises, we explore how these approaches fit with the XP practices.

We All Do It

One of the classic mistakes that development teams often make is to assume that when they get a third-party library it will just work. I am not sure why this belief exists; maybe they believe the marketing hype, or the sales pitch was really good.

The flip side to this is that some developers refuse to touch third-party libraries. These developers are convinced they will definitely not work, in part, because they don't trust any code they didn't write themselves.

Our eXtreme .NET team faces this issue.

Deepak: Hey, I found this cool library that loads and saves time zones for us in an XML file. I reckon we should use it for the application. We're going to need to do this anyway.

Sue: No way. That is easy to write; we can just write our own. Then we don't have to use other people's buggy code.

Eddie: Hey, we can have a look at it. If we write tests for the functionality we want, then we can see if the library does what we need.

Deepak: Okay, that makes sense.

Sue: I am not convinced. Can I pair with someone to write the tests?

Eddie: Sure, let's do it

These misconceptions can be overcome by writing tests around the library, or at least the functionality you need to use. Because you are reading this book, I bet you are thinking of using some third-party development library. How can I be so certain?

The .NET Framework Is a Third-Party Library!

For most of you, the .NET Framework is a third-party library. If you are smart, you will also be highly likely you are using libraries, components, or code developed by other teams. This code might have been developed either in your company or other companies. Why waste your time developing code that someone else has already invested their time and effort into?

Component-Based Software Development Is Here

Microsoft has been working hard on the .NET Framework, and it provides solutions to many of the failings of their previous component-based offering, COM. For many developers, COM was good enough for their component-based applications, but there were issues with scalability to very large systems and cross-platform interoperability. The .NET Framework goes a long way toward solving these problems and opens the doors wider for component-based solutions, leveraging remoting, Web services, and cross-language library integration.

If It Goes Wrong, We're All in the Brown Stuff

The trouble with the increase in utilization of components written by other teams of developers is that we are exposing ourselves to ever-greater unknowns. This is often why developers don't trust anything unless they write it themselves. This lack of trust is not only arrogant, but also commercially unviable. If we are going to use more code that we don't have "control" over, we need to find some way to protect ourselves against issues with that code. We are going to investigate how we can use some of the test-driven development practices to protect ourselves from issues arising through using functionality provided by third-party components.

Put the Alarms in Place

By writing tests for each unit of functionality that you use from a third party, you are doing three things:

1. You are validating your theories as to how the library works.
2. You are building confidence in the use of that library.
3. You are protecting yourself from changes in future versions of the library.

This final one is important. If you have a test suite for a third-party library that tests all the functionality you use from that library, when a new version of the library becomes available, you can run the test suite against that new version. The tests will show you whether the changes will have a detrimental effect on the software you have written.

Step-by-Step Exercises Using a Third-Party Library

In the next exercise, we learn how to build a test suite for a .NET Framework class library in C#. The class library provides some simple functionality for loading and saving collections of time zone information. This library will be useful for the clocks application we first encountered in Chapter 3. This library could have been written by a colleague at work, another department, an external contractor, or bought off the shelf or downloaded from a Web site. Its origins are not important; validation of its functionality is what we care about.

Let's code.

Exercise 8-5: Setting Up NUnit (Again!)

1. Create a new C# console application in Visual Studio called **TimeZones**.

2. As in the previous exercises, add a reference to the NUnit.Framework.dll.

3. Also add a reference to the TimeZoneSerializer.dll (which you can download from http://eXtreme.NET.roodyn.com/Book Exercises.aspx).

4. Create a new class called **TestTimeZoneSerializer.cs** and edit the file, creating a class called **TestTimeZoneSerializer**, using the TestFixture attribute to mark it as a fixture.

```
using System;
using NUnit.Framework;

namespace TimeZones
{
    [TestFixture]
    public class TestTimeZoneSerializer
    {

    }
}
```

We now have a C# console application that has a testing framework ready to test the library we want to use.

Exercise 8-6: The Quick Breadth Test

The first thing we can test is an overall breadth of the functionality we require. If this library doesn't do what we need or operate adequately, we want to know as soon as possible. There is no point in writing detailed tests for each piece of functionality that all succeed, only to find at the end that the overall behavior doesn't match our expectations. Writing a couple of overall breadth of functionality tests first will let us know very quickly whether it is worth continuing and writing some more detailed tests for the functions being used.

1. To test the TimeZoneSerializer, we can make our lives easier by including the namespace in our using list. We also need the System.Globalization namespace to access DateTimeFormatInfo. Add them to the top of the test class file.

```
using TimeZoneSerializer;
using System.Globalization;
```

2. Create a new Test method called **BreadthTest**. In this method, we create a time zones file, add some zones to it, and save it. We then load the file and ensure that it contains the zones we added. This will give us the confidence that the overall functionality is roughly working and does what we need.

```
[Test]
public void BreadthTest()
{
    TimeZonesFile zoneDoc = new TimeZonesFile();

    TimeZoneData zoneLondon = new TimeZoneData();
    zoneLondon.m_strPlace = "London";
    zoneLondon.m_nBias                  = 0;
    zoneLondon.m_nDaylightBias      = -60;
    zoneLondon.m_nStandardBias      = 0;
    zoneLondon.m_DaylightDate = DateTime.Parse(
        "03/31/2002 01:00",
        DateTimeFormatInfo.InvariantInfo);
    zoneLondon.m_StandardDate = DateTime.Parse(
        "10/27/2002 02:00",
        DateTimeFormatInfo.InvariantInfo);
    zoneDoc.AddZone(zoneLondon);

    TimeZoneData zoneSydney = new TimeZoneData();
    zoneSydney.m_strPlace ="Sydney";
    zoneSydney.m_nBias                  =-600;
    zoneSydney.m_nDaylightBias      =-60;
    zoneSydney.m_nStandardBias      =0;
    zoneSydney.m_DaylightDate = DateTime.Parse(
        "10/27/2002 02:00",
        DateTimeFormatInfo.InvariantInfo);
    zoneSydney.m_StandardDate = DateTime.Parse(
        "03/31/2002 03:00",
        DateTimeFormatInfo.InvariantInfo);
    zoneDoc.AddZone(zoneSydney);

    TimeZoneData zoneLA = new TimeZoneData();
    zoneLA.m_strPlace = "L.A.";
```

```
    zoneLA.m_nBias                    =480;
    zoneLA.m_nDaylightBias       =-60;
    zoneLA.m_nStandardBias       =0;
    zoneLA.m_DaylightDate = DateTime.Parse(
        "04/07/2002 02:00",
        DateTimeFormatInfo.InvariantInfo);
    zoneLA.m_StandardDate = DateTime.Parse(
        "10/27/2002 02:00",
        DateTimeFormatInfo.InvariantInfo);
    zoneDoc.AddZone(zoneLA);
    zoneDoc.WriteToFile(
        @"C:\TestTimeZoneSerializer.TestBreadth.xml");

    TimeZonesFile loadedZones = TimeZonesFile.LoadFromFile(
        @"C:\TestTimeZoneSerializer.TestBreadth.xml");
    int zonesLoaded = 0;
    foreach (TimeZoneData tzone in loadedZones.Zones)
    {
        switch (tzone.m_strPlace)
        {
            case "London":
                Assert.AreEqual(zoneLondon, tzone,
                    "London zone is not same as saved");
                zonesLoaded ++;
                break;
            case "Sydney":
                Assert.AreEqual(zoneSydney, tzone,
                    "Sydney zone is not same as saved");
                zonesLoaded ++;
                break;
            case "L.A.":
                Assert.AreEqual(zoneLA, tzone,
                    "L.A. zone is not same as saved");
                zonesLoaded ++;
                break;
        }
    }
    Assert.AreEqual(3,zonesLoaded,
        "Did not loaded all the zones saved");
}
```

3. Compile the program and run the test, using either the NUnit GUI app or the NUnitConsole. The tests should pass, indicating that we are now happy to move on. We can now test each area of functionality more fully without being concerned that we are wasting our time because the whole library does not actually work.

This BreadthTest function is fairly large and takes a bit of time to run. If you have a few test methods like this, the time it takes to run all the tests will start to become annoying to most developers. The developers will stop running the tests on a regular basis. For this reason, it is worth putting tests such as this BreadthTest method in a suite (or fixture) of "long" tests that get run every night only as part of the nightly build process. Of course, a developer can always run these long tests manually if he suspects something might have changed that will cause these tests to fail.

Exercise 8-7: The Functional Depth Test

Now that we have proven that the overall functionality of the library meets our requirements, we can do some deeper testing of the individual units of functionality we want to use. For this example, we write tests only for the static LoadFromFile method of the TimeZonesFile class. This exercise should provide you with enough knowledge to enable you to write your own depth testing methods when you need them.

1. In the same C# console project, create a new class called **TestTimeZonesFile** and set it up as before to be a test fixture using the attribute.

   Add a new Test method to this class called **LoadFromFileTest**.

```
using System;
using System.Globalization;
using TimeZoneSerializer;
using NUnit.Framework;

namespace TimeZones
{
    [TestFixture]
    public class TestTimeZonesFile
    {
        [Test]
        public void LoadFromFileTest()
        {
        }
    }
}
```

2. In the LoadFromFileTest method, we are going to check that the library can load files that exist, handles loading nonexistent files, and is consistent in its

behavior. To write these tests, we need to have some files that we can load. We will write a method called **HelperLoadFromFile**. This method writes out three files: an empty file, a file containing one time zone, and a file containing three time zones. If you are following along with these exercises, you might want to rename the location of your test files. These test files, once created, should become part of your project and be checked into your source control software.

```
[Test]
public void HelperLoadFromFile()
{
    TimeZonesFile zoneDoc = new TimeZonesFile();
    zoneDoc.WriteToFile(
        @"C:\Work\TestFiles\EmptyTimeZoneFile.xml");
    TimeZoneData zoneLondon = new TimeZoneData();
    zoneLondon.m_strPlace = "London";
    zoneLondon.m_nBias                = 0;
    zoneLondon.m_nDaylightBias        = -60;
    zoneLondon.m_nStandardBias        = 0;
    zoneLondon.m_DaylightDate = DateTime.Parse(
        "03/31/2002 01:00",
        DateTimeFormatInfo.InvariantInfo);
    zoneLondon.m_StandardDate = DateTime.Parse(
        "10/27/2002 02:00",
        DateTimeFormatInfo.InvariantInfo);
    zoneDoc.AddZone(zoneLondon);
    zoneDoc.WriteToFile(
        @"C:\Work\TestFiles\SingleTimeZoneFile.xml");

    TimeZoneData zoneSydney = new TimeZoneData();
    zoneSydney.m_strPlace ="Sydney";
    zoneSydney.m_nBias        =-600;
    zoneSydney.m_nDaylightBias        =-60;
    zoneSydney.m_nStandardBias        =0;
    zoneSydney.m_DaylightDate = DateTime.Parse(
        "10/27/2002 02:00",
        DateTimeFormatInfo.InvariantInfo);
    zoneSydney.m_StandardDate = DateTime.Parse(
        "03/31/2002 03:00",
        DateTimeFormatInfo.InvariantInfo);
    zoneDoc.AddZone(zoneSydney);

    TimeZoneData zoneLA = new TimeZoneData();
    zoneLA.m_strPlace = "L.A.";
    zoneLA.m_nBias            =480;
    zoneLA.m_nDaylightBias    =-60;
```

```
        zoneLA.m_nStandardBias  =0;
        zoneLA.m_DaylightDate = DateTime.Parse(
            "04/07/2002 02:00",
            DateTimeFormatInfo.InvariantInfo);
        zoneLA.m_StandardDate = DateTime.Parse(
            "10/27/2002 02:00",
            DateTimeFormatInfo.InvariantInfo);
        zoneDoc.AddZone(zoneLA);

        zoneDoc.WriteToFile(
            @"C:\Work\TestFiles\MultipleTimeZoneFile.xml");
    }
```

3. Compile the program and run the TestTimeZonesFile test fixture. This will run two tests, the empty TestLoadFromFile method and the TestHelperLoad-FromFile. After you have run the test, you can have a look at the files generated. Now comment out the Test attribute from the helper method; hopefully we won't need that again.

   The files we have just created should be fixed and, as mentioned before, checked into your version control system. We can now use these files to test the behavior of the LoadFromFile method.

4. In the TestLoadFromFile method, we can start by loading these files and checking they have the correct number of time zones. This might seem a little simplistic, and people often say, "Why write this test? It doesn't prove anything; it's too simple." There is a lot of benefit to having simple tests. It is often the simple things that point out problems for us. Simple tests that prove the obvious are good, and once written we don't need to revisit them. These tests will just run and run, making sure the obvious doesn't ever get overlooked!

```
[Test]
public void LoadFromFileTest()
{
    TimeZonesFile tzFile = TimeZonesFile.LoadFromFile
        (@"C:\Work\TestFiles\EmptyTimeZoneFile.xml");
    Assert.AreEqual(0,tzFile.Zones.Count,
        "Empty Time Zones File contains a time zone");

    tzFile = TimeZonesFile.LoadFromFile
        (@"C:\Work\TestFiles\SingleTimeZoneFile.xml");
    Assert.AreEqual(1,tzFile.Zones.Count,
      "Single Time Zones File contains incorrect number of time zones");
```

```
    tzFile = TimeZonesFile.LoadFromFile
        (@"C:\Work\TestFiles\MultipleTimeZoneFile.xml");
    Assert.AreEqual(3,tzFile.Zones.Count,
  "Multiple Time Zones File contains incorrect number of time zones");
}
```

5. Compile and run the tests in the TestTimeZoneFile fixture. There should be one test (remember, we commented out the other one), and it should pass.

6. Next we can beef this test up by checking some of the zones we have loaded are as expected.

```
[Test]
public void LoadFromFileTest()
{
    TimeZonesFile tzFile = TimeZonesFile.LoadFromFile
        (@"C:\Work\TestFiles\EmptyTimeZoneFile.xml");
    Assert.AreEqual(0,tzFile.Zones.Count,
        "Empty Time Zones File contains a time zone");

    tzFile = TimeZonesFile.LoadFromFile
        (@"C:\Work\TestFiles\SingleTimeZoneFile.xml");
    Assert.AreEqual(1,tzFile.Zones.Count,
      "Single Time Zones File contains incorrect number of time zones");

    TimeZoneData zoneLondon = new TimeZoneData();
    zoneLondon.m_strPlace = "London";
    zoneLondon.m_nBias           = 0;
    zoneLondon.m_nDaylightBias   = -60;
    zoneLondon.m_nStandardBias   = 0;
    zoneLondon.m_DaylightDate =
    DateTime.Parse("03/31/2002 01:00",
    DateTimeFormatInfo.InvariantInfo);
    zoneLondon.m_StandardDate =
    DateTime.Parse("10/27/2002 02:00",
    DateTimeFormatInfo.InvariantInfo);

    Assert.AreEqual(zoneLondon,tzFile.Zones[0],
        "Time zone loaded from single time zone file incorrect");

    tzFile = TimeZonesFile.LoadFromFile
        (@"C:\Work\TestFiles\MultipleTimeZoneFile.xml");
    Assert.AreEqual(3,tzFile.Zones.Count,
  "Mulitple Time Zones File contains incorrect number of time zones");

    Assert.AreEqual(zoneLondon,tzFile.Zones[0],
      "London time zone loaded from multiple time zone file incorrect");
```

```
TimeZoneData zoneLA = new TimeZoneData();
zoneLA.m_strPlace = "L.A.";
zoneLA.m_nBias              =480;
zoneLA.m_nDaylightBias      =-60;
zoneLA.m_nStandardBias      =0;
zoneLA.m_DaylightDate = DateTime.Parse("04/07/2002 02:00",
    DateTimeFormatInfo.InvariantInfo);
zoneLA.m_StandardDate = DateTime.Parse("10/27/2002 02:00",
    DateTimeFormatInfo.InvariantInfo);

Assert.AreEqual(zoneLA ,tzFile.Zones[2],
    "LA time zone loaded from multiple time zone file incorrect");

}
```

7. Compile and run the tests again; they should pass.

At this point, we have tested that the TimeZonesFile.LoadFromFile method behaves as expected under normal conditions. We have also protected ourselves against future versions of the library not supporting the same file format.

If a new version of the library becomes available, we can run the tests against it. If the tests fail to load these files correctly, it would indicate an issue with backward compatibility. We could make a decision then as to whether we adopt the new version of the library or stay with the existing older version. A new version is likely to have some extra features that are attractive. If many of the tests against that library fail, it could be a strong indicator that the cost of going to the new version of the library means that it is not a viable option.

The next exercise explores how we can handle the exceptional cases and test for behavior outside the boundaries of the method's capabilities.

Exercise 8-8: Testing for Exceptions

We have tested the breadth of the functionality of the library, and we have tested some expected behavior of one particular function (LoadFromFile) in the library. It would be worth testing how this function behaves when given spurious input or in exceptional cases.

1. The first obvious case to test for is when the file doesn't exist. We would expect that the function would throw a standard exception if the file doesn't exist, something like a System.IO.FileNotFound. NUnit supports a C# attribute ExpectedException, which takes the type of exception expected. If the code in the method causes the exception to be thrown, the test passes; otherwise, it fails.

```
[ExpectedException(typeof(System.IO.FileNotFoundException))]
public void TestLoadFromFileNonExistant()
{
        TimeZonesFile tzFile = TimeZonesFile.LoadFromFile
                (@"C:\Work\TestFiles\No such file.xml");
}
```

2. Compile and run the tests; there should be two tests now, and they should both pass.

3. As an exercise for you, think of other cases where the library might fail and write some test methods to confirm your thoughts. (I can think of at least three things to test for.)

After you have finished writing the breadth and depth tests for a library, you can confidently use it with the knowledge that you have protected yourself against any unexpected behavior in this library or any future versions of it. The other thing you have achieved is to have documented the features of the library that you are using. This documentation in the form of executing code is the most valuable documentation I have ever found, because if the tests run it must be right.

Working with Legacy Code

One excuse I hear a lot of when I'm working with companies is this: "Our code doesn't have any tests, and it will be far too hard to put tests in it now." Some of the more keen developers often follow this with, "Great! That means we have to start again and we can throw away all that @*$% code we've been writing for the last *n* months." Actually, no. Unless the code is really bad or doesn't actually do what is required of it,[1] I do not recommend throwing it away and starting again. Instead, leave what works alone. As the saying goes, "If it ain't broke, don't fix it." If, on the other hand, you have an area of code you need to enhance or somewhere there is a bug that needs to be fixed, I recommend fixing it by using the test-first approach.

In the following exercise, we work with a library that was written by a former employee late one night just before he left the company. Needless to say, it has been causing a few problems, and we have been asked to get it working. The library is reasonably simple. It contains one function for calculating some derived data for a stock. You can download the source code for the library from http://www.eXtreme.NET.Roodyn.com/ Book Exercises.aspx.

Exercise 8-9: Examining the Code

Most of the code for this project is in one file, StockData.cs. Examine this code and see how many observations you can make in one minute. Don't try to walk through the functionality; just see what you can spot at first glance.

```
using System;
using System.Globalization;
using System.Xml;
using System.IO;

namespace StockDataLib
{
    public class StockData
    {
        public StockData(){}

        public void CalcDataForDay(string stock, DateTime day,
            ref float open, ref float cloase,ref float high,
            ref float low, ref float average)
        {
            //open the file for the stock
            FileStream file =
                new FileStream(@"c:\stocks\" + stock + ".stk",
                FileMode.Open);

            //read in all the prices
            XmlDocument doc = new XmlDocument();
            doc.Load(file);

            //get the prices for the day
            float[] prices = new float[1024];
            int n = 0;
            foreach (XmlNode price in
                doc.DocumentElement.ChildNodes)
            {
                if (day.Date ==
```

```
                    DateTime.Parse(price["DateTime"].InnerText,
                    DateTimeFormatInfo.InvariantInfo).Date)
            {

                prices[n] =
                  (float)Convert.ToDouble(price["Price"].InnerText);
                 n++;
            }
        }
        // calc the data
        float tmpHigh = 0;
        for (int i = 1; i<prices.Length; i++)
        {
            if (prices[i] > tmpHigh)
            {
                tmpHigh = prices[i];
            }
        }

        float tmpLow = 0;
        for (int i = 1; i<prices.Length; i++)
        {
            if (prices[i] < tmpLow)
            {
                tmpLow = prices[i];
            }
        }

        float tmpAverage = 0;
        for (int i = 1; i<prices.Length; i++)
        {
            tmpAverage += prices[i];
        }
        tmpAverage = tmpAverage/(n-1);

        high = tmpHigh;
        low = tmpLow;
        average = tmpAverage;

    }
  }
}
//struct PriceTime
//{
//    public float price;
//    public DateTime time;
//}
```

Here are a number of things to note about this code:

1. There is no test code.
2. The function is reasonably long.
3. The function does more than one thing.
4. Two of the parameters. (Open and Close aren't used.)
5. The Close parameter is misspelled (indicates a lack of care).
6. There is a PriceTime structure that is commented out. (So why is it there?)
7. It uses hard-coded values (magic numbers), the path for the file, and the size of the prices array.

It would be tempting to get started and change some of the obvious problems (such as the hard-coded values) before dealing with the functionality. I always believe we should code test first and get a solution that meets our customer's needs as quickly as possible and to the highest quality. This means even changing the spelling of one parameter should *not* be done without having a test; the change in the spelling is a refactor and should not be done without a test.

So the first thing we're going to do is write some test code for this function.

Exercise 8-10: Writing a Breadth Test

We need to add a fixture and some test functionality to our library so we can validate its behavior.

1. As in the previous exercises, add a reference to the NUnit.Framework.dll.
2. Add a new StockDataTests class to the project and add the TestFixture attribute to the class.
3. If you now compile the project and run it through the NUnit GUI, you will see that the fixture called StockDataTests turns yellow. This is to indicate that you have an empty fixture, which is something unusual and therefore highlighted.
4. We will create a breadth test first, so create a new test method in the StockDataTests class called **BreadthTestCalcDataForDay**.
5. Next we are going to write the test to use some data from a made-up test stock; edit your StockDataTests class file so it reads as shown.

```
using System;
using System.Globalization;
using NUnit.Framework;

namespace StockDataLib
{
    [TestFixture] public class StockDataTests
    {
        [Test]public void BreadthTestCalcDataForDay()
        {
            StockData sData = new StockData();

            float open = 0.0F;
            float close = 0.0F;
            float high = 0.0F;
            float low = 0.0F;
            float average = 0.0F;
            string stock = "TestStock1";
            DateTime day = DateTime.Parse("03/27/2002 08:58",
                DateTimeFormatInfo.InvariantInfo);

            sData.CalcDataForDay(stock, day,
                ref open, ref close, ref high, ref low, ref average);

            Assertion.AssertEquals(
                "Invalid Open in TestStock1",1.5000,open);
            Assertion.AssertEquals(
                "Invalid Close in TestStock1",1.7000,close);
            Assertion.AssertEquals(
                "Invalid High in TestStock1",1.8000,high);
            Assertion.AssertEquals(
                "Invalid Low in TestStock1",1.4000,low);
            Assertion.AssertEquals(
                "Invalid Average in TestStock1",1.6000,average);
        }
    }
}
```

6. Compile this and run the test through the NUnit GUI. You should see that it fails because it cannot find the file c:\stocks\TestStock1.stk. So we are going to need to create a file for our test stock. This file must contain data that would generate the results we want in the test we have just written.

But how do we know what the format for the stock price file is?

The first port of call should be your customer; this is one of the reasons that an XP practice is the onsite customer. If we couldn't ask the customer a question, we would have to do our best by working out what the file format should be by working through the code or reading the documentation (which doesn't exist!).

The customer for this class library is another development team that needs the library. Asking the customer, we discover that the format is XML (as you probably guessed from looking at the code). This development team provides us with the following example.

```xml
<?xml version="1.0" encoding="utf-8" ?>
<Stock>
    <PriceTime>
        <DateTime>30/01/2002 09:30</DateTime>
        <Price>9.9999</Price>
    </PriceTime>
</Stock>
```

With a PriceTime for each price at a time and saved as the stockname with an .stk extension, this format is not exactly efficient, but we will go with it for the moment. We will create a file that we would expect to give us the results we want from the test.

```xml
<?xml version="1.0" encoding="utf-8" ?>
<Stock>
    <PriceTime>
        <DateTime>03/26/2002 09:30</DateTime>
        <Price>3.5000</Price>
    </PriceTime>
    <PriceTime>
        <DateTime>03/27/2002 09:00</DateTime>
        <Price>1.5000</Price>
    </PriceTime>
    <PriceTime>
        <DateTime>03/27/2002 13:30</DateTime>
        <Price>1.8000</Price>
    </PriceTime>
    <PriceTime>
        <DateTime>03/27/2002 14:45</DateTime>
        <Price>1.4000</Price>
    </PriceTime>
    <PriceTime>
        <DateTime>03/27/2002 16:30</DateTime>
```

```
        <Price>1.7000</Price>
    </PriceTime>
    <PriceTime>
        <DateTime>03/28/2002 14:48</DateTime>
        <Price>2.5000</Price>
    </PriceTime>
    <PriceTime>
        <DateTime>03/28/2002 16:30</DateTime>
        <Price>3.0000</Price>
    </PriceTime>
</Stock>
```

Don't forget to save the file in a directory called stocks on your C: drive (we'll come back to this later) and name it **TestStock1.stk**.

7. Now rerun the test through the NUnit GUI. You should now get a different error: Invalid Open in TestStock1. We can now get about the business of fixing the code.

Exercise 8-11: Getting the Breadth Test Running

In this exercise, we walk through getting part of the test we just wrote to work. Then I leave it to you as an exercise to get the rest of this test running.

We start by fixing the problem reported with the open price. If you look through the code, you will see that the open parameter is not even used, so it is not surprising that it is not correct!

1. The open is the first price of the day. If we look through the code, we can see that there is a loop that walks through all the prices in the file and puts the prices for the day into a prices array. So we need to copy the first value of that array to the open parameter.

```
open = prices[0];
```

2. Compile and run the tests. You should now see that it passes the assert for the open price. The assert for the close price is now failing. You can now fix the rest of this test yourself; the close is the last price of the day, the high is the highest price that day, the low is lowest price of the day, and the average is the sum of all the day's prices divided by the number of prices that day.

Remember to always do the simplest thing that will work and then move on. Work fast and furious.

Your code should look something like this:

```
public void CalcDataForDay(string stock, DateTime day,
    ref float open, ref float close,ref float high,
    ref float low, ref float average)
{
    //open the file for the stock
    FileStream file =
        new FileStream(@"c:\stocks\" + stock + ".stk",
        FileMode.Open);

    //read in all the prices
    XmlDocument doc = new XmlDocument();
    doc.Load(file);

    //get the prices for the day
    float[] prices = new float[1024];
    int n = 0;
    foreach (XmlNode price in doc.DocumentElement.ChildNodes)
    {
        if (day.Date == DateTime.Parse(price["DateTime"].InnerText,
            DateTimeFormatInfo.InvariantInfo).Date)
        {
            prices[n] =
                (float)Convert.ToDouble(price["Price"].InnerText);
            n++;
        }
    }
    open = prices[0];
    close = prices[n-1];

    // calc the data
    float tmpHigh = 0;
    for (int i = 1; i<prices.Length; i++)
    {
        if (prices[i] > tmpHigh)
        {
            tmpHigh = prices[i];
        }
    }

    float tmpLow = float.MaxValue;
    for (int i = 0; i<n; i++)
    {
        if (prices[i] < tmpLow)
        {
            tmpLow = prices[i];
        }
```

```
    }

    float tmpAverage = 0;
    for (int i = 0; i<n; i++)
    {
        tmpAverage += prices[i];
    }
    tmpAverage = tmpAverage/n;

    high = tmpHigh;
    low = tmpLow;
    average = tmpAverage;

}
```

If you did something similar, congratulations! If you did significantly more, you did more than was necessary to fix the test. Pardon me? I thought I heard you say that you can see other problems with the code. Well, yes, there are lots of other problems with this code, and we are going to write new tests to fix those issues.

But why? Why not just fix the stuff that is broken when you can clearly see it is wrong?

The main reason is that the tests will document the code. When we see something that can break the code, we should write a test to break the code and then fix it. So let's do that now. I am emphasizing this point again because it is so important to understand.

Exercise 8-12: Writing a Test to Break the Code

One of the places that looks to be obviously wrong is the calculation of the high. We changed the other two loops for calculating the low and the average, but we did not need to change the loop for the high because it passed the breadth test. We need to think how we can break the code and turn that idea into test code.

1. We'll start by writing a test that will test the high value.

```
[Test]
public void HighTestCalcDataForDay()
{
    StockData sData = new StockData();
```

```
float open = 0.0F;
float close = 0.0F;
float high = 0.0F;
float low = 0.0F;
float average = 0.0F;
string stock = "TestHighFirst";
DateTime day = DateTime.Parse("03/27/2002 08:58",
    DateTimeFormatInfo.InvariantInfo);

sData.CalcDataForDay(stock, day,
    ref open, ref close, ref high, ref low, ref average);

Assert.AreEqual(1.8000,high,
    "Invalid High in TestHighFirst");
}
```

2. Notice that we now have duplicate code that can be refactored into a setup method. We won't do that until we have finished and have this test working. We might change what we have written, and then the refactoring would have been a waste of time.

3. We now must create a file for this new test stock. My suspicion is that the code will fail if the high is the first price of the day, so we create a file that reflects this and save it as **TestHighFirst.stk** in the C:\stocks directory.

```
<?xml version="1.0" encoding="utf-8" ?>
<Stock>
    <PriceTime>
        <DateTime>03/26/2002 09:30</DateTime>
        <Price>3.5000</Price>
    </PriceTime>
    <PriceTime>
        <DateTime>03/27/2002 09:00</DateTime>
        <Price>1.8000</Price>
    </PriceTime>
    <PriceTime>
        <DateTime>03/27/2002 13:30</DateTime>
        <Price>1.7000</Price>
    </PriceTime>
    <PriceTime>
        <DateTime>03/27/2002 14:45</DateTime>
        <Price>1.6000</Price>
    </PriceTime>
    <PriceTime>
        <DateTime>03/27/2002 16:30</DateTime>
```

```
            <Price>1.5000</Price>
        </PriceTime>
        <PriceTime>
            <DateTime>03/28/2002 14:48</DateTime>
            <Price>2.5000</Price>
        </PriceTime>
        <PriceTime>
            <DateTime>03/28/2002 16:30</DateTime>
            <Price>3.0000</Price>
        </PriceTime>
    </Stock>
```

4. Compile and run the test from NUnit, and we discover that sure enough the high is calculated incorrectly. So now we must fix the code.

5. The fix is a simple matter of changing the loop control statement.

```
public void CalcDataForDay(string stock, DateTime day,
        ref float open, ref float close,ref float high,
        ref float low, ref float average)
{
    .
    .
    .

    // calc the data
    float tmpHigh = 0;
    for (int i = 0; i<n; i++)
    {
        if (prices[i] > tmpHigh)
        {
            tmpHigh = prices[i];
        }
    }
    .
    .
    .

}
```

6. Compile the code and run the tests. They should succeed.

   This is a good example of a very simple code change required to fix a bug. The advantage of writing a test is that you have encoded the correct behavior into code that will be run every time the tests are run (which should be often). It is a preventive measure that will protect the code from being broken in the same way again.

7. Now we can refactor the test code to place the duplicate code in a set up method.

Your test class code should read as follows.

```
[TestFixture]
public class StockDataTests
{
    StockData sData;
    float open;
    float close;
    float high;
    float low;
    float average;

    [SetUp]public void Init()
    {
        sData = new StockData();

        open = 0.0F;
        close = 0.0F;
        high = 0.0F;
        low = 0.0F;
        average = 0.0F;
    }

    [Test]
    public void BreadthTestCalcDataForDay()
    {
        string stock = "TestStock1";
        DateTime day = DateTime.Parse("03/27/2002 08:58",
            DateTimeFormatInfo.InvariantInfo);

        sData.CalcDataForDay(stock, day,
            ref open, ref close, ref high, ref low, ref average);

        Assert.AreEqual(1.5000, open,
            "Invalid Open in TestStock1");
        Assert.AreEqual(1.7000,close,
            "Invalid Close in TestStock1");
        Assert.AreEqual(1.8000,high,
            "Invalid High in TestStock1");
        Assert.AreEqual(1.4000,low,
            "Invalid Low in TestStock1");
        Assert.AreEqual(1.6000,average,
            "Invalid Average in TestStock1");
```

```
    }

    [Test]
    public void HighTestCalcDataForDay()
    {
        string stock = "TestHighFirst";
        DateTime day = DateTime.Parse("03/27/2002 08:58",
            DateTimeFormatInfo.InvariantInfo);

        sData.CalcDataForDay(stock, day,
            ref open, ref close, ref high, ref low, ref average);

        Assert.AreEqual(1.8000,high,
            "Invalid High in TestHighFirst");
    }
}
```

We have written a breadth test to validate overall functionality and a test to fix a piece of code that we could see was obviously wrong. Now I want us to return to a problem that you might have noticed when running the tests. When you run the tests multiple times in a row without reloading the assembly, you can get an error: The process cannot access the file…. This is a classic example of a problem that you might encounter in the wild, in that it occurs intermittently. We need to write a test that will force it to happen every time.

Exercise 8-13: Forcing an Intermittent Error

1. It appears that the error occurs when you run the code through its paces several times in a row, so we'll start by writing a simple test that just calls the method multiple times.

```
[Test]
public void MultipleTestCalcDataForDay()
{
    string stock = "TestStock1";
    DateTime day = DateTime.Parse("03/27/2002 08:58",
        DateTimeFormatInfo.InvariantInfo);

    sData.CalcDataForDay(stock, day,
        ref open, ref close, ref high, ref low, ref average);
```

```
        sData.CalcDataForDay(stock, day,
            ref open, ref close, ref high, ref low, ref average);

        sData.CalcDataForDay(stock, day,
            ref open, ref close, ref high, ref low, ref average);
    }
```

2. Compile and run the tests a few times. You should see that while the other two tests sometimes fail, because of this error, this last test always fails. Now we have a test that always fails we can set about fixing the bug.

3. Looking through the code, we can see that the stock file that is opened and the method is never closed, so we can add the following line to the end of the method.

```
file.Close();
```

4. Now compile again and run the tests. You can run the tests a few times and you'll see that we have fixed the bug.

Again this is a simple fix, but we wrote test code to protect ourselves from changes in the future breaking the code again in the same way.

You have seen how to add tests to code that was written without testing in mind and then fix some bugs in that code. We did testing for overall functionality for specific issues that we can spot are incorrect and coping with inconsistent behavior.

Coding with Protection

In the next two exercises, I want you to use a third-party library and protect yourself against changes that might occur in future versions of the library.

Exercise 8-14: Protecting Yourself Against the Change

We are building an application for tourists. This application will provide tourists with information about locations they may want to visit. We are going to use a class library (called WhereIs.dll) that is being written by another team. The first version they give us supports two methods in a Search class:

- FindCity, which returns the capital city if we give it a country name

- FindAttraction, which returns a popular tourist attraction for a capital city

We know that the library is still in development, but we need to start our project now so that we can show something to the customer as soon as possible. You can download the library from http://eXtreme.NET.Roodyn.com/Book Exercises.aspx.

The countries currently supported are Australia, Canada, Denmark, England, France, Japan, and the United States.

We need to create a set of tests to validate the behavior of this library and that will protect us against any changes in future versions breaking our code without us knowing about it. Then use the library to create a simple Windows Forms application to return capital cities and attractions when a user enters a country. I'll help you get started.

1. Create a new C# application called **WhereIsClient**.

2. Add a class called **WhereIsTests** and add the TestFixture attribute to the class.

3. Create a new Test method in the class called **TestFindCapital**.

```
[Test]
public void TestFindCapital()
{
    Search whereis = new Search();
    string city = string.Empty;
    city = whereis.FindCapital("England");
    //fill in the rest here
}
```

I'll leave the rest to you.

Hint: You might need to run the functions to see what they output before completing the tests.

Exercise 8-15: Plugging In the New Changed Library

The team building the WhereIs.dll class library have just released a new version that supports a method to get the next two days of weather for a capital city. The method is called FindWeather and takes a city name. It returns a string containing XML for the next two days' weather. The team tells us that the XML returned looks like this.

```
<Weather>
    <Today>
        Sunny
    </Today>
    <Tomorrow>
        Rain
    </ Tomorrow >
</Weather>
```

You can download the new version of the library from http://eXtreme.NET.Roo-dyn.com/Book Exercises.aspx.

Use the tests we have previously written to check for any changes in the class library. Then write a test (or tests) to validate the behavior of the new method, and then use the method to show the weather in the city displayed.

Conclusion

With the emphasis firmly on the importance of testing in XP, this chapter has provided you with tools you need to tests user interfaces and other people's code. The lesson I hope you take away from this chapter is that you can write tests to cover most eventualities, and you should always start the process of development by writing the tests first. The tests validate the quality of your code and document your assumptions as to how the code will be used. They provide the *communication* and the *feedback* while driving you toward *simpler* solutions. The tests embody these three values that XP holds in high regard.

This chapter explored two techniques you can use to write more testable user interfaces. First, you learned how by encapsulating more functionality in classes away from the user interface, you can develop tests first and build code that is user-interface agnostic. Then this chapter examined how you can use reflection to call methods that are attached to the user interface.

Then this chapter covered how to deal with using third-party libraries and validate that they are performing how we expect and provide the functionality we require. Finally, we walked through some exercises in fixing existing code that contains bugs.

All that's left to do now is put all these practices together. In the next chapter, we do exactly that; we will work on a project using all the practices covered in this book.

---

1 I have more than once made a recommendation to ditch some code that attempted to do far more than was required of it and was not working correctly. Gold plating is one of the evils of software development that eXtreme Programming attempts to remove from the equation.

9

Step-by-Step Development

M UCH OF WHAT XP TEACHES IS ABOUT developing the software one small step at a time. Chapter 3 covered how to break work down into small tasks. Chapter 4 showed the importance of testing. It showed how to develop the code test first and in small, bite-size pieces. Chapter 5, on refactoring, showed how to simplify our code, again taking small steps to achieve the goal. When doing research and experimentation, Chapter 6 covered how to break these spikes into small steps. The automated build techniques examined in Chapter 7 help us to move faster by not having to repeat the same work again and again. This final chapter puts together all these practices covered so far in this book to develop a piece of software.

Step by Step by Step

This development will be done one step at a time. We'll start with an exercise to break the problem down into small units of work or tasks and then exercises to finish each task and integrate the code into the system. There will be an exercise to discover some unknown technology (spiking) and a task that includes integrating a third-party library. Every piece of code in the exercises will be developed in a test-first manner. Refactoring will be carried out as part of many of the exercises. This chapter reinforces all the practices taught in this book and provides a hands-on demonstration to you of how they can be applied together.

One Small Step at a Time

Something that always seems to amaze even the most experienced developers is how small each step in an eXtreme Programming development cycle actually is. At the beginning of 1993, I worked on a C++ project with a team of developers. We did not use XP, but we did use a set of rapid development practices.

The team would take a part of the specification and break it up into small pieces of work. Each of these tasks was estimated to take at most half a day. We listed the tasks on a whiteboard. We compiled the entire system after each task was completed and checked the code into the source control system we were using.

At that time, none of us had heard of unit testing, and the view was that if it compiled then that allowed us to move forward. Every day one of us would run the entire system and manually put it through its paces to check it was working as expected. There were, of course, a few issues, and they became more tasks on the whiteboard.

Because the team was doing well, we recruited a couple of new developers to the team. One of these developers taught us all a very important lesson. The day he started, he read through a section of the specification and then set about coding it. After a week, he declared he was done. I thought that was pretty good until he told us that now he was "ready to compile the code." I was stunned. Did that mean he had written code for a whole week without knowing whether any of it compiled? I wasn't sure I had heard him correctly. I double-checked. Yes, he had written code for a week without doing one compilation.

He compiled it and proudly told us that he only had 197 errors and that he would start getting them fixed up right away. I was still stunned and not sure what to say. A week later and the poor chap was still struggling with a high volume of errors and warnings. He worked hard trying to get the code to work. I tried to sit down and help him, but his ego wouldn't let any help come his way.

In the meantime, the rest of us were working our way through the tasks on the whiteboard one at a time. Another week went by. Although there were certainly fewer errors, our new team member still hadn't managed to get his code to fully compile, let alone work. Needless to say, he didn't last much longer with the team. He had wasted four man weeks of work and had nothing to show for it. The interesting thing was that in the first week or so, the managers thought this new developer was the "best thing since sliced bread." He had just sat quietly at his desk for long hours each day coding away (while the rest of us were constantly talking and making noise and never worked longer than nine hour days). The manager's change in opinion occurred when we showed what we had been delivering and had to explain that the code written by our new friend in the past three weeks had not been included because it broke the system.

Hopefully, the lesson that team learned in 1993 you don't have to learn the hard way.

A Strategy to Lower the Risk of Failure

Breaking everything you do into tiny steps and validating each step increases your chances of success. One of the aims of any software development methodology is to lower the risk of failure. Such a large number of software projects each year fail that it is still the majority case. Of course, many companies twist the story and change the boundaries so as to make the project seem like a success to the shareholders. In reality, very few projects can be considered a success based on the initial project guidelines.

In the following exercise, we work toward delivering a project to the customer. This exercise pulls together all the lessons covered thus far in this book. Because of the scope of even such a small project, this chapter contains only the first iteration of the project. You can download the rest of the iterations from my Web site at http://eXtreme.NET.Roodyn.com.

Step-by-Step Exercise to Demonstrate the Small-Step Approach

As we go through this project, I hope you appreciate the small steps that we are taking at each point and the value of this. I expect that more experienced developers will have the urge to skip through sections of this chapter. Unless you are already comfortable with how to develop in an XP manner, I implore you to stick with the exercises and try to learn from them. In my experience using these exercises in training courses, the experienced developers who do follow the exercises finish them more quickly and feel happier about the results.

The Customer Meeting

We will start off with the first meeting with our customer. In this exercise, our customer is a product manager who is looking for a new component to enhance an existing suite of Windows components. Quick, let's get to the meeting before we are late.

Dr. Neil: You've got this application you want developed; tell me about it.

Product manager: It's an alarm clock; I want an alarm clock for the desktop.

DN: Yep, sounds like a good idea, like Outlook Reminders?

PM: Yes, sort of. But when the alarm rings it should ring until I switch it off, not just once.

DN: Cool idea! What else?

PM: I want to have multiple alarms.

DN: Okay, nice. Do you want the alarms to be set by date as well as time?

PM: Yep, that's right. Also, I want to have a label for the alarm

DN: Okay, like a description?

PM: Yes, and I want to be able to set sounds for an alarm; there should be a default "beep," but I want to choose a tune to play.

DN: Nice.

PM: Oh, and one last thing, I would love it to be able to use different skins so the user can choose how the clock looks.

DN: Okay.

PM: That's it; how long will it take?

DN: Can we create some stories for all of the features you just asked for?

PM: Okay, show me what you're talking about.

The Story Cards

Based on the previous conversation, we can write up the following stories on index cards:

Alarms rings continuously until I switch it off (when date time is reached or soonest time thereafter).

Add alarm for a date and time with a description.

Edit an alarm.

Set custom tune for the alarm.

Custom skin for alarm application.

Delete (remove) an alarm.

Visual feedback that an alarm is ringing.

Option to switch sound and visual feedback on or off (not allowed to have both off).

Options for feedback (visual and sound) per alarm.

DN: Okay, great; these are the stories so far. If you come up with any more, please let us know. Right now I'd like you to sort the cards into three piles: Essential—Must Have, Adds Business Value, and Nice to Have.

PM: Sure.

Essential—Must Have	Adds Business Value	Nice to Have
Add alarm for a date and time	Visual feedback that alarm is ringing	Options for feedback (visual and sound) per alarm
Alarm rings continuously until I switch it off	Option to switch sound and visual feedback on or off	Custom skin for alarm application
Edit and alarm		Set custom tune for the alarm
Delete (remove) an alarm		

DN: Great; now we are going to estimate in ideal programming hours how long it will take to complete these stories. Remember that in a day we may only get three or four ideal programming hours with the amount of disturbance that happens around this office in terms of meetings, e-mail, and other commitments.

Story	Development Cost
Alarms rings continuously until I switch it off (when date time is reached or soonest time thereafter)	2
Add alarm for a date and time with a description	1
Edit an alarm	2
Set custom tune for the alarm	3
Custom skin for alarm application	?
Delete (remove) an alarm	1
Visual feedback that an alarm is ringing	2
Option to switch sound and visual feedback on or off (not allowed to have both off)	2
Options for feedback (visual and sound) per alarm	1

DN: You will notice that the story "Custom skin for alarm application" has a question mark; this is because at this point we don't know how long it will take. We have never developed an application with a skin before.

PM: Okay, well it's not a high priority at the moment, so let's leave that out for the moment.

DN: Fine, based on some previous experience and a bit of guesswork, I think we can deliver four units of development each iteration and our iterations will be a couple of days long. So could you please group the story cards into iterations that contain no more than four units of development each.

PM: So these iterations deliverables are like milestones that I can actually use?

DN: Yep, that's right.

PM: Can I have an iteration with less than four units?

DN: Of course, and you will probably get that iteration delivered a bit earlier.

PM: Okay, sounds good to me; I'd like to see my iterations as follows.

Iteration 1
Add alarm for a date and time
Alarm rings continuously until I shut it off
Delete (remove) an alarm

Iteration 2
Edit an alarm

Iteration 3
Visual feedback that alarm is ringing
Option to switch sound and visual feedback on or off

Iteration 4
Set custom tune for the alarm
Options for feedback (visual and sound) per alarm

Iteration 5
Custom skin for alarm application

DN: Okay, good work; let's get to it and start delivering something as soon as possible.

Iteration 0

Many XP teams start a project with a very short iteration 0 to get everything prepared for the project. In iteration 0, we set up the environment that will enable us to build and ship this application as quickly as possible. This will include setting up the skeleton application, an installer, and an automatic build and test script.

1. In Visual Studio.NET, create a new C# Windows application called **MyAlarm**.

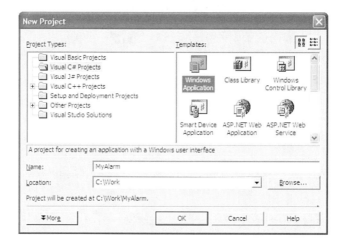

Figure 9-1   Create a new MyAlarm project.

2. In Solution Explorer, right-click the MyAlarm solution and from the pop-up menu select Add/New Project. Then select Setup and Deployment projects and Setup Wizard; we will call the project **MyAlarm Setup**.

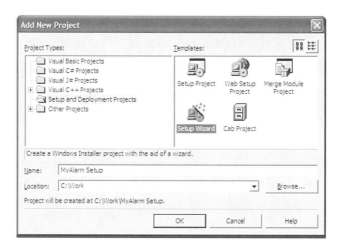

Figure 9-2   Add a new Setup and Deployment project.

3. Follow the wizard and create a setup for a Windows application (see Figure 9-3) and primary output from MyAlarm (see Figure 9-4), then click Finish.

Figure 9-3   Create a Windows application setup.

Figure 9-4   Include the primary output from MyAlarm.

4. Right-click the solution and select Add Solution to Source Control from the pop-up menu. I have created a new Visual SourceSafe database for this project; you might choose to use an existing database.

5. We can now start to set up an automated build and test script. The simplest thing right now is to do it as a batch file. One of the values of XP is simplicity— do the simplest thing that works. We will do this using what we learned in Chapter 7 about automating the build process.

```
@echo off

rem: set the source safe database
set SSDIR=C:\Work\SSDB\MyAlarm

rem: set the working directory for the source safe database root project
ss Workfold $/ C:\Work

rem:change to the directory where all the projects work is
c:
cd Work

rem: get the latest version of the source files from source safe
ss get $/ -R -I-

rem: check that it worked
if errorlevel 1    goto DisplayResult

rem: use the Visual studio cmd line to rebuild the entire solution
devenv /rebuild Debug "C:\Work\MyAlarm\MyAlarm.sln"

rem: check that it worked
if errorlevel 1    goto DisplayResult

rem: run the tests
nunit-console C:\Work\MyAlarm\bin\Debug\MyAlarm.exe

rem: check that they passed
if errorlevel 1    goto DisplayResult

rem: if all the tests passed then rebuild for release
devenv /rebuild Release "C:\Work\MyAlarm\MyAlarm.sln"
if errorlevel 1    goto DisplayResult

:DisplayResult
if errorlevel 1 goto failed
color A1
echo Success!! :-)
goto end
:failed
echo FAILURE :-(
color C1
```

```
:end
rem: for continuous builds the line below
rem: call C:\work\MyAlarm\Build.bat
```

6. Open a command window and run the batch file; because we have no tests in the project yet, you should get the green screen of success.

We have now set up a build and test script along with a simple installer; this will enable us to move faster in the iterations that are to come.

Iteration 1

The Task Breakdown

The stories we have for iteration 1 are as follows:

1. Add alarm for a date and time.
2. Delete (remove) an alarm.
3. Alarm rings continuously until I shut it off.

Let's work through a first attempt at breaking these stories down into tasks using the lessons we learned in Chapter 3.

Story 1: Add Alarm

Task	Estimated Time
Create alarm collection	5 minutes
Check that a new alarm collection is empty	5 minutes
Validate that after adding one alarm to the collection the collection is not empty	10 minutes
Validate that after adding one alarm to the collection there is only one alarm	10 minutes
Validate that after adding three alarms to a new collection there are 3 alarms in the collection	10 minutes
Validate that an alarm added to the collection contains the same date, time, and description as the alarm that was added	10 minutes
Add UI for Adding alarm	15 minutes
Integrate and check in to source control	10 minutes

Story 2: Delete (Remove) an Alarm

Task	Estimated Time
Check that trying to delete an alarm from an empty collection does not cause the system to fail	10 minutes
Check that after deleting an alarm from a collection that contains only that alarm the collection is empty	5 minutes
Check that deleting an alarm from a collection that contains 3 alarms leaves 2 alarms In the collection	10 minutes
Check that the alarm deleted from a collection is the correct alarm	10 minutes
Check that it is not possible to delete an alarm that doesn't exist in a collection	10 minutes
Add UI for deleting alarm	10 minutes
Integrate and check in to source control	10 minutes

Story 3: Alarm Rings Continuously Until I Shut It Off

Task	Estimated Time
Create an alarm ring event	5 minutes
Ensure the event gets called when an alarm should ring	15 minutes
Check that the event does not get called when no alarm should ring	10 minutes
Set up delegate method to play a sound continuously when an alarm rings	10 minutes
Add method to stop sound from playing	10 minutes
Validate that one alarm can ring after another alarm has rung and been switched off	10 minutes
Add UI to allow user to switch alarm sound off	10 minutes
Integrate and check in to source control	10 minutes

We may not have thought of everything, but we are in a good place to start developing this first iteration. So let's get to it.

Story 1: Add Alarm

Task: Create Alarm Collection

1. Add a new class to the MyAlarm project called **AlarmsTests**.

2. Add another new class to the MyAlarm project called Alarms.

3. Okay, we're done! There is nothing to test, and we have an Alarms collection class. Check in to source control.

Task: Check That a New Alarm Collection Is Empty

1. Add a reference to the NUnit.Framework.dll in our MyAlarms project.

2. In the AlarmsTests class, add the using clause for NUnit.Framework and set the TestFixture attribute to the AlarmsTests class.

3. Add a Test method to the AlarmsTests class called TestIsNewCollectionEmpty.

```
[Test]
public void TestIsNewCollectionEmpty()
{
    Alarms alarms = new Alarms();
    Assert.IsTrue(alarms.Empty,
        "New alarms collection should empty");
}
```

4. This will not compile (you should make sure!), so we need to add the Empty property to the Alarms class.

```
public bool Empty
{
    get{ return true;}
}
```

5. Compile this and run the test; it should pass.

6. Once again, we're done for this task. About now you might be looking at the method we just wrote and saying it is pointless. I disagree; we have added the Boolean Empty property to the alarms class. To make our test pass, we did the simplest thing. This might look crazy, but the whole point is to do everything in very small steps. This enables us to focus on getting one thing

right at a time. We know we will have to come back here and change it, but how is that different from any piece of code you write?

7. Check in to source control.

Task: Validate That After Adding One Alarm to the Collection the Collection Is Not Empty

1. Add a new test method to the AlarmsTests class called **TestCollection-NotEmptyAfterAddingAlarm**; sorry about the name, let me know if you can think of a better one.

```
[Test]
public void TestCollectionNotEmptyAfterAddingAlarm()
{
    Alarms alarms = new Alarms();
    Alarm testAlarm = new Alarm();
    alarms.Add(testAlarm);
    Assert.IsFalse(alarms.Empty,
        "Alarms collection should not be empty after adding an alarm");
}
```

2. This will not compile, so add the new Alarm class to the project and the Add method to the alarms class.

```
public void Add(Alarm alarm)
{
}
```

3. Now the code will compile and our new test will fail. So our mission is to make the test pass. At this point we need to make a decision as to how to store the alarms in the collection class. We have a few options here:

- Derive the Alarms class from a .NET collection class.
- Have the Alarms class wrap (contain) a .NET collection class.
- Roll our own collection.

The third option will involve the most work, and I don't see it as the simplest thing we could do. The easiest thing to do would be to derive the Alarms class from a collection. At this point, it is probably also the simplest. If we change our minds, we can always refactor our code later.

4. Add the System.Collections namespace to our using clauses at the top of the file and inherit our Alarms class from ArrayList (we can change this later as well if we need to), and then change the Empty property and remove the Add method. (We don't need it anymore because the base class supports an Add method.)

```
public bool Empty
{
    get
    {
        if (this.Count > 0)
        {
            return false;
        }
        else
        {
            return true;
        }
    }
}
```

5. Compile and run the tests; they should pass.

6. Check in to source control.

Task: Validate That After Adding One Alarm to the Collection There Is Only One Alarm

1. Add a Test called **TestAddingOneAlarm** to the AlarmsTests class.

```
[Test]
public void TestAddingOneAlarm()
{
    Alarms alarms = new Alarms();
    Alarm testAlarm = new Alarm();
    alarms.Add(testAlarm);

    Assert.AreEqual(1, alarms.Count,
        "Alarms collection should have 1 alarm after adding an alarm");
}
```

2. Compile and run the tests; they pass!

We didn't need to write any code for this test to pass. This happens sometimes, but doesn't make the test any less useful; this test will validate that any future changes don't change our assumptions about how the Alarms class works.

3. Check in to source control.

Task: Validate That After Adding Three Alarms to a New Collection There Are Three Alarms in the Collection

1. To the AlarmsTests collection, add the Test method **TestAddingThreeAlarms**.

```
[Test]
public void TestAddingThreeAlarms()
{
    Alarms alarms = new Alarms();
    Alarm testAlarm = new Alarm();
    Alarm testAlarm2 = new Alarm();
    Alarm testAlarm3 = new Alarm();

    alarms.Add(testAlarm);
    alarms.Add(testAlarm2);
    alarms.Add(testAlarm3);

    Assert.AreEqual(3, alarms.Count,
        "Alarms should have 3 alarm after adding 3 alarms");
}
```

2. Compile and run the tests. Again they pass; this is too easy!

3. Check in to source control.

Task: Validate That An Alarm Added to the Collection Contains the Same Date, Time, and Description As the Alarm That Was Added

1. Add a new Test method called **TestAlarmDataIsCorrect** to the AlarmsTests class.

```
[Test]
public void TestAlarmDataIsCorrect()
{
    Alarms alarms = new Alarms();
    DateTime alarmTime = DateTime.Now;
    string alarmDescription = "Test alarm";
    Alarm testAlarm = new Alarm(alarmTime, alarmDescription);

    alarms.Add(alarm);

    Assert.AreEqual(alarmTime, alarms[0].DateTime,
        "Alarm time not equal to that set");
    Assert.AreEqual(alarmDescription, alarms[0].Description,
        "Alarm description not equal to that set");
}
```

2. Try to compile this. Unlike the previous two tasks, this is going to require some work to get it to compile.

3. In the Alarm class, add a new constructor and a couple of properties.

```
public Alarm(DateTime dateTime, string description)
{
}

public DateTime DateTime
{
    get{ return DateTime.Now;}
}

public string Description
{
    get{ return string.Empty;}
}
```

4. This still doesn't compile because the indexer on the Alarms class returns an object and not an Alarm type, so we need to add an indexer method to the Alarms class.

```
public Alarm this[int index]
{
    get
    {
        return base[index] as Alarm;
    }
}
```

5. Now the project compiles, but that last test fails. In the alarm class, add the variables to store the description, date, and time. Then use them in the constructor and the property get methods.

```
private DateTime dateTime;
private string description;

public Alarm(DateTime dateTime, string description)
{
    this.dateTime = dateTime;
    this.description = description;
}
```

```
public DateTime DateTime
{
    get{ return dateTime;}
}

public string Description
{
    get{ return description;}
}
```

6. Compile and run the tests. Yes! Another task done.

7. Check in to source control.

Task: Add UI for Adding Alarm

1. Add a new Windows Form class called AddAlarm to the MyAlarm project (see Figure 9-5).

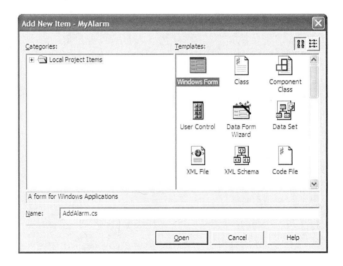

Figure 9-5   Add a new Windows form.

2. Add a new class called **AddAlarmFormTests**.

3. In the new AddAlarmFormTests class file, add a using reference for NUnit.Framework and add the TestFixture attribute to the class.

4. The first test we are going to write will determine the controls we are going to use in our AddAlarm form.

```
[Test]
public void TestFormControls()
{
    AddAlarm testForm;
    BindingFlags flags = BindingFlags.NonPublic|
        BindingFlags.Public|BindingFlags.Static|
        BindingFlags.Instance;
    Type tForm = typeof(AddAlarm);
    testForm = new AddAlarm();
    testForm.Show();

    FieldInfo datePickerInfo =
        tForm.GetField("date",flags);
    MonthCalendar datePicker =
        (MonthCalendar)datePickerInfo.GetValue(testForm);

    Assert.AreEqual(1, datePicker.MaxSelectionCount,
        "Calendar should only allow 1 date selected");

    Assert.AreEqual(DateTime.Now.Date,
        datePicker.SelectionStart.Date,
        "Calendar should initialize to todays date");

    FieldInfo timePickerInfo =
        tForm.GetField("time",flags);
    DateTimePicker timePicker =
        (DateTimePicker)timePickerInfo.GetValue(testForm);

    Assert.AreEqual(DateTimePickerFormat.Custom,
        timePicker.Format,
        "Time picker should be formated to show time only");

    Assert.AreEqual("HH:mm",
        timePicker.CustomFormat,
        "Time picker should be formated to show time only");

    Assert.AreEqual(true,
        timePicker.ShowUpDown,
        "Time picker should show up-down control");

    FieldInfo descriptionInfo =
        tForm.GetField("description",flags);
    TextBox description=
        (TextBox)descriptionInfo.GetValue(testForm);

    Assert.AreEqual(string.Empty,
        description.Text,
```

```
        "Initial description should be blank");

    FieldInfo AddBtnInfo =
        tForm.GetField("AddBtn",flags);
    Button AddBtn=
        (Button )AddBtnInfo.GetValue(testForm);

    testForm.Close();
    testForm.Dispose();
}
```

5. This test will fail because none of the controls are on the form. In the design view for the new form, add a Calendar control, a DateTime picker, a label, a text box, and a button, as shown in Figure 9-6. The values for the properties on the controls that need to be set can be determined from the test.

Figure 9-6   Design the add Alarm dialog.

6. Compile and run the tests; they should all pass. If they do not, it is likely that one of the control properties is not set correctly. We must make sure we get the tests to pass before we move on.

7. We will next write a test to validate the behavior when the Add button is clicked; again we will use the reflection techniques we learned in Chapter 8.

```
[Test]
public void TestAddBtnClick()
{
    AddAlarm testForm;
```

```
BindingFlags flags = BindingFlags.NonPublic|
        BindingFlags.Public|BindingFlags.Static|
        BindingFlags.Instance;
Type tForm = typeof(AddAlarm);
testForm = new AddAlarm();
testForm.Show();

FieldInfo datePickerInfo =
    tForm.GetField("date",flags);
MonthCalendar datePicker =
    (MonthCalendar)datePickerInfo.GetValue(testForm);
datePicker.SelectionStart = new DateTime(2004,12,25);

FieldInfo timePickerInfo =
    tForm.GetField("time",flags);
DateTimePicker timePicker =
    (DateTimePicker)timePickerInfo.GetValue(testForm);
timePicker.Value = DateTime.Parse("08:00");

FieldInfo descriptionInfo =
    tForm.GetField("description",flags);
TextBox description=
     (TextBox)descriptionInfo.GetValue(testForm);
description.Text = "Time to open presents";

MethodInfo clickMethod =
    tForm.GetMethod("AddBtn_Click",flags);
Object[] args = new Object[2];
args[0] = this;
args[1] = new EventArgs();
clickMethod.Invoke(testForm, args);

PropertyInfo alarmInfo =
    tForm.GetProperty("Alarm",flags);
Alarm alarm=
    (Alarm)alarmInfo.GetValue(testForm,null);
Assert.AreEqual(new DateTime(2004,12,25,08,00,00),
    alarm.DateTime,
    "Alarm datetime is not correct");
Assert.AreEqual("Time to open presents",
    alarm.Description,
    "Alarm description is not correct");

testForm.Close();
testForm.Dispose();
}
```

8. The code won't compile. To get it to compile, we need to add an event handler for the Add button and a public property on the form of type Alarm.

```
private void AddBtn_Click(object sender, System.EventArgs e)
{
}

public Alarm Alarm
{
    get
    { return null; }
}
```

9. Compile and run the tests; they fail. We have defined the AddBtn and Alarm property and now need to fill them in.

```
private Alarm alarm;
private void AddBtn_Click(object sender, System.EventArgs e)
{
    alarm = new Alarm(date.SelectionStart +
        time.Value.TimeOfDay,
        description.Text);
}

public Alarm Alarm
{
    get
    {
        return alarm;
    }
}
```

10. Right now I can think of another test we should write. We should check that before the Add button has been clicked, the Alarm property returns null.

```
[Test]
public void TestAlarmBeforeButtonClick()
{
    AddAlarm testForm;
    testForm = new AddAlarm();
    testForm.Show();

    Assert.IsNull(testForm.Alarm,
        "Alarm should be null if add button not clicked");
```

```
    testForm.Close();
        testForm.Dispose();
}
```

11. Compile and run the tests. They all pass. This last test doesn't require any work but prevents any future changes from setting the Alarm to a valid value if the button has not been clicked.

12. There is some refactoring that we can do now in the AddAlarmFormTests class. Let's start by creating a setup and teardown that creates the form and closes and disposes the form.

```
private AddAlarm testForm;
private BindingFlags flags = BindingFlags.NonPublic|
    BindingFlags.Public|BindingFlags.Static|
    BindingFlags.Instance;
private Type tForm = typeof(AddAlarm);

[SetUp]
public void SetUp()
{
    testForm = new AddAlarm();
    testForm.Show();
}

[TearDown]
public void TearDown()
{
    testForm.Close();
    testForm.Dispose();
}
```

I will leave it to you to extract the duplicate code from each of the test methods that now exists in the SetUp and TearDown methods.

13. There is one final thing to do, add a UI to the MyAlarm form to enable the user to add an alarm. We will, of course, do this the test-driven way, so add a new class to the project called **MyAlarmFormTests**. Add the Nunit.Framework namespace to the using clauses at the top of the file and attribute the class as a TestFixture.

At this point I am not sure what the best approach is for calling the Add Alarm dialog, so I ask the customer.

DN: How should the user add an alarm?

PM: From a menu. Is that possible?

DN: Sure.

A quick chat with the customer is the best way to get the answer, and now we know they are expecting a menu to add the alarm. So we can write to test to check that there is a menu item on form to do this.

```
[Test]
public void TestAddAlarmMenuItemExists()
{
    MyAlarmForm testForm;
    BindingFlags flags = BindingFlags.NonPublic|
        BindingFlags.Public|BindingFlags.Static|
        BindingFlags.Instance;
    Type tForm = typeof(MyAlarmForm);
    testForm = new MyAlarmForm();
    testForm.Show();

    FieldInfo menuInfo =
        tForm.GetField("mainMenu",flags);
    MainMenu mainMenu =
        (MainMenu)menuInfo.GetValue(testForm);

    Assert.AreEqual("Alarms",
        mainMenu.MenuItems[0].Text,
        "Alarms menu is not on the main menu");
    Assert.AreEqual("Add",
        mainMenu.MenuItems[0].MenuItems[0].Text,
        "Add menu is not on the Alarms menu");

    testForm.Close();
    testForm.Dispose();
}
```

14. Compile the code and run the tests. They fail. In the design view, we need to add a MainMenu control to our MyAlarm form. Then add an Alarms menu item and an Add menu item to the Alarms menu. Rerun the tests; they should pass.

15. At this point we know the AddAlarm form behaves as expected because we have tested it, and we know that the Alarms collection class passes all the

tests, so we should feel comfortable plugging them together in the menu click event code.

```
private Alarms alarms;
public MyAlarmForm()
{
    InitializeComponent();

    alarms =  new Alarms();
}

private void AlarmsAddMenu_Click(object sender,
        System.EventArgs e)
{
    AddAlarm alarmFrm = new AddAlarm();
    alarmFrm.ShowDialog();
    if (alarmFrm.Alarm != null)
    {
        alarms.Add(alarmFrm.Alarm);
    }
}
```

16. Compile and run the tests again just to be sure we haven't broken anything. We must be nearly done now. There are a couple of things left to do. The alarm we add doesn't get used at the moment, we need to display a list on the form, and there is a small bug in one of our forms.

17. To the MyAlarmFormTests class, add a new test method called **TestAddAlarm**. Time to ask the customer another question:

DN: How do you want to see the alarms?

PM: Like in Outlook, in a list with description first, then time and date.

Let's code a test for this.

```
[Test]
public void TestAddAlarm()
{
    MyAlarmForm testForm;
    BindingFlags flags = BindingFlags.NonPublic|
        BindingFlags.Public|BindingFlags.Static|
        BindingFlags.Instance;
    Type tForm = typeof(MyAlarmForm);
```

```
testForm = new MyAlarmForm();
testForm.Show();

FieldInfo alarmListInfo =
    tForm.GetField("alarmsList",flags);
ListView alarmList =
    (ListView)alarmListInfo.GetValue(testForm);

Assert.AreEqual(0, alarmList.Items.Count,
    "There should be no alarms on a new form");

FieldInfo alarmsInfo=
    tForm.GetField("alarms",flags);
Alarms alarms =
     (Alarms)alarmsInfo.GetValue(testForm);

DateTime testDateTime =
    new DateTime(2005, 12, 25, 08, 00, 00);
alarms.Add(new Alarm(testDateTime, "Christmas"));

MethodInfo refreshMethod =
    tForm.GetMethod("RefreshAlarmList",flags);
refreshMethod.Invoke(testForm, null);

Assert.AreEqual(1, alarmList.Items.Count,
    "There should be 1 alarm after adding it");

Assert.AreEqual("Christmas",
    alarmList.Items[0].Text,
    "The new alarm description is not correct");

testForm.Close();
testForm.Dispose();
}
```

18. Run the test we just wrote. As we get more tests into the system, we don't want to have to run all the tests after we have written a new one, especially if we expect our new test to fail. We should run all the tests when we have got this test to pass. To get this test to pass, we need to add a ListView called **alarmsList** to our form and a method called **RefreshAlarmList** that updates the list view.

```
protected void RefreshAlarmList()
{
    alarmsList.Items.Clear();
```

```
    foreach(Alarm alarm in alarms)
    {
        alarmsList.Items.Add(
            new ListViewItem(
            new string[] {alarm.Description,
                alarm.DateTime.ToShortDateString(),
                alarm.DateTime.ToShortTimeString()})
                );
    }
    this.Refresh();
}
```

19. Rerun the test; it should pass, and we can check that all the tests pass, which they should because we haven't broken anything.

20. Finally, we can plug this new method into the menu click event.

```
private void AlarmsAddMenu_Click(object sender,
    System.EventArgs e)
{
    AddAlarm alarmFrm = new AddAlarm();
    alarmFrm.ShowDialog();
    if (alarmFrm.Alarm != null)
    {
        alarms.Add(alarmFrm.Alarm);
        RefreshAlarmList();
    }
}
```

21. We should now run all the tests and make sure they pass. Then we should run the application we have written; we should just do a quick run through and make sure it behaves as expected. There is one main thing we should notice. The Add button doesn't close the AddAlarm dialog form. That is not how we would expect the program to work. So we will write a test to highlight this bug and then fix it.

```
    [Test]
    public void TestAddBtnClosesForm()
    {
        MethodInfo clickMethod =
            tForm.GetMethod("AddBtn_Click",flags);
        Object[] args = new Object[2];
        args[0] = this;
        args[1] = new EventArgs();
```

```
        clickMethod.Invoke(testForm, args);

        Assert.AreEqual(null, Form.ActiveForm,
            "There should be no active form after add btn clicked");
        Assert.IsFalse(testForm.Visible,
            "After add click form should not be visible");
    }
```

22. The test should fail to fix this one line of code, but don't forget the value in the test is to make sure that correction remains encoded in the system.

```
private void AddBtn_Click(object sender,
    System.EventArgs e)
{
    alarm = new Alarm(date.SelectionStart +
        time.Value.TimeOfDay,
        description.Text);
    this.Close();
}
```

23. Run all the tests and check that nothing else has been broken. Then run the application again. There is one other small thing that we need to think about. The ListView by default shows the items using the LargeIcon view, but the customer wanted to see them "like in Outlook," as a list with the description first. Let's code a test to enforce the ListView uses the Details View mode. While we are here, we can check that there are three columns, for the description, date, and time.

```
[Test]
public void TestAlarmsListView()
{
    MyAlarmForm testForm;
    BindingFlags flags = BindingFlags.NonPublic|
        BindingFlags.Public|BindingFlags.Static|
        BindingFlags.Instance;
    Type tForm = typeof(MyAlarmForm);
    testForm = new MyAlarmForm();
    testForm.Show();

    FieldInfo alarmListInfo =
        tForm.GetField("alarmsList",flags);
    ListView alarmList =
        (ListView)alarmListInfo.GetValue(testForm);
```

```
        Assert.AreEqual(View.Details, alarmList.View,
            "Alarms list should display Details");

        Assert.AreEqual(3, alarmList.Columns.Count,
            "there should be 3 columns");

        testForm.Close();
        testForm.Dispose();
    }
```

24. Run this test; it should fail until we set up the ListView to display a Details view and have three columns (which we can do from the Properties window on the design view of the form).

25. There is more refactoring that we can do now in the MyAlarmFormTests class. In the same way as we did with the AddAlarmFormTests, we should extract the repeated form initialization and destruction code into SetUp and TearDown methods.

26. Check in to source control.

Task: Integrate and Check In to Source Control

1. The first thing we should do is check that everything is still good with our automated batch file to build and test the project. Run the batch file; we should get the green screen of joy. We are nearly done.

2. Check in the files to source control. If we were working on a project where other people were accessing the same source control database, I would suggest running the batch file again now to ensure that nothing has changed and that the version of the code in the source control compiles and all the tests run.

That is the first story complete, yippee, high fives all around and a general feeling of "we've done it" and "we're making progress." Let's take a small break, and then get started with the next story.

Story 2: Delete (Remove) an Alarm

Task: Check That Trying to Delete an Alarm from an Empty Collection Does Not Cause the System to Fail

1. By now I'm sure you know we need to write the test first. We will do this in the AlarmsTests class; we have introduced the ExpectedException attribute here to enable us to get the test to pass only when the exception is thrown.

```
[Test,
ExpectedException(typeof(ArgumentOutOfRangeException))]
public void TestRemoveFromEmptyList()
{
    Alarms alarms = new Alarms();
    alarms.RemoveAt(0);
}
```

2. Compile and run the test. It passes. Because we have inherited the alarms class from the ArrayList, it supports this functionality "out of the box." Time to move to the next task.

3. Check in to source control.

Task: Check That After Deleting an Alarm from a Collection That Contains Only That Alarm the Collection Is Empty

1. Test first again.

```
[Test]
public void TestRemove()
{
    Alarms alarms = new Alarms();
    alarms.Add(new Alarm());
    alarms.RemoveAt(0);
    Assert.IsTrue(alarms.Empty,
        "After removing an item the list should empty");
}
```

2. Compile and run the test. It works. Good. Check in to source control and let's move on.

Task: Check That Deleting an Alarm from a Collection That Contains Three Alarms Leaves Two Alarms in the Collection

1. The test.

```
[Test]
public void TestListContainsItemsNotRemoved()
{
    Alarms alarms = new Alarms();
    alarms.Add(new Alarm(DateTime.Now, "One"));
    alarms.Add(new Alarm(DateTime.Now, "Two"));
    alarms.Add(new Alarm(DateTime.Now, "Three"));
    alarms.RemoveAt(0);
    Assert.AreEqual(2, alarms.Count,
        "After removing an item the list should not be empty");
}
```

2. Test passes. Okay. Check in to source control. Next task. Are you getting the feeling that we are starting to move faster now?

Task: Check That the Alarm Deleted from a Collection Is the Correct Alarm

1. The test.

```
[Test]
public void TestRemoveTakesCorrectAlarm()
{
    Alarms alarms = new Alarms();
    alarms.Add(new Alarm(DateTime.Now, "One"));
    alarms.Add(new Alarm(DateTime.Now, "Two"));
    alarms.Add(new Alarm(DateTime.Now, "Three"));
    alarms.RemoveAt(1);
    Assert.AreEqual("One", alarms[0].Description);
    Assert.AreEqual("Three", alarms[1].Description);
}
```

2. Compile and run the tests. All still good and green. Check in to source control. Next task, please.

Task: Check That It Is Not Possible to Delete an Alarm That Doesn't Exist in a Collection

1. This is cool; we are nearing the end of this story, and it has been so easy to validate the functionality. Once again, the test comes first.

```
[Test,
ExpectedException(typeof(ArgumentOutOfRangeException))]
```

```
public void TestRemoveNonExistantAlarm()
{
    Alarms alarms = new Alarms();
    alarms.Add(new Alarm(DateTime.Now, "One"));
    alarms.Add(new Alarm(DateTime.Now, "Two"));
    alarms.Add(new Alarm(DateTime.Now, "Three"));
    alarms.RemoveAt(4);
}
```

2. Then we compile and run the tests. Yes, all good; check in to source control. Let's get this story done!

Task: Add UI for Deleting Alarm

Before we start this, I hope you have refactored out the SetUp and TearDown methods in the MyAlarmFormTests because we need them now.

1. In the MyAlarmFormTestsClass, we'll start with a test to validate the control we want for deleting an alarm is on the form.

```
[Test]
public void TestDeleteMenuExists()
{
    FieldInfo menuInfo =
        tForm.GetField("mainMenu",flags);
    MainMenu mainMenu =
        (MainMenu)menuInfo.GetValue(testForm);

    Assert.AreEqual("Delete",
        mainMenu.MenuItems[0].MenuItems[1].Text,
        "Delete menu is not on the Alarms menu");
}
```

2. Compile and run the test. It looks like we have to do some work here. We need to add a Delete menu item to the Alarms menu in the design view.

3. The next test we write will check that if no alarm is selected in the list then the delete menu should be disabled. This test does require that we have an understanding of how menus work. We can set up a popup event delegate to get called just before a menu gets displayed. We want to validate that one exists for the alarms menu and that after it has been fired it sets the Enabled property of our Delete menu to false when there are no selected items in the ListView.

```
        [Test]
        public void TestDeleteDisabled()
        {
            FieldInfo menuInfo =
                tForm.GetField("mainMenu",flags);
            MainMenu mainMenu =
                (MainMenu)menuInfo.GetValue(testForm);

            MethodInfo menuPopupMethod =
                tForm.GetMethod("AlarmsMenu_Popup",flags);
            Object[] args = new object[2];
            args[0] = testForm;
            args[1] = null;
            menuPopupMethod.Invoke(testForm, args);

            Assert.IsFalse(
                mainMenu.MenuItems[0].MenuItems[1].Enabled,
                "Delete menu should be disabled by default");
        }
```

4. Compile and run this test. It will fail because there is no AlarmMenu_Popup method. We should add this to the code in the MyAlarmForm. You can get an event handler skeleton generated for you by selecting the events from the Properties window of the Alarms menu item and double-clicking the Popup event.

```
private void AlarmsMenu_Popup(object sender, System.EventArgs e)
{
    if (0 <= alarmsList.SelectedItems.Count)
    {
        mainMenu.MenuItems[0].MenuItems[1].Enabled = false;
    }
    else
    {
        mainMenu.MenuItems[0].MenuItems[1].Enabled = true;
    }
}
```

5. Compile and run the test again. We should be seeing green for go.

6. We should also write a test to validate that the menu is enabled when an alarm is selected.

```
[Test]
public void TestDeleteEnabled()
```

```
{
    FieldInfo alarmListInfo =
        tForm.GetField("alarmsList",flags);
    ListView alarmList =
        (ListView)alarmListInfo.GetValue(testForm);

    FieldInfo alarmsInfo=
        tForm.GetField("alarms",flags);
    Alarms alarms =
        (Alarms)alarmsInfo.GetValue(testForm);

    DateTime testDateTime =
        new DateTime(2005, 12, 25, 08, 00, 00);
    alarms.Add(new Alarm(testDateTime, "Christmas"));

    MethodInfo refreshMethod =
        tForm.GetMethod("RefreshAlarmList",flags);
    refreshMethod.Invoke(testForm, null);

    alarmList.Items[0].Selected = true;
    alarmList.Select();

    FieldInfo menuInfo =
        tForm.GetField("mainMenu",flags);
    MainMenu mainMenu =
        (MainMenu)menuInfo.GetValue(testForm);

    MethodInfo menuPopupMethod =
        tForm.GetMethod("AlarmsMenu_Popup",flags);
    Object[] args = new object[2];
    args[0] = testForm;
    args[1] = null;
    menuPopupMethod.Invoke(testForm, args);

    Assert.IsTrue(
        mainMenu.MenuItems[0].MenuItems[1].Enabled,
        "Delete menu should be enabled");
}
```

7. Compile and run the test. It fails. Hold on a minute; shouldn't it pass? Didn't we just write the code in the Popup event method to ensure this test would pass? Let's look at that method again. Notice anything? We've put a less than where we should have a greater than sign! Let's change that and run the tests again. This is a good example of how tests can help us when we are going too fast.

8. Now let's write a test to check that we can delete a selected alarm from the list.

```
[Test]
public void TestDelete()
{
    FieldInfo alarmListInfo =
        tForm.GetField("alarmsList",flags);
    ListView alarmList =
        (ListView)alarmListInfo.GetValue(testForm);

    FieldInfo alarmsInfo=
        tForm.GetField("alarms",flags);
    Alarms alarms =
        (Alarms)alarmsInfo.GetValue(testForm);

    DateTime testDateTime =
        new DateTime(2005, 12, 25, 08, 00, 00);
    alarms.Add(new Alarm(testDateTime, "Christmas"));

    MethodInfo refreshMethod =
            tForm.GetMethod("RefreshAlarmList",flags);
    refreshMethod.Invoke(testForm, null);

    alarmList.Items[0].Selected = true;
    alarmList.Select();

    Assert.AreEqual(1,
        alarmList.Items.Count,
        "Alarm list should contain 1 alarm");

    FieldInfo menuInfo =
        tForm.GetField("mainMenu",flags);
    MainMenu mainMenu =
        (MainMenu)menuInfo.GetValue(testForm);

    mainMenu.MenuItems[0].MenuItems[1].PerformClick();

    Assert.AreEqual(0,
        alarmList.Items.Count,
        "Alarm list should be empty");
}
```

9. Compile and run the test. It fails. We need to add some code in a click event for the Delete menu.

```
private void AlarmsDeleteMenu_Click(object sender, System.EventArgs e)
{
    foreach(int index in alarmsList.SelectedIndices)
    {
        alarms.RemoveAt(index);
    }
    RefreshAlarmList();
}
```

10. Compile and run the run the tests. All 21 tests should pass. That's correct, we have written 21 tests already. Pretty good going, that's 21 ways that we have protected the system from failing. Check in to source control.

Task: Integrate and Check In to Source Control

1. Run the batch file; we should get the green screen.

2. Check in the files to source control.

3. Take a break.

Story 3: Alarm Rings Continuously Until I Shut It Off
Task: Create an Alarm Ring Event

1. Test first.

```
[Test]
public void TestAlarmEventExists()
{
    Alarms alarms = new Alarms();
    alarms.AlarmRing +=
        new AlarmRingEventHandler(AlarmRing);
}

private void AlarmRing(Object obj,
    AlarmRingEventArgs args)
{    }
```

2. The code doesn't compile, so we need to add the delegate and event declarations to the Alarms class.

```
public class AlarmRingEventArgs: EventArgs {}

public delegate void AlarmRingEventHandler(Object obj,
    AlarmRingEventArgs args);
```

```
public class Alarms:ArrayList
{
    public event AlarmRingEventHandler AlarmRing;
    .
    .
    .
```

3. Compile the code and run the tests. Check in to source control.

Task: Ensure the Event Gets Called When an Alarm Should Ring

1. This task is the hardest one we have seen to date, and that is not surprising because it really specifies the core functionality of the software we are writing. We will code the test first, of course. We will use an AutoResetEvent from the Threading namespace to indicate when an alarm has gone off.

```
using System.Threading;
.
.
.
private void AlarmRing(Object obj,
    AlarmRingEventArgs args)
{
    alarmRung.Set();
}

private AutoResetEvent alarmRung;

[Test]
public void TestAlarmRings()
{
    Alarms alarms = new Alarms();
    alarmRung = new ManualResetEvent(false);
    alarms.AlarmRing +=
        new AlarmRingEventHandler(AlarmRing);
    alarms.Add(new Alarm(DateTime.Now, "Test Alarm") );

    Assert.IsTrue(alarmRung.WaitOne(1500, false),
        "Alarm didn't ring");
}
```

2. Compile and run the test. It will fail. From here there are a few ways we can go about making this test pass. We will use a worker thread to run in the background and monitor the alarms and then raise the event when an alarm

should ring. I have used a common design for threads with a monitor to ensure the thread ends when the object gets disposed.

```csharp
using System.Threading;
public class Alarms:ArrayList, IDisposable
{
    ManualResetEvent monitorAlarms;
    Thread monitorThread;
    public void Dispose()
    {
        monitorAlarms.Reset();
    }

    public Alarms()
    {
        monitorAlarms = new ManualResetEvent(true);
        monitorThread = new Thread(new
            ThreadStart(this.AlarmMonitorThread));
        monitorThread.Start();
    }

    protected void AlarmMonitorThread()
    {
        while (monitorAlarms.WaitOne())
        {
            foreach(Alarm alarm in this)
            {
                if (alarm.DateTime <= DateTime.Now)
                {
                    AlarmRing(this, new AlarmRingEventArgs());
                }
            }
            Thread.Sleep(500);
        }
    }
    .
    .
    .
```

3. We should write a test to ensure we have coded our thread termination correctly. This is an example where we have jumped ahead of ourselves. We could have written a simpler version of the thread function with a while (true) loop. From experience, we should know that this will cause us trouble and do it the correct way, but we should also protect our code from being

changed in some way that would prevent the thread from exiting when the object is disposed.

```
[Test]
public void TestAlarmThreadTerminates()
{
    Alarms alarms = new Alarms();
    alarmRung = new ManualResetEvent(false);
    alarms.AlarmRing +=
        new AlarmRingEventHandler(AlarmRing);
    alarms.Dispose();
    alarms.Add(new Alarm(DateTime.Now, "Test Alarm") );
    Assert.IsFalse(alarmRung.WaitOne(1000, false),
        "Alarm rings after dispose");
}
```

4. Compile and run this test; it should pass because we jumped ahead and wrote the code for this for the previous test to pass. Now make sure you run all the tests. You should see that this test fails when the other tests run. We have introduced a dependency in the tests. This is not good. The issue is that Dispose isn't getting called. The best way to fix this would be to Refactor the AlarmsTests class to contain a SetUp and TearDown method.

```
public class AlarmsTests
{
    Alarms alarms;

    [SetUp]
    public void SetUp()
    {
        alarms = new Alarms();
    }

    [TearDown]
    public void TearDown()
    {
        alarms.Dispose();
    }
    .
    .
    .
```

5. Compile and run the tests; again, they all pass. Check in to source control. Let's move on with our next task.

Task: Check That the Event Does Not Get Called When No Alarm Should Ring

1. The test for this will be similar to the previous test.

```
[Test]
public void TestAlarmDoesntRing()
{
    alarmRung = new ManualResetEvent(false);
    alarms.AlarmRing +=
        new AlarmRingEventHandler(AlarmRing);
    alarms.Add(new Alarm(DateTime.Now +
        new TimeSpan(1,0,0), "Test Alarm") );
    Assert.IsFalse(alarmRung.WaitOne(1000, false),
        "Alarm rings when it shouldn't");
}
```

2. Compile and run the tests; they all pass, so the code we wrote for the alarm ringing seems to be good. Check in to source control.

Task: Set Up Delegate Method to Play a Sound Continuously When an Alarm Rings

1. The .NET Framework does not currently support playing sound files. So for playing sounds, we are going to use a third-party library that I have made available for download from my Web site (http://eXtreme.NET.Roodyn.com/ Book Exercises.aspx). This library provides access to the MultiMedia Windows function to play a sound via a static method in a class. To test this, we are just going to write a test that makes sure the method is there and it doesn't crash. This will protect us from any changes to library that might occur in the future. Because it is a user-interface feature, we will write the test in the MyAlarmFormTests class.

```
[Test]
public void TestPlaySound()
{
    SoundPlay.Player.PlaySound(@"Ringin.wav");
}
```

2. To get this to compile, we need to add a reference to the DLL to our MyAlarm project and place the Ringin.wav file somewhere that it can be accessed. We should add the Ringin.wav file to our source control system also.

3. We can then hook together the parts we need to get the alarm sound to play in the user interface.

```
public MyAlarmForm()
{
    InitializeComponent();

    alarms = new Alarms();
    alarms.AlarmRing +=
        new AlarmRingEventHandler(alarms_AlarmRing);
}

private void alarms_AlarmRing(Object obj,
    AlarmRingEventArgs args)
{
    SoundPlay.Player.PlaySound(@"Ringin.wav");
}
```

4. Make sure the tests pass. Check in to source control.

Task: Add Method to Stop Sound from Playing

1. If we run the MyAlarms application, we can set an alarm and it will ring continuously as per the code and tests we have written. There is no way to stop the alarm. Until we put a call to the Dispose method of the Alarms class in the MyAlarmForm Dispose method, even trying to close the application will not stop the alarm from ringing!

```
protected override void Dispose( bool disposing )
{
    if( disposing )
    {
        if (components != null)
        {
            components.Dispose();
        }
        alarms.Dispose();
    }
    base.Dispose( disposing );
}
```

2. We need a test to ensure that the alarm can stop ringing.

```
[Test]
public void TestSwitchAlarmOff()
{
    alarmRung = new ManualResetEvent(false);
    alarms.AlarmRing +=
        new AlarmRingEventHandler(AlarmRing);
```

```
    alarms.Add(new Alarm(DateTime.Now, "Test Alarm") );
    alarms[0].Off = true;
    alarmRung.Reset();
    Assert.IsFalse(alarmRung.WaitOne(1000, false),
        "Alarm rings when it has been switched off");
}
```

3. This doesn't compile; we need to put an Off property on the Alarm class.

```
public bool Off
{
    get{return true;}
    set{     }
}
```

4. Compile and run the test; it fails. We need to put code into the Off property and use it to indicate whether the alarm should ring.

```
public class Alarm
{
    .
    .
    .
    private bool off;
    .
    .
    .
    public bool Off
    {
        get{return off;}
        set{off = value;}
    }
}

public class Alarms:ArrayList, IDisposable
{
    protected void AlarmMonitorThread()
    {
        while (monitorAlarms.WaitOne())
        {
            foreach(Alarm alarm in this)
            {
                if (!alarm.Off &&
                    alarm.DateTime <= DateTime.Now)
                {
                    AlarmRing(this, new AlarmRingEventArgs());
```

```
            }
        }
        Thread.Sleep(500);
    }
}
.
.
.
```

5. Compile and run the test. It passes, so we must check all the tests in case we have broken anything else. Yes, looks good. Check in to source control.

Task: Add UI to Enable User to Switch Alarm Sound Off

We must now enable users to switch an alarm off from the UI. We are not sure as to the best way to do this, and the product manager is not available. We manage to find a potential user elsewhere in the company; her name is Kris.

DN: Kris, we have been working on this Alarm program for our product manager, I think you know about it?

Kris: Yes, I have discussed this with the PM.

DN: Will you help us, please? We need to know how an alarm should be switched off when it is ringing. We can demo the application so far.

K: Sure, let's see.

<demo application to user>

K: I think it should show a box with the description of the alarm and a button to switch it off.

DN: Okay; can the box be dismissed without switching the alarm off?

K: No, it shouldn't be possible.

DN: What if more than one alarm is ringing?

K: There has to be a separate box for each alarm.

DN: Okay, thanks

K: You're welcome.

1. This sounds like it might be a larger job than we initially thought. We can start by creating a Test class for our new form, AlarmNotificationFormTests, and adding a test to assert that a button on the form switches an alarm off.

```
using System;
using System.Windows.Forms;
using NUnit.Framework;
using System.Reflection;

namespace MyAlarm
{
    [TestFixture]
    public class AlarmNotificationFormTests
    {
        [Test]
        public void TestSwitchOffAlarm()
        {
            Alarm alarm = new Alarm();
            alarm.Off = false;
            AlarmNotificationForm testForm =
                new AlarmNotificationForm(alarm);
            testForm.Show();
            BindingFlags flags = BindingFlags.NonPublic|
                BindingFlags.Public|BindingFlags.Static|
                BindingFlags.Instance;
            Type tForm = typeof(AlarmNotificationForm);
            FieldInfo btnInfo =
                tForm.GetField("OffBtn",flags);
            Button offBtn =
                (Button)btnInfo.GetValue(testForm);

            offBtn.PerformClick();

            Assert.IsTrue(alarm.Off,
                "Alarm should be switched off");
        }
    }
}
```

2. This doesn't compile because we haven't created the Form class yet, so let's do that. Add a button called OffBtn to the form in the design view, and then in the code we need to change the constructor so that it takes a parameter of type Alarm.

```
public AlarmNotificationForm(Alarm alarm)
{
    .
    .
    .
```

3. The code will now compile, and we can run the test, which fails. We need to put some code behind the OffBtn click event that switches the alarm off. To do this, we need to keep a reference to the alarm in the class.

```
Alarm alarm;
public AlarmNotificationForm(Alarm alarm)
{
    InitializeComponent();

    this.alarm = alarm;
}

private void OffBtn_Click(object sender, System.EventArgs e)
{
    alarm.Off = true;
    this.Close();
}
```

4. Compile and run the test; it passes, so we must run all the tests. They all pass. Now we need to call the dialog the first time an alarm rings. We can start with a method that displays the dialog. Because the dialog is related to one alarm, we should put that method in the Alarm class. I am not convinced this is a great idea, but it is simple and we can refactor it later if the need arises.

```
internal void ShowNotificationForm()
{
    AlarmNotificationForm frm =
        new AlarmNotificationForm(this);
    frm.ShowDialog();
}
```

Note

We have given this method the internal access modifier; this allows only files within our assembly to see the method as public. The very fact we have used the internal modifier is a good indicator that we should look at it later for refactoring.

5. For this method to be called, we need to know which alarm is to ring when we raise the AlarmRing event. We can write a test for this in the AlarmsTests class.

```
private void AlarmRingCheckAlarm(Object obj,
    AlarmRingEventArgs args)
```

```
{
    checkAlarm = obj as Alarm;
    alarmRung.Set();
}


private Alarm checkAlarm;

[Test]
public void TestCorrectAlarmRings()
{
    alarmRung = new ManualResetEvent(false);
    alarms.AlarmRing +=
        new AlarmRingEventHandler(AlarmRingCheckAlarm);
    Alarm testAlarm =
        new Alarm(DateTime.Now, "Test Alarm");
    alarms.Add(testAlarm );

    Assert.IsTrue(alarmRung.WaitOne(1000, false),
        "Alarm should ring");
    Assert.AreSame(testAlarm, checkAlarm,
        "Alarms should be the same");
}
```

6. Compile and run the test. It fails. We need to set the alarm as the first parameter of the delegate method that gets called by the event. This is in the Alarms class.

```
protected void AlarmMonitorThread()
{
    while (monitorAlarms.WaitOne())
    {
        foreach(Alarm alarm in this)
        {
            if (!alarm.Off &&
                alarm.DateTime <= DateTime.Now)
            {
                AlarmRing(alarm, new AlarmRingEventArgs());
            }
        }
        Thread.Sleep(500);
    }
}
```

7. Compile and run the tests; they should all pass.

8. We now need to use this alarm in the delegate that gets called on an alarm ringing in the MyAlarmForm class. We only want the form to display once for each alarm, and the event gets called repeatedly until the alarm is switched off. We will use a flag to indicate whether this is the first time the alarm has started ringing. We will put this as a property on the alarm.

```
public class Alarm
{
    .
    .
    .

    private bool started =false;
    public bool StartedRinging
    {
        get{return started;}
    }

    internal void ShowNotificationForm()
    {
        started = true;

        AlarmNotificationForm frm =
            new AlarmNotificationForm(this);
        frm.ShowDialog();
    }
}
public class MyAlarmForm : System.Windows.Forms.Form
{
    .
    .
    .

    private void alarms_AlarmRing(Object obj,
        AlarmRingEventArgs args)
    {
        Alarm alarm = obj as Alarm;
        if (!alarm.StartedRinging)
        {
            Thread thread = new Thread(
                new ThreadStart(alarm.ShowNotificationForm));
            thread.Start();
        }
        SoundPlay.Player.PlaySound(@"Ringin.wav");
    }
}
```

9. Compile and run the tests to check we haven't broken anything, and then run the program and "user test" it. The alarm should ring, and we can switch it off by clicking the button in the notification form that displays. Check in to source control.

Task: Validate That One Alarm Can Ring After Another Alarm Has Rung and Been Switched Off

1. We can do this with a test in the AlarmsTests class.

```
[Test]
public void TestOneAlarmAfterAnother()
{
    alarmRung = new ManualResetEvent(false);
    alarms.AlarmRing +=
        new AlarmRingEventHandler(AlarmRingCheckAlarm);
    Alarm testAlarm =
        new Alarm(DateTime.Now, "Test Alarm");
    Alarm testAlarm2 =
        new Alarm(DateTime.Now, "Test Alarm2");
    alarms.Add(testAlarm);
    alarms.Add(testAlarm2);
    Assert.IsTrue(alarmRung.WaitOne(1000, false),
        "Alarm should ring");
    testAlarm.Off = true;
    alarmRung.Reset();

    Assert.IsTrue(alarmRung.WaitOne(1000, false),
        "Alarm2 should ring");
    Assert.AreSame(testAlarm2, checkAlarm,
        "Alarms should be the same");
}
```

2. Compile and run the test; it should pass.

3. There is one other thing we should test here: that two alarms can ring at the same time.

```
private void AlarmsRinging(Object obj,
    AlarmRingEventArgs args)
{
    if (!ringingAlarms.Contains(obj))
    {
        ringingAlarms.Add(obj);
    }
    if (ringingAlarms.Count == 2)
```

```
    {
        alarmRung.Set();
    }
}

private ArrayList ringingAlarms;

[Test]
public void TestTwoAlarmsRinging()
{
    ringingAlarms = new ArrayList();
    alarmRung = new ManualResetEvent(false);
    alarms.AlarmRing +=
        new AlarmRingEventHandler(AlarmsRinging);
    Alarm testAlarm =
        new Alarm(DateTime.Now, "Test Alarm");
    Alarm testAlarm2 =
        new Alarm(DateTime.Now, "Test Alarm2");
    alarms.Add(testAlarm);
    alarms.Add(testAlarm2);

    Assert.IsTrue(alarmRung.WaitOne(1000, false),
        "Both alarms should ring");

    Assert.IsTrue(ringingAlarms.Contains(testAlarm),
        "Alarm1 should ring");
    Assert.IsTrue(ringingAlarms.Contains(testAlarm2),
        "Alarm2 should ring");
}
```

4. Compile and run the test. It works! All 31 tests that we have written should now run and pass. We have nearly completed our first iteration. Check in to source control.

Task: Integrate and Check In to Source Control

1. We need to make sure the WAV file we added to our project gets shipped, so we should include that in the setup project. This is a good example of making sure we are always ready to ship.

2. Run the batch file; we should get the green screen.

3. Check in the files to source control.

4. Send a copy of the alarms setup to our product manager.

Customer Meeting

The day after we sent a copy of the setup file, we have a meeting with our customer, the product manager. I'm keen to find out what they have to say.

 Dr. Neil: Did you get the setup program? Have you had time to look at it?

Product manager: Yes, it looks okay. Not bad at all.

DN: Are all the stories from the first milestone complete as far as you're concerned?

PM: Yes, sort of, but I want the application to start automatically.

DN: Okay, that's not too hard; we'll put that down as a story. There is something else we realized that we haven't included.

PM: What's that?

DN: It doesn't save and load the alarms.

PM: That's kind of important!

DN: Yeah, we just didn't think about it when we were sitting down the first time, doh! I'll create three new story cards, Save, Load, and AutoStart

PM: Okay, great.

DN: Let me put some costs for delivery on those.

Story	Development Cost
Save alarms	1
Load alarms	1
Autostart application	1/2

PM: Great.

DN: You had a short iteration 2 scheduled next, so we could put some of that in there.

PM: I want it all in; then we have something that starts to be marketable.

DN: Does it make sense to have save and load as separate stories?

PM: Not really

DN: Okay, let's rip those cards up and replace them with one that reads "Load and Save Alarms" with a development cost of two.

PM: Fine, but I want those in this next iteration's deliverable.

DN: Okay, that will be a slightly longer-than-normal iteration, and seeing as it is only an extra half point on the development cost, I will let it pass. But remember, this milestone will be delivered later than normal.

PM: Sure.

DN: Great, we're done and ready to go.

At the end of this meeting, the stories for the next iteration are as follows:

1. Edit an alarm.
2. Save and Load an alarm.
3. Autostart the application.

Following Iterations

In order to finish this project, you can download the rest of the iterations from the Web site http://eXtreme.NET.Roodyn.com/Book Exercises.aspx. Each iteration will take you a step closer to the completed Alarm clock. At any time, you can stop following the exercises and carry on by yourself. You might then find it interesting to compare your work with that in the suggested iteration available on the Web site.

Conclusion

If you can take on all of these lessons and code using the techniques taught so far, you will not necessarily be developing in an XP environment, but I have no doubt you will gain in many ways. Your code will be more robust, you will feel more comfortable with delivering what you have, and the code will be more malleable and therefore easier to refactor. Of course, the only way to know for sure is to show the courage discussed in Chapter 1. Go ahead, try it. You'll like it!

While writing this chapter, I had an interesting conversation with Jim McCarthy on the merits of writing the code this way. Jim was in many ways one of the leaders toward an agile approach to software development. Jim worked for Microsoft for many years and directed the Visual C++ team at the beginning of the 1990s.

I would like to share the theme of the conversation. Jim put across the point that the tests are in some ways the specification for the software. By writing the tests first, you are encoding the specification into the system. As far as the deliverable is concerned, Jim didn't care whether the tests were done before or after the software, but it's pretty damn hard to deliver the software without having the specification! The collection of small practices presented in this book require us, as developers, to code to a more rigid specification that we have clearly defined before writing the code, and yet the code is still very flexible. The tests provide the framework that enables us to refactor the code with less concern that we might break something. We can use tests to document spikes and remain in the source as a reference of the information discovered.

I hope that you have learned to appreciate the value of using the techniques presented in this book. Now have the courage to take these lessons with you and develop some great code.

◼ APPENDIX I ◼

Guideline Solutions for Task Breakdown Exercises in Chapter 3

Exercise 3-4: The Shopping Cart

This exercise is reasonably straightforward. You answers should look something like this.

Stories:

1. Add item to shopping cart
2. Remove item from shopping cart
3. Show running total for cart

Tasks for Story 1: Add Item to Shopping Cart

Task	Estimated Time
Test for adding normal item to cart	10 minutes
Test for adding null item to cart	10 minutes
Test for adding non existent item to cart	10 minutes
Code to make tests run	20 minutes
User interface to add items	15 minutes
Connect user interface to code	10 minutes
Check into source control and integrate with rest of system	5 minutes

Tasks for Story 2: Remove Item from Shopping Cart

Task	Estimated Time
Test for removing item from cart that is in cart	10 minutes
Test for removing null item from cart	10 minutes
Test for removing item from cart that is not in cart	10 minutes
Code to make tests run	20 minutes
User interface to remove items from the cart	15 minutes
Connect user interface to code	10 minutes
Check into source control and integrate with rest of system	5 minutes

Tasks for Story 3: Show Running Total for Cart

Task	Estimated Time
Test for running total being zero when cart is empty	10 minutes
Test for cart with one item in	10 minutes
Test for cart with 1,000 items in	10 minutes
Test for cart with multiples of the same item	10 minutes
Code to make tests run	20 minutes
User interface to display running total of items in the cart	15 minutes
Connect user interface to code	10 minutes
Check into source control and integrate with rest of system	5 minutes

Exercise 3-5: Derived Stock Market Data

This exercise is a little more difficult than the first because some unknowns need to be investigated before we can give certain timeframes.

Stories:

1. Spike the existing software to understand how to access the portfolio data
2. Spike on how to collect all the quote prices for the day
3. Calculate open price

   Calculate the high price

   Calculate the low price

   Calculate the close price

   Calculate the profit made on a stock

Tasks for Story 1: Spike the Existing Software to Understand How to Access the Portfolio Data

Task	Estimated Time
Does the existing software provide a .NET interface? Web service? Remoting?	30 minutes
Does the existing software provide a COM interface?	30 minutes
Examine the files saved by the existing software	1 hour

Tasks for Story 2: Spike on How to Collect All the Quote Prices for the Day

Task	Estimated Time
Does the existing software provide a mechanism for accessing this data?	30 minutes
What other software does the customer have that would allow us to gather the data	1 hour
Search for a Web service that can provide the data	1 hour

Tasks for Story 3: Calculate Open Price

Task	Estimated Time
Test that the open on a non trading day is not calculated	15 minutes
Test open is calculated correctly based on some hard-coded data	10 minutes
Test software performs as expected when no data is obtained for that day	10 minutes
Write code to make tests pass	20 minutes
Design user interface to display open price	15 minutes
Connect user interface to code	10 minutes
Check into source control and integrate with rest of system	5 minutes

Tasks for Story 4: Calculate the High Price

Task	Estimated Time
Test that the high on a non trading day is not calculated	15 minutes
Test high is calculated correctly based on some hard coded data	10 minutes
Test software performs as expected when no data is obtained for that day	10 minutes
Write code to make tests pass	20 minutes
Design user interface to display high price	15 minutes
Connect user interface to code	10 minutes
Check into source control and integrate with rest of system	5 minutes

Tasks for Story 5: Calculate the Low Price

Task	Estimated Time
Test that the low on a non trading day is not calculated	15 minutes
Test low is calculated correctly based on some hard-coded data	10 minutes
Test software performs as expected when no data is obtained for that day	10 minutes
Write code to make tests pass	20 minutes
Design user interface to display low price	15 minutes
Connect user interface to code	10 minutes
Check into source control and integrate with rest of system	5 minutes

Tasks for Story 6: Calculate the Close Price

Task	Estimated Time
Test that the close on a non trading day is not calculated	15 minutes
Test close is calculated correctly based on some hard-coded data	10 minutes
Test software performs as expected when no data is obtained for the previous day	10 minutes
Write code to make tests pass	20 minutes
Design user interface to display close price	15 minutes
Connect user interface to code	10 minutes
Check into source control and integrate with rest of system	5 minutes

Tasks for Story 7: Calculate the Profit Made on a Stock

Task	Estimated Time
Obtain stock volume held from portfolio data	? (Depends on outcome of the spikes)
Obtain stock purchase price from portfolio data	? (Depends on outcome of the spikes)
Obtain current stock price	? (Depends on outcome of the spikes)
Test that a positive profit is calculated correctly	15 minutes
Test that a negative profit is calculated correctly	15 minutes
Test software performs as expected when no data is obtained from the portfolio	10 minutes
Test software performs as expected when the current price cannot be obtained	10 minutes
Write code to make tests pass	20 minutes

Task	Estimated Time
Design user interface to display profit made on a stock	15 minutes
Connect user interface to code	10 minutes
Check into source control and integrate with rest of system	5 minutes

Exercise 3-6: What's the Weather Like?

This exercise has an interesting feature in that it has a potentially repeatable story. For every site that the portal connects to, the tasks will be the same.

Stories:

1. Spike for weather Web sites with data we can use
2. Spike for severe weather warning information on the Web
3. Create a Web site with a world map that can be clicked
4. For every weather source on the Web, provide a clickable area on the world map to access that source's data
5. Display sever weather warnings on the Web page

Tasks for Story 1: Spike for Weather Web Sites with Data We Can Use

Task	Estimated Time
Do a Web search for world weather sites	1 hour
Search for Web services that supply weather information	1 hour

Tasks for Story 2: Spike for Severe Weather Warning Information on the Web

Task	Estimated Time
Do a Web search for sites containing severe weather warnings	1 hour
Search for news sites that might supply severe weather warnings	1 hour

Tasks for Story 3: Create a Web Site with a World Map That Can Be Clicked

Task	Estimated Time
Create a basic ASPX Web application	5 minutes
Add a map of the world image to the index page	10 minutes
Add a frame on the page to display the weather for the area clicked	10 minutes
Create an image map for the world map image	10 minutes
Change the test at the top of the frame to indicate which area has been clicked	10 minutes
Check into source control	5 minutes

Tasks for Story 4: For Every Weather Source on the Web, Provide a Clickable Area on the World Map to Access That Source's Data

Task	Estimated Time
Associate an area of the world map with the weather source	10 minutes
Display the data from the source in the frame (weather for the area)	20 minutes
Check into source control	5 minutes

Tasks for Story 5: Display Sever Weather Warnings on the Web Page

Task	Estimated TIme
Create a frame on the page for severe weather warnings	10 minutes
Display the data from the source in the frame	20 minutes
Check into source control	5 minutes

Exercise 3-7: The Unfinished Solution

This is such a common scenario that I had to include it as one of the exercises. The real problem here is that you do not really know what you are starting with, and the customer has already gone through explaining what he wants and does not want to go through the whole thing again.

Stories:

1. Validate existing code
2. Allow user to enter message
3. Allow user to add tags to message
4. Send message to each contact in list
5. Customize e-mail message for each contact based on tags in profile and e-mail message

Tasks for Story 1: Validate Existing Code

Task	Estimated Time
Skim through existing code to understand classes	20 minutes
Write tests to validate any theories about how the code works	30 minutes
Check into source control and integrate with existing system	5 minutes

Tasks for Story 2: Allow User to Enter Message

Task	Estimated Time
Test to disallow a blank e-mail	10 minutes
Test to validate correct processing of non character input to the message	20 minutes
Test for a message of maximum length (string length?)	10 minutes
Code to pass tests	20 minutes
User interface to allow user to type the message	10 minutes
Connect code to user interface	10 minutes
Check into source control and integrate with existing system	5 minutes

Tasks for Story 3: Allow User to Add Tags to Message

Task	Estimated Time
Test that a tag in any profile can be added to the message	15 minutes
Test that a tag that doesn't exist in any profile cannot exist in a message	10 minutes
Test that a message can contain no tags	15 minutes
Test that a message can contain only tagged input	15 minutes
Code to pass tests	20 minutes
User interface to allow user to select a tag for input	10 minutes
Connect code to user interface	10 minutes
Check into source control and integrate with existing system	5 minutes

Tasks for Story 4: Send Message to Each Contact in List

Task	Estimated Time
Test that each contact in the list is sent the message	10 minutes
Test when the contact list is empty	10 minutes
Test when the contact list contains a maximum number of contacts (have to autogenerate contacts)	15 minutes
Test when message is empty	10 minutes
Code to pass tests	20 minutes
User interface to allow user to send message (button?)	10 minutes
Connect code to user interface	10 minutes
Check into source control and integrate with existing system	5 minutes

Tasks for Story 5: Customize E-mail Message for Each Contact Based on Tags in Profile and E-mail Message

Task	Estimated Time
Test that a profile with no tags is not sent a message containing only tags	10 minutes
Test that a profile with all the tags receives the correct message	10 minutes
Test that a known (hard-coded) profile receives the correct message from a hard-coded tagged message	15 minutes
Test when message is empty	10 minutes
Code to pass tests	20 minutes
Integrate code with user interface from story 4	10 minutes
Check into source control and integrate with existing system	5 minutes

■ APPENDIX II ■

Building Your Own Simple Test Framework with Excel

One of the issues with NUnit is it is focused specifically on testing .NET solutions. In the real world, you might have Visual Basic, C++ solutions as well as .NET C# and VB.NET code. I like to have one place where I can run all the tests for the entire system. Using Excel is fairly generic, and most languages can expose a COM interface for Excel to work with. In the following exercise, we will build a simple framework with C# and VBA in Excel.

In this exercise, we build a test framework for a .NET class library using Excel as the main engine and tests that are exposed in the form of a COM interface. So let's get into it:

1. Create a new C# class library called **ExcelTestLibrary**.

2. In the Class1.cs file, create a class that supports a COM interface so that we can call it from Excel. We can use the ClassInterface attribute, as shown:

```
using System;
using System.Runtime.InteropServices;

namespace ExcelTestLibrary
{
    [ClassInterface(ClassInterfaceType.AutoDual)]
    public class Tests
    {
        public int TestCount
        {
            get
```

```
        {
            return 2;
        }
    }

    public string[] RunTests()
    {
        string[]results = new string[2];
        results[0] = Test1();
        results[1] = Test2();
        return results;
    }

    private string Test1()
    {
        return "Success: Test1 Ran";
    }

    private string Test2()
    {
        return "Failure: Test2 Ran";
    }
  }
}
```

3. In Solution Explorer, right-click the project and select Properties to bring up the Property Pages dialog box. In the Configuration Properties / Build section, set the Register for COM Interop Output to True, as shown in Figure A-1. This will generate a type library and register it in the system Registry.

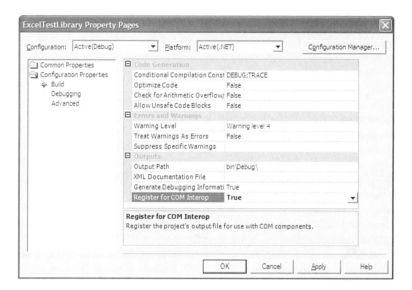

Figure A-1   Register for COM Interop.

4. Build the library. Now we can fire up Excel and call the COM interface to run the tests.

5. Load Excel with a blank spreadsheet. Press Alt+F11 to fire up the Visual Basic Editor to enter a macro. Double-click ThisWorkbook in the project view in the upper-right corner. This brings up a blank Code Entry sheet. In this, we create a macro called **RunTests**, as shown:

```
Sub RunTests()
    Dim testLib As New ExcelTestLibrary.Tests

    Dim results() As String
    results = testLib.RunTests()

    Dim nTest As Integer
    Dim result As String
    Dim resultRow As Range
    For nTest = 0 To testLib.TestCount - 1
        result = results(nTest)
        Set resultRow = Range(Sheet1.Cells(nTest + 1, 1),
        Sheet1.Cells(nTest + 1, 10))
        If Left(result, 7) = "Success" Then
            resultRow.Interior.Color = RGB(0, 255, 0)
        Else
            resultRow.Interior.Color = RGB(255, 0, 0)
```

```
        End If
        Sheet1.Cells(nTest + 1, 1) = result
    Next

End Sub
```

6. Run the macro and have a look at the spreadsheet. You should see the results highlighted in Figure A-2.

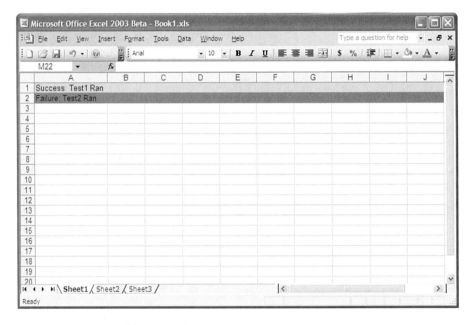

Figure A-2   Results of Our Tests in Excel.

7. (Optional) Enhancing the solution. There are a number of things you can do to make this framework more useful.

   a. Save the sheet after the tests have run into an archive so that you can track the progress of tests through the project life cycle.

   b. Format the sheet with headings so that it is presentable to management as an output of the build and test process.

   c. Create a mechanism to return the success or failure output as a Boolean separately from a results string.

   d. Think of how you can incorporate this into your solution at work.

■ APPENDIX III ■
Recommended Reading

Important Books for Software Developers Working in Teams

Rapid Development, by Steve McConnell (Microsoft Press, 1996)

Dynamic of Software Development, by Jim McCarthy (Microsoft Press, 1995)

Software Craftsmanship, by Pete McBreen (Pearson Education, 2001)

The Pragmatic Programmer, by Andrew Hunt and David Thomas (Addison-Wesley, 1999)

Software for Your Head, by Jim and Michele McCarthy (Addison-Wesley, 2001)

XP-Specific Books

Extreme Programming Explained, by Kent Beck (Addison-Wesley 1999)

Planning Extreme Programming, by Kent Beck and Martin Fowler (Addison-Wesley 2000)

Extreme Programming Installed, by Ron, Jeffries, Ann Anderson, and Chet Hendrickson (Addison-Wesley 2000)

Extreme Programming Explored, by Bill Wake (Pearson Education 2001)

Questioning Extreme Programming, by Pete McBreen (Addison-Wesley 2002)

Testing Extreme Programming, by Lisa Crispin and Tip House (Addison-Wesley 2002)

XP Adventures in C#, by Ron Jeffries (Microsoft Press 2004)

XP-Specific Web Sites

http://www.extremeprogramming.org/

http://www.xprogramming.com/

http://groups.yahoo.com/group/extremeprogramming/

Agile Techniques Books

User Stories Applied, by Mike Cohn (Pearson Education, 2004)

Test Driven Development for Microsoft .NET, by Jim Newkirk and Alexei Vorontsov (Microsoft Press, 2004)

Test Driven Development, by Kent Beck (Addison-Wesley, 2002)

Refactoring, by Martin Fowler (Addison-Wesley, 1999)

Refactoring Workbook, by William Wake (Addison-Wesley, 2003)

Refactoring to Patterns, by Joshua Kerievsky (Pearson Education, 2004)

Puir Programming Illuminated, by Laurie Williams (Addison-Wesley, 2002)

Agile Web Sites

http://www.userstories.com/

http://www.Refactoring.com/

http://dotnetrefactoring.com/

http://www.agilealliance.org/

http://www.testdriven.com/
http://groups.yahoo.com/group/testdrivendevelopment/
http://groups.yahoo.com/group/agiledotnet/

Agile Tools Web Sites

http://www.xtreme-simplicity.net/CSharpRefactory.html
http://www.NUnit.org/

A Book About Change

The Tipping Point, by Malcolm Gladwell (Back Bay Books, 2002)

Index

A

add alarm story (step-by-step development exercise), 229-245
agile development movement, 3
alarm exercise. *See* step-by-step development
answers. *See* solutions to exercises
automating the build process
  batch file exercise, 145-151
  MSBuild, 159
  NAnt exercise, 151-159
  reasons for, 144-145
  step-by-step development
    exercise, 226-227

B

batch file creation exercise, 145-151
Beck, Kent (*Extreme Programming Explained*), 17
breadth test exercise (stock data example), 202-207
breaking code with tests exercise (stock data example), 207-211
bug-free code, 62
bugs, writing tests to fix, 77-81

build process, 141-142
  automating
    batch file exercise, 145-151
    MSBuild, 159
    NAnt exercise, 151-159
    reasons for, 144-145
    step-by-step development
      exercise, 226-227
  build file components, 153
  disadvantages of F5 function
    key, 143
business, pace of change in, 2-3
business logic, inserting into user
  interface, 75-77, 86-87

C

calculator project (test-driven development example), 66-91
change in business, pace of, 2-3
classes, extracting for refactoring, 108-110
coach (team member role), 5
coding standards (XP practice), 16
collective ownership (XP practice), 16

COM interfaces, exposing tests, 281-284

communication (XP value), 18-19
  and refactoring, 99

complex solutions, problems with, 44

conditionals, replacing during refactoring, 118-120

confidence level, increasing by spiking, 126

constant refactoring. *See* refactoring (XP practice)

continuous alarm story (step-by-step development exercise), 252-265

continuous integration (XP practice), 13-14

courage (XP value), 23-24

currency-converter exercise (refactoring), 103-120

customer (team member role), 4
  paying for testing, 65-66

customer meeting (step-by-step development exercise), 220-221, 266-267

customer user stories. *See* stories

D

delete alarm story (step-by-step development exercise), 246-252

derived stock market data exercise, 57
  solutions, 271-274

design and XP, 20

developer (team member role), 4

drag and drop with Rich Text control exercise (spiking), 139

E

embrace change (XP practice), 17

enumerated types, replacing during refactoring, 113-118

event-oriented code, 162-163

Excel, building test frameworks with, 281-284

exceptions test exercise (testing third-party libraries), 198-200

exercises
  batch file creation, 145-151
  business logic into user interface, 75-77, 86-87
  currency-converter (refactoring), 103-120
  derived stock market data, 57
    solutions, 271-274
  drag and drop with Rich Text control (spiking), 139
  exceptions test (testing third-party libraries), 198-200
  extracting functionality from user interface, 87-91
  functional depth test (testing third-party libraries), 194-198
  NAnt (automating the build process), 151-159
  NUnit setup, 191

perfection game (pair programming), 29-31

protecting against changes (testing third-party libraries), 212-214

quick breadth test (testing third-party libraries), 191-194

reflection for GUI testing, 175-188

running NUnit, 67-71

screen saver (pair programming), 31-40
  refinements to, 40-41

session state (spiking), 139

shopping cart, 56
  solutions, 269-271

step-by-step development, 220-267
  add alarm story, 229-245
  continuous alarm story, 252-265
  customer meeting, 220-221, 266-267
  delete alarm story, 246-252
  iteration 0 (setup), 223-227
  iteration 1 (task breakdown), 227-229
  stories, 221-223

stock data (testing third-party libraries)
  breadth test, 202-207
  breaking code with tests, 207-211
  examining code, 200-202
  forcing intermittant errors, 211-212

story breakdown into subtasks, 50-55

story definitions, 48-50

test-driven development
  with tests, 92-93
  without tests, 91-92

thin GUI layer (testing), 163-175

time zone data (spiking), 127-134

unfinished solution, 59-60
  solutions, 277-279

weather information, 58
  solutions, 275-276

Web services (spiking), 139

writing tests
  adding functionality, 71-75
  adding methods, 81-83
  extracting methods, 83-85
  fixing bugs, 77-81

experimentation. See spiking (XP practice)

extracting
  classes for refactoring, 108-110
  functionality from user interface, 87-90
  methods
    exercise, 83-85
    for refactoring, 103-108

eXtreme .NET, xix

Extreme Programming Explained (Beck), 17

eXtreme Programming. See XP

F

F5 function key, disadvantages, 143

feedback (XP value), 21-23
  and refactoring, 99

fixed working week (XP practice), 15

fixtures, 70

functional depth test exercise (testing third-party libraries), 194-198

functions. *See* methods

G-H

genuis in problem-solving, 44-45
exercises, 56-60
problem breakdown example, 45-47
story breakdown, 50-55
story definitions, 48-50

go with instincts (XP practice), 17

GUI. *See* user interface

honesty and openness (XP practice), 17

I-J

incremental change (XP practice), 17

integration build batch file creation exercise, 145-151

integration machine, 142

intellectual property, 62

intermittent errors exercise (stock data example), 211-212

iteration 0 (setup), step-by-step development exercise, 223-227

iteration 1 (task breakdown), step-by-step development exercise, 227-229

job descriptions, 61

K-L

leave baggage behind (XP practice), 16

legacy code, 199

libraries, testing third-party libraries, 188-214, 256-257

M

McCarthy, Jim, 267

metaphor (XP practice), 15

methodology, xviii

methods
extracting for refactoring, 103-108
moving during refactoring, 110-113
writing tests
to add, 81-83
to extract, 83-85

Microsoft .NET Framework. *See* .NET

moving methods during refactoring, 110-113

MSBuild, 159

N

NAnt, automating the build process, 151-159

.NET, xviii, 3
building test frameworks with Excel, 281-284
integration with XP, 3-5

NUnit, 66
  functionality
    adding, 71-75
    extracting from user interface,
      87-90
    business logic into user interface,
      75-77, 86-87
  fixing bugs, 77-81
  methods
    adding, 81-83
    extracting, 83-85
  running, 67-71
  setup exercise, 191

O-P

on-site customer (XP practice), 6-7

pace of change in business, 2-3

pair programming (XP practice),
  8-9, 27-41
  perfection game exercise, 29-31
  professional attitude, importance
    of, 28
  screen saver exercise, 31-40
    refinements to, 40-41
paying for testing, 65-66
perfection game exercise (pair
  programming), 29-31
planning game (XP practice), 7-8
play to win (XP practice), 17
playing sound files, 256-257
polymorphism, replacing
  conditionals during refactoring,
  118-120

practices (XP), 6-18
  coding standards, 16
  collective ownership, 16
  constant refactoring, 11-12, 97-121
  continuous integration, 13-14
  embrace change, 17
  go with instincts, 17
  honesty and openness, 17
  incremental change, 17
  leave baggage behind, 16
  metaphor, 15
  pair programming, 8-9, 27-41
  planning game, 7-8
  play to win, 17
  quality work, 16
  short releases, 16
  simple design, 16
  spiking, 12-13, 51, 125-139
  stand-up meetings, 14-15
  sustainable pace, 15
  teach learning, 17
  test-driven development, 9-11,
    61-93
  whole team, 6-7
problem breakdown example, 45-47
  story breakdown, 50-55
  story definitions, 48-50
problem-solving, 43-44
  simplicity, 44-45
    exercises, 56-60
    problem breakdown example,
      45-55
professional attitude, importance
  of, 28
protecting against changes exercise
  (testing third-party libraries),
  212-214

Q

quality software. *See* bug-free code
quality work (XP practice), 16
quick breadth test exercise (testing third-party libraries), 191-194

R

refactoring (XP practice), 11-12, 97-121
  benefits of, 98-102
  and communication, 99
  currency-converter exercise, 103-120
  defined, 97
  extracting
    classes, 108-110
    methods, 103-108
  and feedback, 99
  moving methods, 110-113
  replacing
    conditionals, 118-120
    enumerated types, 113-118
  and simplicity, 99
  and teamwork, 102
  and testing, 98
  tools for, 121
  when not to refactor, 121
  when to do, 98
Refactory (refactoring tool), 121
reflection (GUI testing exercise), 175-188

replacing
  conditionals during refactoring, 118-120
  enumerated types during refactoring, 113-118
research. *See* spiking (XP practice)
respect (XP value), 24-25
Rich Text control drag and drop exercise (spiking), 139
roles. *See* team member roles

S

screen saver exercise (pair programming), 31-40
  refinements to, 40-41
session state exercise (spiking), 139
SetUp method (NUnit), 71
shopping cart exercise, 56
  solutions, 269-271
short releases (XP practice), 16
  feedback, 22
simple design (XP practice), 16
simplicity (XP value), 19-21
  in problem-solving, 44-45
    exercises, 56-60
    problem breakdown example, 45-55
  and refactoring, 99
"smelly" code, 87
software development problem. *See* problem-solving

solutions to exercises. *See also*
    problem-solving
  derived stock market data
      exercise, 271-274
  shopping cart exercise, 269-271
  unfinished solution exercise,
      277-279
  weather information exercise,
      275-276
sound files, playing, 256-257
source control software, 142
specialization, dangers of, 125-126
spiking (XP practice), 12-13, 51,
    125-139
  confidence level, increasing, 126
  drag and drop with Rich Text
      control exercise, 139
  session state exercise, 139
  specialization, dangers of, 125-126
  and testing, 135-138
  time zone data exercise, 127-134
  Web services exercise, 139
stand-up meetings (XP practice),
    14-15
  feedback, 22
step-by-step development, 217
  example exercise, 220-267
    add alarm story, 229-245
    continuous alarm story, 252-265
    customer meeting, 220-221,
        266-267
    delete alarm story, 246-252
    iteration 0 (setup), 223-227

  iteration 1 (task breakdown),
      227-229
  stories, 221-223
  importance of, 218-219
stock data exercise (testing third-
    party libraries)
  breadth test, 202-207
  breaking code with tests, 207-211
  examining code, 200-202
  forcing intermittant errors, 211-212
stories
  breakdown into subtasks, 50-55
  defining, 48-50
  feedback, 21
  in step-by-step development
      exercise, 221-223
    add alarm story, 229-245
    continuous alarm story, 252-265
    delete alarm story, 246-252
    task breakdown, 227-229
sustainable pace (XP practice), 15

T

task breakdown (step-by-step
    development exercise), 227-229
TDD. *See* test-driven development
    (XP practice)
teach learning (XP practice), 17
team member roles, 4-5
teamwork
  importance of, 24-25
  and refactoring, 102
TearDown method (NUnit), 71

test frameworks, building with Excel, 281-284

test-driven development (XP practice), 9-11, 61-93. *See also* testing

  bug-free code, 62

  exercise with tests, 92-93

  exercise without tests, 91-92

  feedback, 21

  NUnit, 66

    adding functionality, 71-75

    adding methods, 81-83

    business logic into user interface, 75-77, 86-87

    extracting functionality from user interface, 87-90

    extracting methods, 83-85

    fixing bugs, 77-81

    running, 67-71

  paying for testing, 65-66

  reasons for using, 63-65

  unit testing, 63

TestFixture attribute (NUnit), 70

testing. *See also* test-driven development (XP practice)

  importance of, 161

  and refactoring, 98

  and spiking, 135-138

  third-party libraries, 188-190

    breaking code with tests exercise, 207-211

    exceptions test exercise, 198-200

    functional depth test exercise, 194-198

    intermittent errors exercise, 211-212

    NUnit setup exercise, 191

    protecting against changes exercise, 212-214

    quick breadth test exercise, 191-194

    step-by-step development exercise, 256-257

    stock data exercise, 200-207

  user-interface testing, 161-162

    reflection for GUI testing exercise, 175-188

    step-by-step development exercise, 234-245

    thin GUI layer exercise, 163-175

thin GUI layer exercise (testing), 163-175

third-party libraries, testing, 188-190

  breaking code with tests exercise, 207-211

  exceptions test exercise, 198-200

  functional depth test exercise, 194-198

  intermittent errors exercise, 211-212

  NUnit setup exercise, 191

  protecting against changes exercise, 212-214

  quick breadth test exercise, 191-194

  step-by-step development exercise, 256-257

  stock data exercise, 200-207

threads, 254-255
tidying code. *See* refactoring
time zone data exercise (spiking),
    127-134
tools for refactoring, 121

U

UI. *See* user interface
unfinished solution exercise, 59-60
    solutions, 277-279
unit testing, 63
user interface
    event-oriented code, 162-163
    extracting functionality from,
        87-90
    inserting business logic, 75-77,
        86-87
    testing, 161-162
        reflection for GUI testing
            exercise, 175-188
        step-by-step development
            exercise, 234-245
        thin GUI layer exercise, 163-175

V

values (XP), 18-25
    communication, 18-19, 99
    courage, 23-24
    feedback, 21-23, 99
    respect, 24-25
    simplicity, 19-21, 99
virtuous cycle, 5
Visual SourceSafe, 142
Visual Studio 2005, refactoring
    tools, 121

W

weather information exercise, 58
    solutions, 275-276
Web services exercise (spiking), 139
whole team (XP practice), 6-7
Windows time zone data exercise
    (spiking), 127-134

X-Z

XP (eXtreme Programming), xvii, 1-2
    integration with .NET, 3, 5
    learning from, 4
    practices, 6-18
        coding standards, 16
        collective ownership, 16
        constant refactoring, 11-12,
            97-121
        continuous integration, 13-14
        embrace change, 17
        go with instincts, 17
        honesty and openness, 17
        incremental change, 17
        leave baggage behind, 16
        metaphor, 15
        pair programming, 8-9, 27-41
        planning game, 7-8
        play to win, 17
        quality work, 16
        short releases, 16
        simple design, 16
        spiking, 12-13, 51, 125-139
        stand-up meetings, 14-15
        sustainable pace, 15
        teach learning, 17

test-driven development, 9-11,
   61-93

whole team, 6-7

team member roles, 4-5

values, 18-25

communication, 18-19, 99

courage, 23-24

feedback, 21-23, 99

respect, 24-25

simplicity, 19-21, 99

zero-defect software. *See*
   bug-free code

Microsoft .NET Development Series

.NET Framework
Standard Library
Annotated Reference
Volume 1:

Microsoft .NET Framework
Class Libraries Team
Brad Abrams, Editor

0321154894

.NET Web Services
Architecture and Implementation

Keith Ballinger

0321113594

A First Look at
SQL Server 2005
for Developers

Bob Beauchemin
Niels Berglund
Dan Sullivan

0321180593

Essential .NET
Volume 1
The Common Language Runtime

Don Box
with Chris Sells

0201734117

Graphics
Programming
with GDI+

Mahesh Chand

0321160770

The C#
Programming
Language

Anders Hejlsberg
Scott Wiltamuth
Peter Golde

0321154916

A First Look at
ADO.NET and
System Xml v 2.0

Alex Homer
Dave Sussman
Mark Fussell

0321228391

Essential ASP.NET
with Examples in C#

Fritz Onion

0201760401

Essential ASP.NET
with Examples in Visual Basic .NET

Fritz Onion

0201760398

The Visual Basic
.NET Programming
Language

Paul Vick

0321169514

For more information go to
www.awprofessional.com/msdotnetseries/

0321228960

0321154932

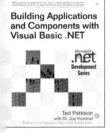

0201734958

0321116208

0321125193

0201770180

0201745682

0321174038

0321174046

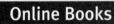